MOUNTAIN
BIKE
PARK CITY

Previous page: *Approaching a rock garden on the Mid Mountain Trail at Park City Mountain.* **Above:** *Rounding a banked, wood berm on Speedbag (Route 16).* **Below:** *Crooked aspens on the Flagstaff Loop (Route 8) at Deer Valley.*

Above: *Riding through a burst of fall colors on the Flying Dog Loop (Route 23) can feel like going through a tunnel of fire.* **Below:** *An aspen grove erupts with autumn yellows on the 9K Trail (Route 16) below Jupiter Peak.*

Ascending Tour des Suds (Route 8) among wildflowers in summer.

Above: *The jewel-blue waters of Lake Desolation provide a stunning backdrop on the Wasatch Crest Trail (Route 36).* **Below:** *Speeding through a straightaway on the Mid Mountain Trail.*

Above: *Sweeping views of the Wasatch Back surround mountain bikers on the WOW Trail (Route 38).* **Below:** *Rolling through Round Valley on Tin Man en route to descend Pulp Friction (Route 31).*

Above: *Wildflowers in Park City's mountains offer splashes of delicate color in summer.* **Below:** *The WOW Trail (Route 38) bends through mountain meadows at its upper elevations.* **Next page:** *Pedaling through October aspen leaves at the Deer Valley Bike Park (Route 12).*

MOUNTAIN BIKE PARK CITY

47 SELECT SINGLETRACK ROUTES

JARED HARGRAVE

MOUNTAINEERS BOOKS

For Callista and Ridge—Pedal, pedal, pedal. Pedal all the way!

MOUNTAINEERS BOOKS is dedicated to the exploration, preservation, and enjoyment of outdoor and wilderness areas.

1001 SW Klickitat Way, Suite 201, Seattle, WA 98134
800.553.4453, www.mountaineersbooks.org

Copyright © 2021 by Jared Hargrave

All rights reserved. No part of this book may be reproduced or utilized in any form, or by any electronic, mechanical, or other means, without the prior written permission of the publisher.

Mountaineers Books and its colophon are registered trademarks of The Mountaineers organization.

Printed in the United States of America
Distributed in the United Kingdom by Cordee, www.cordee.co.uk

First edition, 2021

Copyeditor: Cooper Lee Bombardier, Indigo Editing
Design and layout: Heidi Smets
Cartographer: Pease Press
All photographs by the author unless credited otherwise
Cover photograph: *Riding through a grove of scrub oak at High Star Ranch in Kamas* (Photo by Jay Dash)

The background maps for this book were produced using the online map viewer CalTopo. For more information, visit www.caltopo.com.

Library of Congress cataloging-in-publication data for this title is on file at https://lccn.loc.gov/2020032365. The ebook record is available at https://lccn.loc.gov/2020032366.

Mountaineers Books titles may be purchased for corporate, educational, or other promotional sales, and our authors are available for a wide range of events. For information on special discounts or booking an author, contact our customer service at 800-553-4453 or mbooks@mountaineersbooks.org.

Printed on FSC-certified materials

ISBN (paperback): 978-1-68051-234-2
ISBN (ebook): 978-1-68051-235-9

An independent nonprofit publisher since 1960

CONTENTS

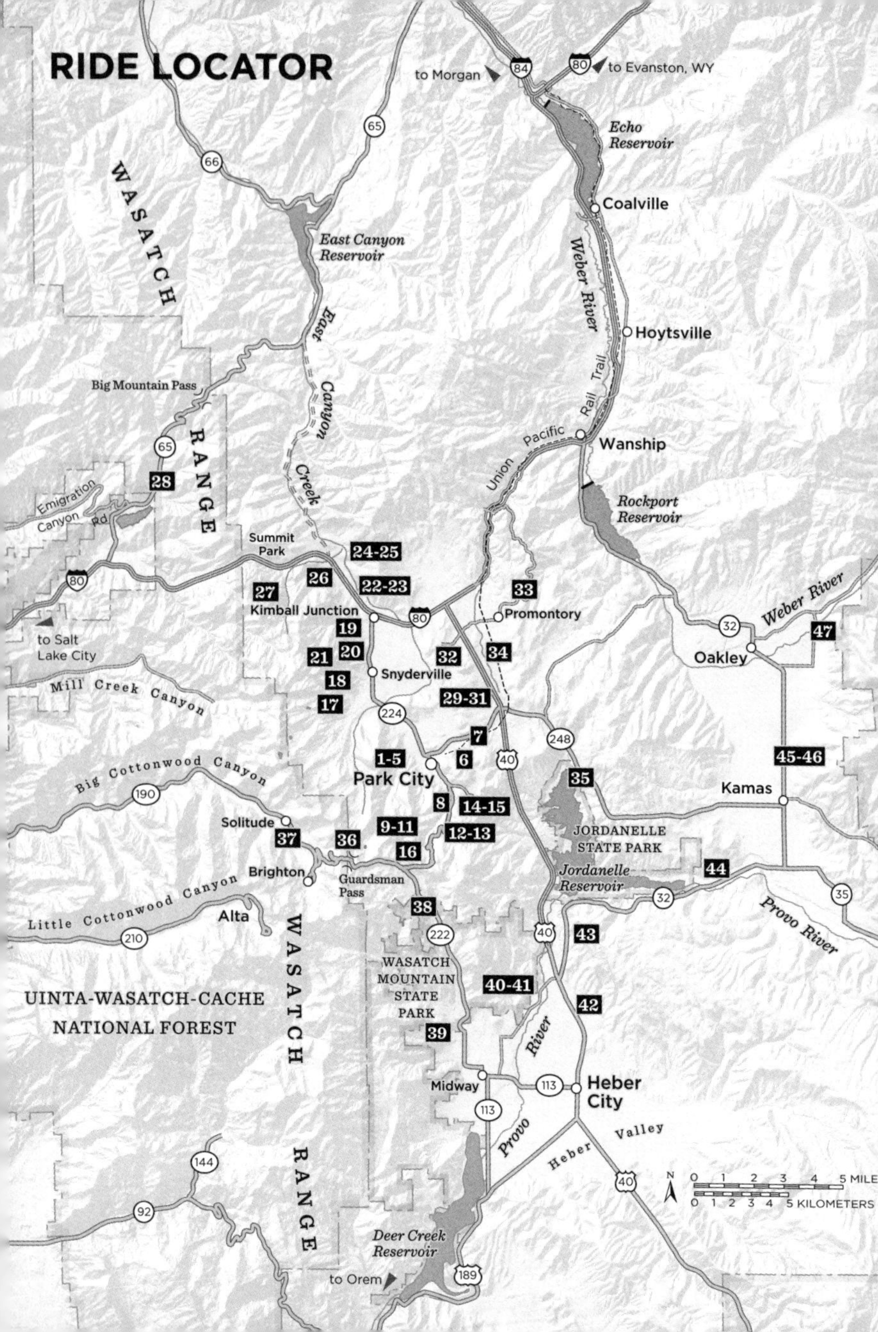

RIDE LOCATOR
WASATCH RANGE
WASATCH RANGE
UINTA-WASATCH-CACHE NATIONAL FOREST
to Morgan
to Evanston, WY
to Salt Lake City
to Orem
Echo Reservoir
East Canyon Reservoir
East Canyon Creek
Rockport Reservoir
Jordanelle Reservoir
Deer Creek Reservoir
Weber River
Weber River
Provo River
Provo River
Big Mountain Pass
Emigration Canyon Rd
Mill Creek Canyon
Big Cottonwood Canyon
Little Cottonwood Canyon
Summit Park
Kimball Junction
Snyderville
Park City
Solitude
Brighton
Alta
Guardsman Pass
Coalville
Hoytsville
Wanship
Promontory
Oakley
Kamas
Midway
Heber City
Heber Valley
Union Pacific Rail Trail
JORDANELLE STATE PARK
WASATCH MOUNTAIN STATE PARK
28
27
26
24-25
22-23
19
21
20
18
17
1-5
9-11
16
8
36
37
38
39
40-41
42
43
44
45-46
47
35
33
34
32
29-31
7
6
14-15
12-13
N
0 1 2 3 4 5 MILE
0 1 2 3 4 5 KILOMETERS

ROUTES AT A GLANCE

	Route	Mileage	Ride Type	Technical Difficulty	Fitness Intensity
1.	**Armstrong to Spiro**	10	Loop	Intermediate	Moderate
2.	**Shadow Lake**	16	Loop	Intermediate	Strenuous
3.	**Park City IMBA Super Epic**	32	Loop	Advanced	Very strenuous
4.	**Jenni's to Mojave to CMG**	10.8	Loop	Intermediate	Moderate
5.	**Old Town Loop**	8	Loop	Advanced	Moderate
6.	**Lost Prospector Loop**	7.1	Loop	Intermediate	Easy
7.	**Union Pacific Rail Trail**	28	Shuttle or out-and-back	Beginner	Strenuous
8.	**Tour des Suds**	6	Shuttle or out-and-back	Intermediate	Moderate
9.	**Corvair to Payroll**	2.3	Lariat loop	Advanced	Easy
10.	**Bowhunter Loop**	7.7	Loop	Intermediate	Moderate
11.	**Lower Empire Canyon**	5.6	Loop	Intermediate	Easy
12.	**Deer Valley Bike Park**	Up to 27	Network	Intermediate–expert	Easy–strenuous
13.	**Mid Mountain Trail**	26.2	Shuttle	Intermediate	Very strenuous
14.	**Snowtop to Solamere Loop**	4	Loop	Intermediate	Moderate
15.	**Spin Cycle**	6	Loop	Advanced	Moderate
16.	**9K Trail to Black Forest**	5.3	Shuttle	Advanced	Easy
17.	**Canyons Village Downhill Trails**	Up to 10	Network	Intermediate–advanced	Moderate
18.	**Rob's to Ambush Loop**	8.7	Loop	Intermediate	Moderate
19.	**RTS Network**	Up to 3	Network	Beginner–intermediate	Easy
20.	**Iron Bill and Legacy Loop**	6	Lariat loop	Advanced	Moderate
21.	**UOP Bobsled**	6	Loop	Intermediate	Moderate
22.	**Glenwild Loop**	8.3	Loop	Intermediate	Moderate
23.	**Flying Dog Loop**	16.5	Loop	Intermediate	Strenuous

	Route	Mileage	Ride Type	Technical Difficulty	Fitness Intensity
24.	Bob's Basin	Up to 12.4	Network	Intermediate–advanced	Easy–moderate
25.	Flying Dog via Preserve Connector	12.7	Loop	Intermediate	Moderate
26.	Road to Arcylon	6.2	Lariat loop	Advanced	Easy
27.	Road to WOS	5	Lariat loop	Intermediate	Easy
28.	Mormon Pioneer Trail	12	Shuttle or out-and-back	Intermediate	Moderate
29.	Round Valley Easy Loop	6.3	Loop	Beginner	Easy
30.	Round Valley Classic Loop	11.2	Loop	Intermediate	Moderate
31.	Pulp Friction	3	Loop	Intermediate	Easy
32.	Trailside Bike Park	Up to 4	Network	Beginner–expert	Easy
33.	Princess Di	14.5	Loop	Advanced	Strenuous
34.	South Canyon	9	Loop	Intermediate	Easy
35.	Ross Creek	3.2	Loop	Beginner	Easy
36.	Wasatch Crest	14	Shuttle	Advanced	Moderate
37.	Solitude Mountain Resort	6	Loop	Advanced	Moderate
38.	WOW Trail	10	Shuttle	Intermediate	Moderate
39.	Wasatch Mountain State Park	4.7	Loop	Intermediate	Strenuous
40.	Dutch Hollow Short Loop	4.4	Loop	Beginner	Easy
41.	Dutch Hollow Big Loop	9.5	Loop	Intermediate	Moderate
42.	Riverview Loop	13.1	Loop	Intermediate	Moderate
43.	Coyote Canyon	19.5	Loop	Advanced	Strenuous
44.	Rocky Top	8	Out-and-back	Intermediate	Easy
45.	High Star Ranch Advanced Loop	8.2	Loop	Advanced	Moderate
46.	High Star Ranch Intermediate Loop	5.6	Loop	Intermediate	Easy
47.	Oakley Trail Park	Up to 3	Network	Intermediate	Easy

WELCOME TO PARK CITY

Park City, nestled in Utah's Wasatch Mountains, is world famous for luxury ski resorts and the Sundance Film Festival. But what visitors to this bustling winter destination don't realize is that Park City is also home to some of the best mountain bike trails in the world. The town even has an award to prove it. In 2012, Park City was named the world's first Gold Ride Center by the International Mountain Bicycling Association (IMBA). To become a Gold Ride Center, Park City had to meet a set of criteria that took into account the following: number of trail miles, quality of trails, quality of hotel rooms and restaurants, bike shops, trailhead facilities, bike parks, brew pubs, and cooperation among local government, businesses, and land owners to create a vast, interconnected trail network.

Variety of trails is also very important. Park City has it all, from beginner loops to rugged backcountry epics and downhill-only gravity trails. Over 400 miles of nonmotorized trail are continuous, connected, and easy to access. The network spans two ski resorts and beyond, from low-elevation sagebrush desert to old-growth evergreen and aspen forests, to breathtaking alpine terrain above tree line.

Also, Park City isn't the only trail destination in this guide. Nearby towns along the Wasatch Back, such as Heber City, Kamas, and Oakley, each have rapidly expanding singletrack networks of their own. Park City truly is a mountain biking paradise.

PARK CITY OVERVIEW

The Wasatch Mountains are the most prominent range in Northern Utah, stretching 160 miles from the Utah–Idaho border south to the center of the

Dead leaves crunching under tires and cool temperatures make autumn a favorite time of year to ride Park City. (Photo by Sean Zimmerman-Wall)

state. Situated right in the middle of the range in the Central Wasatch and located only 33 miles from downtown Salt Lake City (and its international airport), Park City is super easy to get to via Interstate 80 up Parleys Canyon. In fact, mountain bikers can be on the trails at Summit Park or Glenwild with just a 30-minute drive from the capital city.

At 7000 feet in elevation, Park City is definitely a mountain destination. Anyone arriving from sea level would be wise to acclimate for a few days before tackling the trails. Because of the high-alpine locale, the diverse terrain allows for excellent mountain biking from spring through autumn.

The Glenwild area (Routes 22–25), located just north of Park City near Kimball Junction, is at a lower elevation with trails mostly on south-facing slopes. These rides are among the first to dry out in the spring. You'll find bitterbrush and sage down low and an alpine transition zone higher up with maples and scrub oak. Round Valley (Routes 29–35), which is closer to town, is similar and is another good option for spring riding. In Heber City, Kamas, and Midway (Routes 39–47), where the elevation is between 5000 and 6000 feet, the Dutch Hollow, Riverview, and High Star Ranch trails are also dry and ready to ride in the spring.

As summer begins and the snow line performs its slow disappearing act up the mountainsides, mid-elevation trails above Park City open up. Most of these trails are located in ski resorts like Deer Valley and Park City Mountain (Routes 1–18). Here, the mountain biking is on smooth singletrack that winds through aspen groves and stands of fir and pine. Solitude Mountain in Big Cottonwood Canyon (Route 37), the WOW Trail (Route 38), Utah Olympic Park (Routes 19–21), and Road to WOS (Route 27) are other trails that are ready to ride by summertime.

Finally, from midsummer through fall, the highest trails above tree line reveal themselves from under the melting snow. Deer Valley and Park City Mountain have many high-elevation rides, like the Bowhunter Loop (Route 10), 9K Trail (Route 16), and Shadow Lake (Route 2). But the most popular and highest ride, at an elevation of 9800 feet, is the Wasatch Crest Trail (Route 36). Ride this classic when you can, because the window of opportunity can be short depending on how long it takes for the snow to melt.

LOCAL MOUNTAIN BIKING HISTORY

Park City was settled in 1868 after silver ore was discovered. The town was incorporated in 1884 and it boomed as mines tunneled into the mountainsides. But by the 1950s, silver mines shut down and the town lost most of its population. Skiing saved the economy in the 1960s and '70s, and today Park City is booming once again, with tourism as a primary economic driver.

But skiing is a winter sport, and back in the '70s there wasn't much happening in the summer months. So, in the early 1980s, when mountain biking was in its infancy, Tom Noaker opened the town's first bike shop, New Park Cyclery. Back then, riders pedaled on old mining roads. In 1985, Charlie and Kathy Sturgis started their shop, White Pine Touring. To create actual singletrack trails, Charlie began the Thursday Night Ride series, an event that doubled as a pirate trail-building mission.

Meanwhile, Deer Valley started cutting mountain bike trails with the goal of creating an interconnected network. In 1992, the ski resort opened Utah's first lift-served mountain biking off the Sterling chairlift. Around this time, other local mountain bikers banded together to create the Mountain Trails Foundation. This nonprofit worked with private landowners, public lands administrators, and the ski resorts to build the massive singletrack network we enjoy today. Their crowning achievement was the completion of the Mid Mountain Trail, which became a 23-mile hub that connects Deer Valley to Park City Mountain Resort's Canyons Village.

Over the years, other nonprofits have stepped up to meet the growing demand of multiple-use singletrack trails. Basin Recreation has built and now maintains 145 miles of trail in Snyderville Basin and Summit Park. They've also been instrumental in creating open space on the outskirts of town. The South Summit Trails Foundation has been constructing trails in eastern Summit County. And the Wasatch Trails Foundation has turned the Wasatch Back towns of Heber City and Midway into mountain biking destinations with singletrack that is every bit as good as Park City's world-class riding.

What's unique about Park City is that most of its trails are located on private property. But due to the partnerships Mountain Trails Foundation and Basin Recreation have forged with landowners, mountain bikers are free to enjoy the singletrack through public easements. That's why it's important to stay on the trails, not litter, and be respectful of other trail users.

WEATHER AND CLIMATE

Utah's Wasatch Mountains are famous for getting a ton of the "Greatest Snow on Earth." Park City Mountain's average annual snowfall is 360 inches, which precipitates from late October through April. As a result, mountain bike season is generally from April through October in the lower elevations,

Cornering through a break in the rock fin on Glenwild Loop (Route 22)

and more like June through September above 8000 feet. After big snow years, trails like the Wasatch Crest might not be rideable until July!

Springtime is mud season. As the snow melts and trails reappear, cooped-up mountain bikers are excited to ride. But pedaling in the mud damages the trails in many ways. First, bike tires leave ruts behind, which channel water to low spots that create puddles. Then trail users go around those puddles, which eventually widens the trail. Keep singletrack single! Wait for trails to dry out before riding. A good rule to live by: If mud is sticking to your tires, it's time to turn around.

In the summer, Park City's weather is very pleasant. The trails are dry, even dusty, and the temperature rarely gets above 90 degrees. Likewise, overnight lows stay well above freezing. However, with trails at elevations from 5000 feet to nearly 10,000 feet, there is a lot of variability in temperature range and weather. Although it doesn't rain very much in Park City, afternoon thunderstorms are common, especially during late summer's monsoon season. It's important to check the weather forecast before heading out for a ride. Skies could be sunny and warm when you hit the trail down low, then turn into a nightmare of hail and lightning as soon as you top out on an exposed mountaintop (I know this from experience). The high elevation also means the sun can be quite intense, making a cool day feel a lot hotter than it really is. Be sure to drink plenty of water and slather on that sunscreen.

Autumn is my favorite time of year to ride, with cooler temperatures and brilliant fall leaves to enjoy. A little more rainfall leaves behind tacky trails that bike tires stick to. We call it "hero dirt." Unfortunately, the autumn window is far too short, and winter always arrives too soon.

SKILLS AND FITNESS

Mountain biking is a serious workout, especially at an elevation of 8000 feet. Even the easiest beginner trails at this altitude can throw your cardio system into max–heart rate territory. Before you embark on your first singletrack adventure, it's a good idea to be sure that your body is up to the task. Same goes with skills. It's best to start on level, smooth trails before tackling steep drops and rock gardens. Practice and get fit on short, easy rides, then work your way up to longer and more challenging routes.

WILDLIFE

The mountains around Park City are teeming with wildlife, and you have a good chance of encountering animals along the trail. Moose are perhaps the most common. It's important to give moose a very wide berth, especially if a mother and her calves are hanging out on the trail. I've had a few experiences with an angry moose where it was best to simply turn around and ride back the way I came. These large mammals weigh on average 1800 pounds when full grown and can sprint at speeds of up to 35 miles per hour. If they feel threatened, they can be dangerous to humans.

Along with moose you may see deer and elk, especially in the fall during the rut. Autumn is also hunting season, so wear bright colors out on trails this time of year. There aren't many places around Park City where hunting is legal, but it's best to be safe. Also, you may encounter cows on private land where cattle are free to graze.

TRANSPORTATION

Each featured route includes driving directions and parking locations, but you can mountain bike many of Park City's trails without ever using your car. Park City Transit is a free bus system, and its entire fleet is fueled by biodiesel. The bus routes and stops can drop you off at or near several popular trailheads. Eleven bus routes go from Summit Park to Deer Valley and all points between. Log onto the Bus Tracker page online at www.parkcity.org /departments/transit-bus or use the MyStop mobile app to track buses in real time.

The buses are bike friendly from early June until September 1. Only six bikes are allowed on the bus at a time (three on the front bike rack and three on board). The Park City Transit buses are so convenient that locals frequently do "bus laps," where we can ride the bus over 1000 vertical feet above town, descend singletrack back to the bus stop, then do it all over again. It's like a lift-served bike park, only with a bus, and it's free.

The purple and orange routes to Deer Valley and Empire Pass offer the best options for a variety of mountain bike skill levels. Hop on the bus and ride it to Empire Pass (purple route) or Silver Lake at Deer Valley (orange route) and choose the ride down that's right for you. Bus laps may be lazy, but sometimes we like to get our gravity fix without earning it.

GEAR

So you want to be a mountain biker? Then you need to carry the right gear. First of all, you need a mountain bike. In this modern era there is no shortage in the variety of bikes you can ride. There are three wheel sizes—26, 27.5, and 29 inches. You can ride a hardtail bike or a full suspension one. Frames come in aluminum or carbon fiber. Mountain bikes are even categorized as downhill, enduro, trail, or cross-country. What bike you choose is really up to your personal style and preference. But for Park City's trails, which are mostly buff and fast singletrack with a few technical sections, I suggest a full suspension trail or enduro bike. However, many of the smoother trails can be a lot of fun on a basic hardtail. Really, the most fun bike is the one you are currently riding.

Besides the bike, you'll most likely need some specialized gear:

- Helmet
- Sunglasses
- Bike gloves
- Mountain bike shoes (either clipless or flats)
- Padded shorts or chamois
- Multitool that includes Allen wrenches, screwdrivers, etc.
- Spare tire tube
- Patch kit
- Tire levers
- Tire plugs (if you run tubeless tires)
- Air pump or CO_2 cartridges
- Chain lube
- Chain tool and extra link
- First-aid kit
- Water bottle or hydration bladder

Tire-level view of the RTS Loop (Route 19)

It's a good idea to carry all of these items, just to be prepared for any bike mechanical failures such as broken chains or flat tires. I like to carry a small backpack or hip pack, but you can divide these items up into frame bags. I also bring a packable rain shell in case of cloudburst or unexpected chilly weather.

In addition to the above mountain biking gear, it's always a good idea to pack the Ten Essentials, a list developed by The Mountaineers. The point of this list has always been to answer two basic questions: Can you prevent emergencies and respond positively should one occur (items 1–5)? And can you safely spend a night—or more—outside (items 6–10)? Use this list as a guide and tailor it to the needs of your outing:

1. Navigation
2. Headlamp
3. Sun protection
4. First aid
5. Knife
6. Fire
7. Shelter
8. Extra food
9. Extra water
10. Extra clothes

Obviously, these lists are comprehensive. Packing everything on them would be overkill on short three- to six-mile rides. If the weather is perfect and the forecast looks clear, some food, water, sunscreen, and your repair kit are all you're likely to need. It feels great to ride without the weight of a pack on your shoulders. But if you're setting off on a longer ride that covers many miles and most of the day, then it's best to be self-sufficient and bring all of the above items. Being prepared is especially important if you're alone or planning on exploring trails at higher elevations and in more remote areas.

When you're recreating at high elevation, drinking enough water is important, especially while mountain biking. A single water bottle on your bike frame is often not enough on long rides. The Institute of Altitude Medicine recommends drinking 1 to 1.5 liters of water daily when you're above 5000 feet. Therefore, carrying a pack with a hydration bladder ensures that you have enough hydration for longer rides.

E-BIKES

Electric bikes, or e-bikes, have become very popular in recent years. In fact, e-bikes are the fastest growing category in cycling. But new technology can cause controversy. And in the mountain biking world nothing has been more controversial than e-bikes. So, what's the problem? Basically, the trails in Park City are nonmotorized and many people consider e-bikes motorized vehicles. As I write this, e-bikes are prohibited in Park City on natural surface trails and are limited to paved bike trails. However, the ordinance allows people 65 and older, or those with mobility issues, to ride e-bikes on all trails. This ordinance may change in the near future; check with any Park City bike shop or contact Mountain Trails Foundation or Basin Recreation to find out more.

E-bikes are allowed on some trails in this book, including all trails inside Utah State Parks (Wasatch Mountain and Jordanelle) and the High Star Ranch trail system. Until state or national laws are passed allowing e-bikes on all trails, it's best to check with the appropriate land agency to determine if e-bikes are allowed on your chosen route.

FAT BIKES

Fat bikes are becoming very popular for riding in the snow. Park City is an awesome place to fat bike and many of the trails in this book can be ridden in the winter. Mountain Trails Foundation and Basin Recreation groom the trails for multiuse in certain areas.

Perhaps the best venue for fat biking is Round Valley. All four trailheads are open in the winter, and signs point the way for the trail's preferred use. Other fat biking areas include Willow Creek between Park City and Kimball Junction, Ecker Hill Middle School, and The Woods of Parleys Lane near Summit Park.

Outside established, groomed areas, you can always fat bike other single-track as long as the snow isn't too deep or soft. Anything that's not within a ski resort's boundary is fair game. The Glenwild area, Rail Trail, and the East Park City trails like Lost Prospector are good options when snow conditions are primo.

RULES OF THE TRAIL

The International Mountain Bicycling Association (IMBA) launched its Rules of the Trail to educate mountain bikers and serve as a pro-bike advocacy tool. The trails in Park City are extremely popular and sometimes crowded, especially with hikers and other trail users like equestrians. Be courteous and follow these guidelines for responsible riding to ensure that mountain bikers keep access to trails for years to come.

Respect the Landscape

Respect your local trail builders and be a good steward of the physical environment. Keep singletrack single by staying on the trail. Practice Leave No

High-speed approach to a banked berm on Tidal Wave (Route 12) in Deer Valley Bike Park (Photo by Justin Lozier)

Trace principles. Do not ride muddy trails because it causes rutting, widening, and maintenance headaches. Ride through standing water, not around it. Ride on (or walk) technical features, not around them.

Share the Trail

Most of the trails we ride are multiuse. Mountain bikers yield to horses and foot traffic, and descending riders yield to climbing riders. This yield triangle has been formally adopted by land managers since the late 1970s and is a significant reason why we have the access we do. There are some regional differences and unique rules on single-use, directional mountain bike trails—know the code where you ride. Be nice. Say hi.

Ride Open, Legal Trails

Poaching trails, building illegal singletrack, or adding unauthorized trail features are detrimental to our access. Poorly built features could also seriously injure other trail users. If you believe there aren't enough trails or variety near you, it's time to get involved. Your engagement will be welcomed because it takes a village to create, enhance, and protect great places to ride.

Ride in Control

Speed, inattentiveness, and rudeness are the primary sources of trail conflict among user groups. Slow down, ring a bell, or verbally announce yourself if you need to pass, and then wait until the other trail user is out of the path. Use extra caution around horses, which are unpredictable. Be extra aware when riding trails with poor sight lines and blind corners and make sure you can hear what's going on around you.

Plan Ahead

Be prepared and self-sufficient. Every mountain biker should carry what they need for the ride they're undertaking and know how to fix a flat tire and make minor repairs. Download a GPS trail app on your phone for navigation or carry a map in unfamiliar locations. Ride with a partner or share your riding plan with someone if you're heading out solo.

Mind the Animals

When it comes to wildlife, live and let live. In some places, running cattle and disturbing wildlife are serious offenses. If you want to ride with your dog, first find out whether it's allowed by looking up the leash laws. Be prepared to take care of your dog. Ensure your companion is obedient enough to not cause problems for you, other trail users, or wild animals.

ENJOY THE RIDE

The most important thing to remember while mountain biking in Park City is to have fun! The vast network of trails has rides for all skill levels, so there is an endless amount of options to curate your personal two-wheeled adventure. I honestly can't imagine another mountain bike destination in the world that is more friendly, accessible, and entertaining (both on and off the trail) than Park City, Utah.

HOW TO USE THIS GUIDE

This guidebook features 47 routes, starting with Park City and radiating out to surrounding areas from Deer Valley, Canyons Village, and the Utah Olympic Park to Parleys Canyon/Glenwild, Round Valley, and Guardsman Pass. Beyond the Park City core, I include trail networks in neighboring towns like Heber City, Midway, Kamas, and Oakley.

Each route begins with basic information such as elevation gain, mileage, ride type, technical difficulty, and fitness intensity. I then offer a basic overview of the ride, driving directions to the trailhead, and a mileage log of the route marking every major intersection and point of interest. At the end of each route, a final section highlights options or ways you can tailor the featured route to match your preferences or, in some cases, skill level or available time. And, of course, there is a map highlighting the main route and intersecting trails, parking areas, and major roads. Here's a breakdown of what you'll find in each route description.

RIDE TYPE

I've categorized the routes into five types: a loop, lariat loop, out-and-back, shuttle, or network.

Loop

Just as it sounds, a loop starts and ends at the same trailhead by going around in a circle. Loops use different ascent and descent trails to make the ride circle back to end where it started.

Lariat Loop

Also known as a lollipop loop, a lariat loop is a cross between an out-and-back and a loop.

Out-and-Back

An out-and-back route follows the same trail up and down, with a turnaround point at some sort of high point or cool destination.

Shuttle

Almost always downhill, shuttle rides are one-way routes for those who want all the gravity thrills without earning it by pedaling uphill. You leave a vehicle at the bottom, then drive to the top of the trail for a bike ride back down.

Network

In Park City, almost every trail is part of a network where I feature a particular loop or ride within the singletrack system. For this book, I use the network category for places like the Deer Valley Bike Park, where I don't focus on a single route but feature every trail. You can choose your own adventure within a given network.

TRAIL TYPE

Trail type describes the type of trail or trails in a route, such as singletrack, doubletrack, etc. I give a percentage of each trail type in a given route.

DISTANCE

This category outlines the mileage of each route. I've rounded the mileage to the nearest tenth of a mile, so you may find your GPS mileage is a bit off from my route descriptions.

ELEVATION GAIN/LOSS

This category indicates the amount of uphill and downhill elevation loss or gain you can expect on a route, given in vertical feet and rounded to the nearest ten. The vast majority of routes in this book (loops) have the same elevation gain and loss. Shuttle rides and lift-served mountain biking have a significant difference, with elevation loss outpacing the gain.

Opposite: *Trailside Bike Park (Route 32) is a great place to learn technical skills and practice bike handling on manmade features.*

HIGH POINT

High point indicates the highest point above sea level of every ride. This fig-ure sometimes (but not always) indicates the turnaround point for out-and-back rides.

RIDE TIME

Ride time is subjective, as every mountain biker goes at their own pace. I consider myself a mountain biker of average fitness, so for this book I used a range between my own "moving time" and the total ride time that includes time spent stopped for photos, snacks, and simply enjoying the view.

DIFFICULTY RATINGS

The overall difficulty of these rides is broken down into two parts: technical difficulty and fitness intensity. This category is also subjective, as one rider may have no problem banging out a 30-mile ride with 4000 feet of elevation gain, but cringes at the thought of rock drops or steep, rooty sections. On the other hand, many gravity riders don't blink an eye at launching off giant wood features at the bike park, but are incapable of pedaling an epic backcountry

A NOTE ABOUT SAFETY

Safety is an important concern in all outdoor activities. No guide-book can alert you to every hazard or anticipate the limitations of every reader. Therefore, the descriptions of roads, trails, routes, and natural features in this book are not representations that a particular place or excursion will be safe for your party. When you follow any of the routes described in this book, you assume responsibility for your own safety. Under normal conditions, such excursions require the usual attention to traffic, road and trail conditions, weather, terrain, the capabilities of your party, and other factors. Because many of the lands in this book are subject to development and/or change of own-ership, conditions may have changed since this book was written that make your use of some of these routes unwise. Always check for cur-rent conditions, obey posted private property signs, and avoid con-frontations with property owners or managers. Keeping informed on current conditions and exercising common sense are the keys to a safe, enjoyable outing.

—Mountaineers Books

Sharing the Union Pacific Rail Trail (Route 7) with cows as the route passes through a working ranch (Photo by Eric Ghanem)

route. Use these ratings to match your technical skill and fitness to find rides that you will consider most enjoyable.

Technical Difficulty

Routes are categorized into one of four levels of difficulty: beginner, intermediate, advanced, and expert. It is very important to know your own skill level when choosing a route to ride. However, sometimes the technical sections of any given trail are short, and you can walk your bike around them. The Spine on the Wasatch Crest (Route 36) is a great example. Most of the Wasatch Crest is intermediate, but I label it advanced because of that one technical section. It's up to you to decide what is rideable and what warrants a dismount to hike-a-bike.

Beginner: Easy rides with few or no obstacles. The trails are wide, smooth, and flat. There are also no steep sections.

Intermediate: Routes are rougher and narrower, with smaller, unavoidable obstacles that are easy to roll over. Intermediate trails can also be steeper. The vast majority of routes in Park City fall under this category.

Advanced: Narrow and uneven trail tread combined with steeper grades and larger obstacles like rock drops, large roots, and tight corners with loose soil. These routes require advanced skills to clean safely.

Expert: The most difficult trails with very steep grades, continuous uneven tread, large drops, challenging rock gardens, and big, unavoidable jumps. These types of routes are mostly found in lift-served bike parks where body armor and full-face helmets are recommended.

Fitness Intensity

This category is based on a scale of effort to complete a route, quantified by mileage and elevation gain. Some trails are short but steep, while others are very long, but without much climbing. To come up with the fitness rating, I always choose the more difficult rating between mileage and vertical. Again, these ratings are subjective and dependent on a rider's individual fitness level.

- **Easy:** 10 miles or less and/or 1000 or less feet of vertical gain
- **Moderate:** 10–15 miles and/or 1000 to 2000 feet of vertical gain
- **Strenuous:** 15–25 miles and/or 2000 to 3000 feet of vertical gain
- **Very Strenuous:** 25–plus miles and/or over 3000 feet of vertical gain

SEASON

Because of Park City's elevation and mountainous terrain, bike season generally runs from late spring until mid-autumn. Some lower-elevation trails are rideable in early spring, while the highest trails don't open until July. I've indicated the best time of year to ride each route, but that may vary based on the weather and snowpack of any given year.

MAP

Each route in this book includes a simple topographic map, but it's always a good idea to supplement with other maps. Every year, Mountain Trails Foundation publishes an updated trail map of the entire Park City network; it's the best map to bring on your ride if you want to link the routes in this book with other trails. The Adventure Maps Salt Lake City, Park City, and the Wasatch is another good resource. If you cannot find another resource, I've included the name of the USGS 7.5-minute TOPO maps that encompass each route.

GPS COORDINATES

The GPS coordinates listed in this category are for a route's trailhead. Each coordinate is listed in degrees, minutes, and decimal seconds using the WGS84 datum (for example: 40°36'24.65"N, 111°33'17.95"W).

BEYOND THE ROUTE DATA

The **Overview** section describes the route and what you can expect. **Getting There** provides basic driving directions from a major intersection in the nearest town. The **Mileage Log** details every intersection and point of interest on the route. **Options** offers alternatives to the highlighted route.

Park City and the surrounding area are lousy with singletrack. There are over 400 miles of nonmotorized trails for mountain bikers to enjoy. If you look at a trail map, you'll get heart palpitations trying to figure out what to ride. So in this book, I've highlighted what I consider to be the best rides within this massive, mind-boggling network. However, with so many cross trails and options, there is no limit to how these trails can be explored. I offer this guidebook as a starting point. Use it to learn the trails, then go out and discover your own favorite ways to ride the best mountain biking trail system in the world.

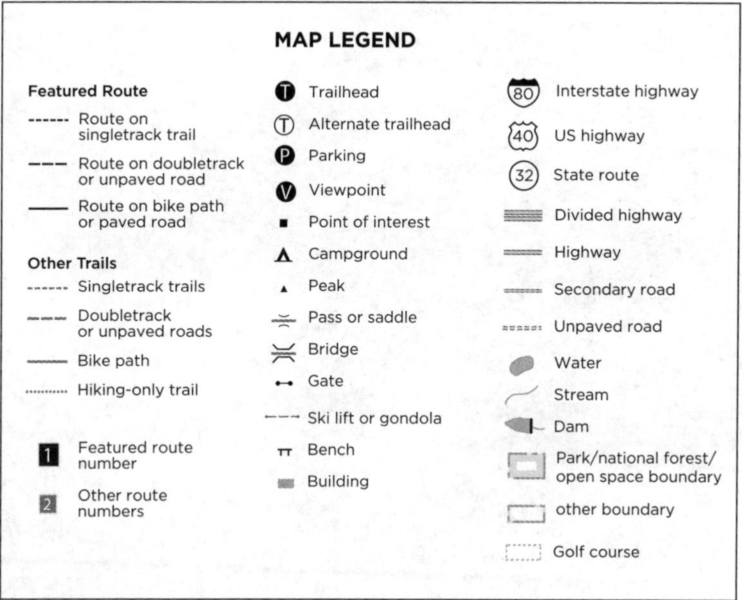

PARK CITY

The center of mountain biking in Park City is, of course, the city itself. The routes in this region cover downtown trails as well as the singletrack network on Park City Mountain ski resort. The trailheads in town are the most centrally located, which makes Park City the hub of the entire network. You can connect to Deer Valley, Canyons Village, and the Utah Olympic Park trails from here or even climb to the Wasatch Crest. Overall, the riding in Park City central is on buff singletrack with few technical sections, so these trails are ideal for intermediate riders seeking stout climbs and fun descents.

Don't forget to check out the mining ruins. Signs at each timeworn relic about the silver boom from days past are very informative. Plus, when you're finished with a ride, you're only a few pedal strokes away from one of Park City's numerous restaurants and bars for a post-ride celebratory beverage.

In general, the trails in this region are open from early summer through mid-autumn, depending on snowpack. Lower elevation trails, like Lost Prospector (Route 6) and the Rail Trail (Route 7), are usually dry in the spring.

1 ARMSTRONG TO SPIRO

LOOP

Trail Type: 95% singletrack, 5% doubletrack
Distance: 10 miles
Elevation Gain/Loss: 1650/1650 feet
High Point: 8365 feet
Ride Time: 2–3 hours
Technical Difficulty: Intermediate
Fitness Intensity: Moderate

Season: Summer–fall
Maps: Mountain Trails Foundation Summer Map; Adventure Maps Salt Lake City, Park City, and the Wasatch; USGS 7.5-minute Park City West
GPS: 40°39'10.54"N, 111°30'31.08"W
Land Manager: Park City Mountain

Opposite: *Traversing a wide open ski run on Jenni's Trail (Route 4)*

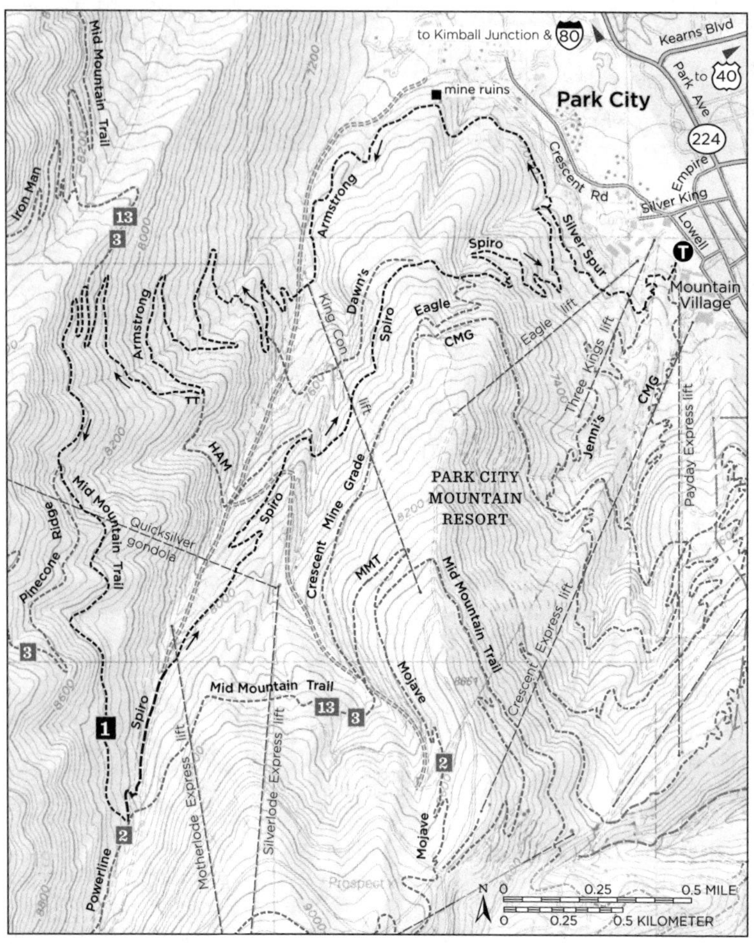

OVERVIEW

If I had to venture a guess, I'd say the Armstrong–Spiro loop is the most crowded route on Park City Mountain. But don't let that deter you—its overwhelming popularity is well deserved. First of all, Armstrong is four miles of uphill-only climbing. I bet you won't find a more leisurely and enjoyable ascent anywhere else in the Wasatch. At the top, Armstrong connects with the Mid Mountain Trail (MMT), a classic in its own right. In fact, many consider the two-mile section of MMT to be the best part. Finally, the loop has a grand finale with a descent of Spiro. Just about everybody uses this ultimate, classic Park City trail. And when the singletrack is in good condition, it's among the most fun downhills around.

This intermediate-level loop is the perfect length for a quick fix, but there are options to make it shorter (via the HAM Trail) or longer (with an out-and-back on Pinecone) as time allows. Start from The Mountain Village base at Park City Mountain and begin the ride on Silver Spur.

GETTING THERE

From the intersection of Park Avenue and Kearns Boulevard in Park City, drive south on Park Avenue for 0.3 mile. Turn right onto Empire Avenue, following the signs to Park City Mountain. Empire Avenue curves back south for 0.1 mile to Silver King Drive, where you turn right again. After only a few hundred feet, turn left on Lowell Avenue and park in the Park City Mountain Village parking lot. The singletrack trails begin on the southwest side of the lot at the bottom of the ski resort's beginner runs.

MILEAGE LOG

0.0 From the parking lot, go to the southwest end by a lodge. Get on the singletrack marked by signs that read "Jenni's Trail and Silver Spur." Begin pedaling up into the ski resort.

0.2 At the intersection of Jenni's and Silver Spur, go right on Silver Spur. From here the trail traverses through a large Gambel oak grove toward Armstrong. The trail gets narrow in the trees and there are a lot of hikers, so be aware.

0.6 Silver Spur intersects with the Spiro Trail. Go right while following the signs for Armstrong. Soon after, begin the uphill-only Armstrong Trail. Armstrong traverses northwest on a bench overlooking town. Stop and check out the mining ruins crumbling just off the trail. After the ruins, Armstrong goes west into a forest so shady you'll want to take off your sunglasses. This section is one of my favorite parts of the climb.

1.9 The trail exits the forest into a large meadow at the base of the King Con chairlift. Stay below the lift and ignore the doubletrack that goes uphill. The Armstrong Trail continues into the woods on the other side of the meadow.

2.2   At a fork, stay right on Armstrong (left is the uphill-only Dawn's Trail).

3.6   After consistent switchbacking up through evergreen forests, you'll come to a fork with the HAM Trail, which connects on the left. A good place to take a breather or eat a snack, this junction has a bench and an excellent view. For a shortcut option, you may follow HAM and connect to a lower section of Spiro. Otherwise, for the longer loop described here, stay right on Armstrong.

Mine ruins along the trail at the beginning of the climb up Armstrong

4.2 On this most technical part of Armstrong, you must negotiate a chunky rock garden, followed by a very tight switchback, followed by yet another chunky rock garden.

4.5 Armstrong ends at the Mid Mountain Trail (MMT). Go left on MMT and follow the signs for Pinecone Ridge and Spiro.

5.0 After a few switchbacks and a traverse south, the Mid Mountain Trail intersects with Pinecone Ridge. This fantastic 4-mile, 1600-foot climb to the Wasatch Crest is also a banger downhill, with fast flow and even some opportunities to get some air. If you have the time, you may want to extend this loop with an out-and-back on Pinecone. For the featured route, stay left on Mid Mountain. From here the trail descends easily through smooth berms and fast, straight sections.

6.2 Mid Mountain intersects with Powerline. Go left where a sign indicates the direction for Spiro. Enjoy a couple of fun berms before the single-track connects with a doubletrack. This dirt road is part of Spiro. Go left (downhill) and hang on for a fast and loose ride. But don't go too fast or you'll blow right past the turnoff onto the singletrack.

6.6 Exit the road onto the Spiro singletrack on the right. From here it's a killer ride with some flow, corners, rock gardens, and straightaways where you can go fast. Spiro pretty much throws everything at you.

7.5 The bottom of the HAM Trail comes in on the left. Stay right on Spiro to climb for a bit before traversing over a rock garden known to have caused many pinch flats.

8.1 Pass the bottom of Dawn's Trail on the left. Stay right on Spiro.

8.3 Go left on Spiro at the next fork (right is Eagle).

9.3 You're back at the intersection with Armstrong and Silver Spur. Go right on Silver Spur and take it back to the Park City Mountain Village.

10.0 You've returned to the parking lot.

OPTIONS

You may use HAM to create a shorter version of the loop. On the other hand, tacking on an out-and-back on Pinecone from the Mid Mountain Trail adds 8 miles and 1600 feet of climbing, and downhill makes this ride much more epic—I highly recommend that option if you have the time and energy!

2 SHADOW LAKE

LOOP

Trail Type: 90% singletrack, 10% doubletrack
Distance: 16 miles
Elevation Gain/Loss: 2620/2620 feet
High Point: 9125 feet
Ride Time: 4–5 hours
Technical Difficulty: Intermediate
Fitness Intensity: Strenuous

Season: Summer–fall
Maps: Mountain Trails Foundation Summer Map; Adventure Maps Salt Lake City, Park City, and the Wasatch; USGS 7.5-minute Park City West
GPS: 40°39′10.54″N, 111°30′31.08″W
Land Manager: Park City Mountain

OVERVIEW

Sometimes you need a destination to go with your ride, and lakes are always a good choice. Shadow Lake at Park City Mountain is an ideal spot to take your bike. This small, natural lake is nestled beneath Jupiter Hill just above the bottom of the Jupiter lift.

If you ask people for directions to Shadow Lake, you will likely get a few different answers. I prefer the route described here because it combines a steep ascent (read: a good workout) and very fun descent with huge alpine views. There's also much to see, like well-preserved mining-era ruins, and of course Shadow Lake itself. This ride may be best served in the hot summer months, as the high elevation and shady evergreens keep you cool. Plus, you can make like a local and energize your ride with a cold-water swim.

Shadow Lake attracts more than just mountain bikers and hikers. Watch for wildlife around the water. Moose are especially common, so keep your distance if you encounter one.

GETTING THERE

From the intersection of Park Avenue and Kearns Boulevard in Park City, drive south on Park Avenue for 0.3 mile. Turn right onto Empire Avenue while following the signs to Park City Mountain. Empire Avenue curves back south for 0.1 mile to Silver King Drive. Turn right. After only a few hundred feet, turn left on Lowell Avenue and park in the Park City Mountain Village

The Shadow Lake Loop passes a high-alpine lake on a trail with nice views.

parking lot. The singletrack trails begin on the southwest side of the lot at the bottom of the ski resort's beginner runs.

MILEAGE LOG

0.0 Go to the southwest end of the parking lot by a lodge. Get on the singletrack marked by signs that say "Jenni's Trail and Silver Spur." Begin pedaling up into the ski resort.

0.2 At the intersection of Jenni's Trail and Silver Spur, go right on Silver Spur. From here the trail traverses through a large Gambel oak grove toward Armstrong. The trail gets narrow through the trees and there are a lot of hikers, so be aware.

0.6 Silver Spur intersects with the Spiro Trail. Stay right on Silver Spur while following the signs for Armstrong. This is the start of the uphill-only Armstrong Trail, which traverses northwest with a view overlooking town. Be sure to stop and check out the mining ruins crumbling just off of the trail. After the ruins, Armstrong goes west into a forest so shady you'll want to take off your sunglasses—one of my favorite parts of the climb.

1.9 The trail exits the forest into a large meadow at the base of the King Con chairlift. Stay below the lift, ignoring the doubletrack that goes uphill. The Armstrong Trail continues into the woods on the other side of the meadow.

2.2 At the next fork, stay right on Armstrong (left is the uphill-only Dawn's Trail).

3.6 After consistent switchbacking up through evergreen forests, you'll come to a fork with the HAM Trail, which connects on the left. There's a bench to sit on and an excellent view to enjoy—take a breather or eat a snack. To continue, stay right on Armstrong.

4.2 This is the most technical part of Armstrong, where you must negotiate chunky rock garden, followed by a very tight switchback, followed by yet another chunky rock garden.

4.5 Armstrong ends at the Mid Mountain Trail (MMT). Go left on MMT while following the signs for Pinecone Ridge and Spiro.

5.0 After a few switchbacks and a traverse south, the MMT intersects with Pinecone Ridge. (A fantastic optional out-and-back that's 4 miles long with a 1600-foot climb to the Wasatch Crest, Pinecone Ridge is a banger downhill, with fast flow and even places to get some air.) For Shadow Lake, stay left on the MMT. From here the trail descends with an easy drop through smooth berms and fast, straight sections.

6.2 Mid Mountain intersects with Powerline on the right and Spiro on the left. Go right (uphill) on Powerline. The next few miles are the steepest part of the ride, since the trail basically goes straight uphill. Dig deep and grind it out in granny gear.

6.8 Powerline ends at the Comstock Mine Road. Soon after you pedal up this doubletrack, you'll see the old Comstock Mine building on your left. Silver was mined here from 1885 to 1925. This building is among the most well-preserved in Park City and you won't be able to resist pulling out the camera and taking a look around. Right after the mine, Comstock Mine becomes singletrack. Continue up.

7.3 Comstock Mine ends at a dirt road, also called Comstock. Go right on this road, while continuing uphill. A sign here indicates the way to Shadow Lake.

7.5 Stay on Comstock Mine Road as you pass the Jupiter chairlift loading station. At a switchback, stay right on the doubletrack Wasatch Crest Connector, which heads uphill underneath the lift. A few yards later, you'll come to Shadow Lake. Enjoy the scene, soak your feet, or cool off with a swim in the cold water. When you're ready, get back on Wasatch Crest Connector on the northwest side of the lake and pedal up the doubletrack—the ride's high point waits ahead.

8.3 Leave the road by going left on the Shadow Lake Loop singletrack (if you stay right, you'll end up at Scotts Pass.) A few dozen yards later, stay left on Shadow Lake Loop (on the right is Blazing Saddles,

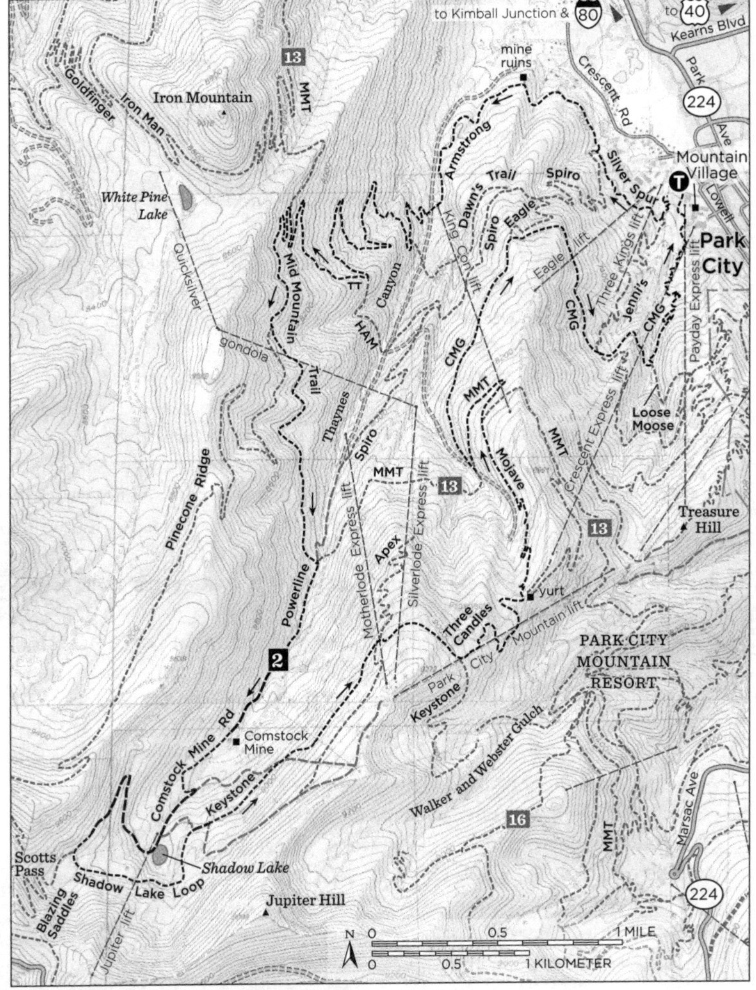

which also goes up to Scotts Pass). Shadow Lake Loop goes downhill from here, looping above the lake. The descent is really fun, with some technical features and nice flow.

9.2   Shadow Lake Loop ends at a doubletrack. Take the right fork, basically staying straight. You are now on Keystone. It doesn't take long for the doubletrack to become singletrack once again. This is another nice trail with good flow.

10.2   At an intersection with Apex, stay straight on Keystone.

10.6   At a three-way intersection, leave Keystone and go left onto Three Candles. This is another fun downhill with berms and good flow. But this trail is also a popular connection for uphill riders, so keep your speed in check.

11.3   Three Candles ends at the yurt on Thaynes Road. Go left on the road and immediately go right onto Mojave. This is downhill-only and great fun. You must negotiate some rock features, but the difficulty remains intermediate.

12.3   Mojave Trail ends at the Mid Mountain Trail. Go left on the MMT.

12.9   MMT comes to a dirt road called Claim Jumper. Take a hard right onto the Crescent Mine Grade (CMG) singletrack. This part of your descent is much different than Mojave. Instead of berms and flow, you'll experience a more rough-and-tumble trail that is equal parts fast and rough. There are few corners, as CMG traverses much of Park City Mountain's ski runs.

13.9   At a fork, stay right on CMG (left is Eagle). Soon after this intersection, CMG goes under the Eagle chairlift.

14.6   CMG intersects with Jenni's Trail. Stay left (straight) on CMG. From here CMG is downhill-only, so open 'er up and enjoy the ride.

15.1   CMG intersects with Loose Moose on the right. Stay left and continue downhill on CMG. Near the bottom there is a series of very fun berms with nice flow. It's a great way to end the loop.

15.7   At the bottom of CMG, get off your bike and walk it through the Park City Mountain Village base area. Walking your bike through here is a requirement per resort operations. Once you've cleared the roller coasters and throngs of children, get back on your bike and ride it to the parking lot.

16.0   End of ride.

OPTIONS

There are so many ways to get to Shadow Lake from Park City that it's impossible to detail them all. I suggest you use the Mountain Trails Foundation Summer Map to piece together alternative routes. You'll probably never ride to Shadow Lake the same way twice.

3 PARK CITY IMBA SUPER EPIC

LOOP

Trail Type: 95% singletrack, 5% doubletrack
Distance: 32 miles
Elevation Gain/Loss: 4100/4100 feet
High Point: 9880 feet
Ride Time: 5–6 hours
Technical Difficulty: Advanced
Fitness Intensity: Very Strenuous
Season: Summer–fall

Maps: Mountain Trails Foundation Summer Map; Adventure Maps Salt Lake City, Park City, and the Wasatch; USGS 7.5-minute Park City West, Brighton
GPS: 40°39'10.54"N, 111°30'31.08"W
Land Manager: Park City Mountain, Uinta-Wasatch-Cache National Forest

OVERVIEW

Park City is an International Mountain Bicycling Association (IMBA) Gold Ride Center. With over 450 miles of singletrack accessible from town, you can create a ride for any length or skill level that your mind can conjure up. One such ride is the Park City IMBA Super Epic.

IMBA has created a list of "Epics," rides that meet specific criteria, found around the world. At least 20 miles long, Epics are demanding, technically and physically challenging, mostly singletrack trails in a remote backcountry setting. The route outlined here is not the "official" Park City IMBA Epic Loop, which is 23 miles and includes paved bike trails; rather, this "super" version—a 32-mile bruiser of mostly singletrack—is a much more satisfying ride. The loop begins at the base of Park City Mountain and climbs to the Wasatch Crest. It traverses to the Canyons side of the resort,

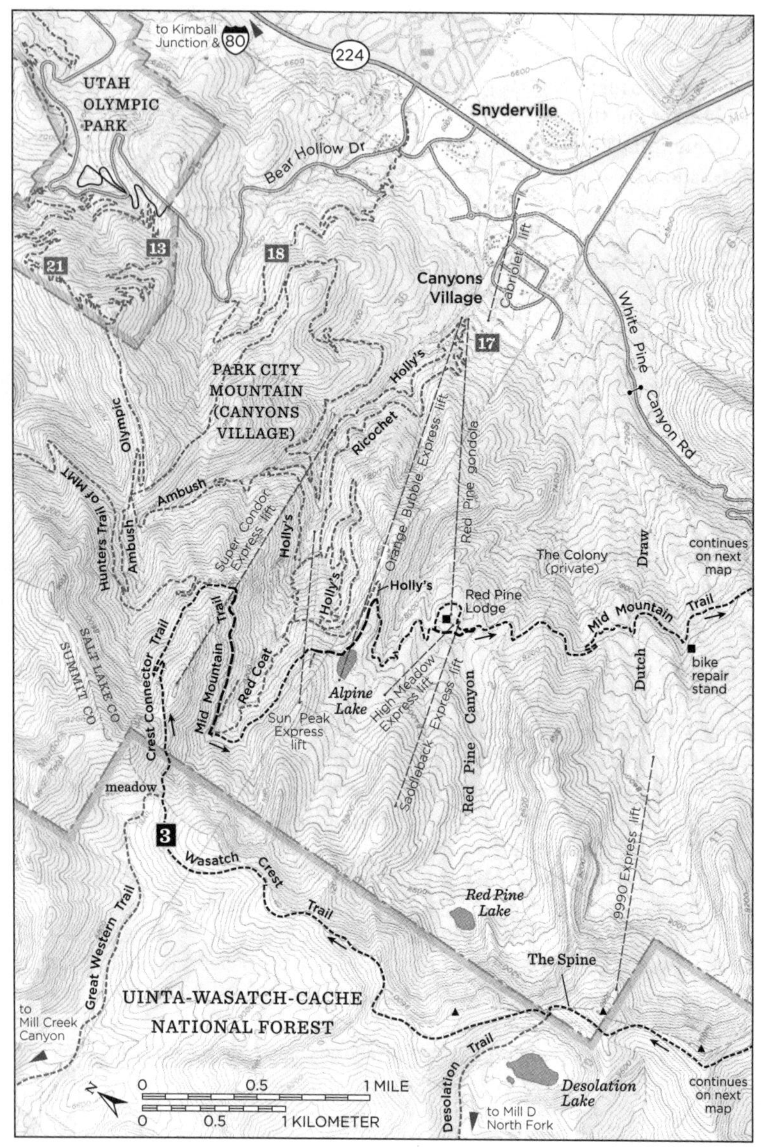

to Kimball Junction & 80
224
UTAH OLYMPIC PARK
Snyderville
Bear Hollow Dr
13
21
18
Canyons Village
Cabriolet lift
17
PARK CITY MOUNTAIN (CANYONS VILLAGE)
Holly's
Ricochet
White Pine Canyon Rd
Olympic
Orange Bubble Express lift
Red Pine gondola
Ambush
Ambush
Hunters Trail
Jo of Mmt Trail
The Colony (private)
continues on next map
Super Condor Express lift
Holly's
Holly's
Holly's
Red Pine Lodge
Mid Mountain Trail
Crest Connector Trail
SALT LAKE CO
SUMMIT CO
Mid Mountain Trail
Red Coat
High Meadow Express lift
Dutch Draw
bike repair stand
Alpine Lake
Sun Peak Express lift
Saddleback Express lift
Red Pine Canyon
meadow
3
9990 Express lift
Wasatch Crest Trail
Great Western Trail
Red Pine Lake
The Spine
to Mill Creek Canyon
UINTA-WASATCH-CACHE NATIONAL FOREST
Desolation Trail
Desolation Lake
continues on next map
N
0   0.5   1 MILE
0   0.5   1 KILOMETER
to Mill D North Fork

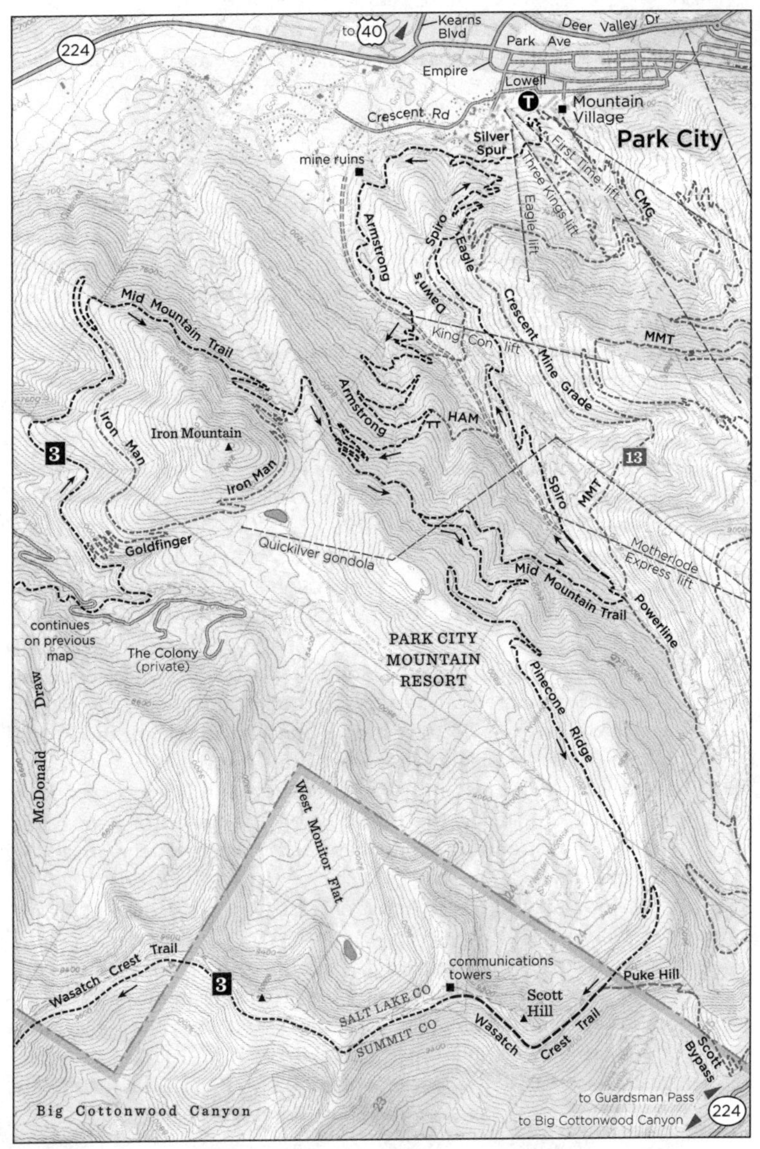
to 40
224
Kearns Blvd
Deer Valley Dr
Park Ave
Empire
Lowell
T
Mountain Village
Park City
Crescent Rd
Silver Spur
First Time lift
Three Kings lift
Eagler lift
CMG
mine ruins
Armstrong
Spiro
Eagle
Dawn's
Mid Mountain Trail
King Con lift
Crescent Mine Grade
MMT
Iron Man
Iron Mountain
Armstrong
TT
HAM
13
3
Iron Man
Spiro
MMT
Goldfinger
Quicksilver gondola
Motherlode Express lift
Mid Mountain Trail
Powerline
continues on previous map
PARK CITY MOUNTAIN RESORT
The Colony (private)
McDonald Draw
Pinecone Ridge
West Monitor Flat
Wasatch Crest Trail
3
communications towers
Puke Hill
Scott Hill
SALT LAKE CO
SUMMIT CO
Wasatch
Crest Trail
Scott Bypass
Big Cottonwood Canyon
to Guardsman Pass
to Big Cottonwood Canyon
224

then returns to Park City Mountain via Mid Mountain Trail. The loop finishes with a descent on Spiro back to town for a leg-crushing 4100 feet of elevation gain, 32 miles, and a whole lot of scenery to take in.

GETTING THERE

From the intersection of Park Avenue and Kearns Boulevard in Park City, drive south on Park Avenue for 0.3 mile. Turn right onto Empire Avenue while following the signs to Park City Mountain. Empire Avenue curves back south for 0.1 mile to Silver King Drive. Turn right. After only a few hundred feet, turn left on Lowell Avenue and park in the Park City Mountain Village parking lot. The singletrack trails begin on the southwest side of the lot at the bottom of the ski resort's beginner runs.

MILEAGE LOG

0.0   From the parking lot, go to the southwest end by a lodge. Get on the singletrack marked by signs that say "Jenni's Trail and Silver Spur." Begin pedaling up into the ski resort.

0.2   At the intersection of Jenni's Trail and Silver Spur, go right on Silver Spur. From here the trail traverses through a large Gambel oak grove toward Armstrong. The trail narrows through the trees and there are a lot of hikers, so be aware.

0.6   Silver Spur intersects with the Spiro Trail. Go right while following the signs for Armstrong. This is the start of the uphill-only Armstrong Trail, which traverses northwest on a bench overlooking town. After the mine ruins, Armstrong goes west into a forest.

1.9   The trail exits the forest into a large meadow at the base of the King Con chairlift. Stay below the lift and ignore the doubletrack that goes uphill. The Armstrong Trail continues into the woods on the other side of the meadow.

2.2   At the fork, stay right on Armstrong (to the left is the uphill-only Dawn's Trail).

3.6   After consistent switchbacking up through evergreen forests, you'll come to a fork with the HAM Trail, which connects on the left. This is a good place to take a breather, eat a snack, and enjoy the view. When you've finished with your break, stay right on Armstrong.

4.5   Armstrong ends at the Mid Mountain Trail (MMT). Go left on MMT while following the signs for Pinecone Ridge and Spiro.

With striking vistas, it's no wonder why "The Crest" is so popular.

5.0   After a few switchbacks and a traverse south, MMT intersects with Pinecone Ridge, a fantastic 4-mile, 1600-foot climb to the Wasatch Crest. Go right onto Pinecone Ridge and enjoy this epic ascent.

9.1   Pinecone Ridge ends at the Wasatch Crest where it intersects with the top of Puke Hill. Take in the view, then go right (west) on the Wasatch Crest Trail.

9.5   Pass the communications towers on Scott Hill. At this point the doubletrack ends and the singletrack begins. This next section is among the most scenic, as you're treated with views of Big Cottonwood Canyon's row of high-alpine peaks. It's mostly a mellow, rolling downhill save for one decent climb (I call it the "red dirt climb"). Don't forget to stop and take in the scenery from time to time.

13.0   Welcome to The Spine: a fin of sharp, steep rocks that only the best and bravest mountain bikers can ride. There is an easier route to the left of The Spine's crest, but it's still very technical. Because of the difficulty and the high possibility of injury from a crash, most riders choose to walk this part, and there is no shame in doing so.

13.3   At the bottom of The Spine, come to a fork. Stay right on the Wasatch Crest Trail, toward Mill Creek Canyon and Park City Mountain (the left fork goes to Desolation Lake and the Desolation Trail, which leads to Mill D North Fork). After taking the right fork, climb for a bit before descending over several technical rock gardens. They're nowhere as scary as The Spine but still may challenge you.

15.4 The Wasatch Crest Trail ends in a large meadow at a three-way inter-section. Left is the Great Western Trail, which falls into Mill Creek Canyon (open to mountain bikers on even-numbered days only). Instead, go right on the Crest Connector (also called Ridge Connector) into Park City Mountain.

16.6 Crest Connector ends at the Mid Mountain Trail. Go right on MMT.

17.0 MMT intersects a doubletrack. Go left (downhill) on the road, which is still part of the MMT.

17.3 At the bottom of the hill, you'll see Red Coat on the left. Leave the doubletrack by going right on MMT, which is now singletrack again.

18.0 MMT runs into a dirt road near Alpine Lake beneath the Orange Bubble Express chairlift. Stay left on the MMT singletrack.

18.3 MMT makes a sharp right turn where it once again ends up on a dirt road. To cut the IMBA Super Epic short, you can take a left here on Holly's down to Canyons Village. Otherwise, stay right on MMT.

19.1 Mid Mountain Trail comes to Red Pine Lodge and the top terminal of the Red Pine gondola, which provides lift-served mountain biking. The lodge, open in summer, is a great place to stop and refuel. If you need to get back to town, you may ride the gondola down to Canyons Village.

   To continue your super epic, pass the lodge and continue on MMT. At this point you enter The Colony—an exclusive, mansion-filled neighborhood. You must stay on the trail for the next two miles, as you are now surrounded by private property. You're not even allowed to ride on the neighborhood streets. You will cross several paved roads. MMT is easy to pick up on the other side of each road crossing.

22.2 Goldfinger enters in on the right—stay left on MMT. Goldfinger switch-backs up to Iron Man, which eventually reconnects with Mid Mountain Trail, so this is another option to change up this route.

24.2 Mid Mountain Trail makes a hard left turn, where it connects with Iron Man. Take that hard left and continue on MMT.

25.7 At a fork, the other end of Iron Man is on the right. Stay left on MMT.

26.2 Mid Mountain Trail connects with Armstrong. Congrats! You've completed a huge loop. But you're not going downhill yet. As Armstrong is uphill only, you must stay right on MMT and go toward Spiro.

26.7 You're back at the bottom of Pinecone Ridge. This time, stay left on MMT (unless you really want to do another loop).

28.0 MMT runs into an intersection with Powerline. Go left here, where a sign indicates the direction for Spiro. There are a couple of fun berms here before the singletrack connects with a doubletrack. This dirt road is part of Spiro. Go left (downhill) and hang on for a fast and loose ride. But don't go too fast or you'll blow right past the turnoff onto the singletrack.

28.4 Exit the road onto the Spiro singletrack on the right. From here it's a killer ride with some flow, corners, rock gardens, and straightaways where you can go fast. Spiro pretty much throws everything at you.

29.3 The bottom of the HAM Trail comes in on the left. Stay right on Spiro. At this point, Spiro climbs for a bit before traversing over a rock garden that has been known to cause many pinch flats.

30.0 You'll see the bottom of Dawn's Trail on the left. Stay right on Spiro.

30.2 The trail forks. Go left on Spiro (right is Eagle).

31.4 Here you're back at the intersection with Armstrong and Silver Spur. Go right on Silver Spur and take it back to the Park City Mountain Village.

32.0 You're back at the parking lot and at the end of a super epic ride!

OPTIONS

You can ride the official IMBA Epic, which is a shorter variation, by descending to Canyons Village from the Wasatch Crest, then pedaling the paved bike trail back to town. For an even shorter version, use a shuttle service to drop you off at Guardsman Pass to cut out the uphill part of the ride. But to earn bragging rights, stick to the route above and experience the best riding Park City has to offer.

4 JENNI'S TO MOJAVE TO CMG

LOOP

Trail Type: 95% singletrack, 5% doubletrack

Distance: 10.8 miles

Elevation Gain/Loss: 1870/1870 feet

High Point: 8646 feet

Ride Time: 2–3 hours

Technical Difficulty: Intermediate

Fitness Intensity: Moderate

Season: Summer–fall

Maps: Mountain Trails Foundation Summer Map; Adventure Maps Salt Lake City, Park City, and the Wasatch; USGS 7.5-minute Park City West

GPS: 40°39'10.54"N, 111°30'31.08"W

Land Manager: Park City Mountain

OVERVIEW

The Jenni's to Mojave to CMG loop offers a great overview of the Park City Mountain trail network. In fact, after one lap, you'll understand why Park City was named a Gold-Level IMBA Riding Area. Of the dozens of singletrack options in this area, this one is particularly popular among locals.

The loop begins at the resort base area and goes up Jenni's Trail. This uphill-only section is the best and preferred way to access all the trails on this part of the mountain, with a pleasant climb through shaded aspen forests that alternate with open ski runs. A final climb up Tommy's Two Step puts riders atop Mojave, a downhill-only trail with great flow and fast cornering. Below that, the Mid Mountain Trail (MMT) connects with Crescent Mine Grade (CMG) for a straight and speedy final descent. You'll encounter very few corners, so you can let off the brakes and go scary fast. After losing a ton of elevation, CMG winds down through evergreen forests and the lower ski runs, where a fun berm section returns you to the base.

If you're allergic to pedaling uphill, taking the Crescent Express chairlift will get you close to Mojave and the downhill section of this route.

GETTING THERE

From the intersection of Park Avenue and Kearns Boulevard in Park City, drive south on Park Avenue for 0.3 mile. Turn right onto Empire Avenue while following the signs to Park City Mountain. Empire Avenue curves back south for 0.1 mile to Silver King Drive. Turn right. After only a few hundred feet, turn left on Lowell Avenue and park in the Park City Mountain Village parking lot. The singletrack trails begin on the southwest side of the lot at the bottom of the ski resort's beginner runs.

MILEAGE LOG

0.0 From the parking lot, go to the southwest end by a lodge. Get on the singletrack marked by signs that say "Jenni's Trail and Silver Spur." Begin pedaling up into the ski resort.

0.2 At the fork, stay left on Jenni's. The right fork is Silver Spur. Jenni's really starts climbing and crosses a few doubletracks as it switchbacks beneath the Three Kings chairlift. Cross the roads and continue. Jenni's is uphill for only the first 1.5 miles.

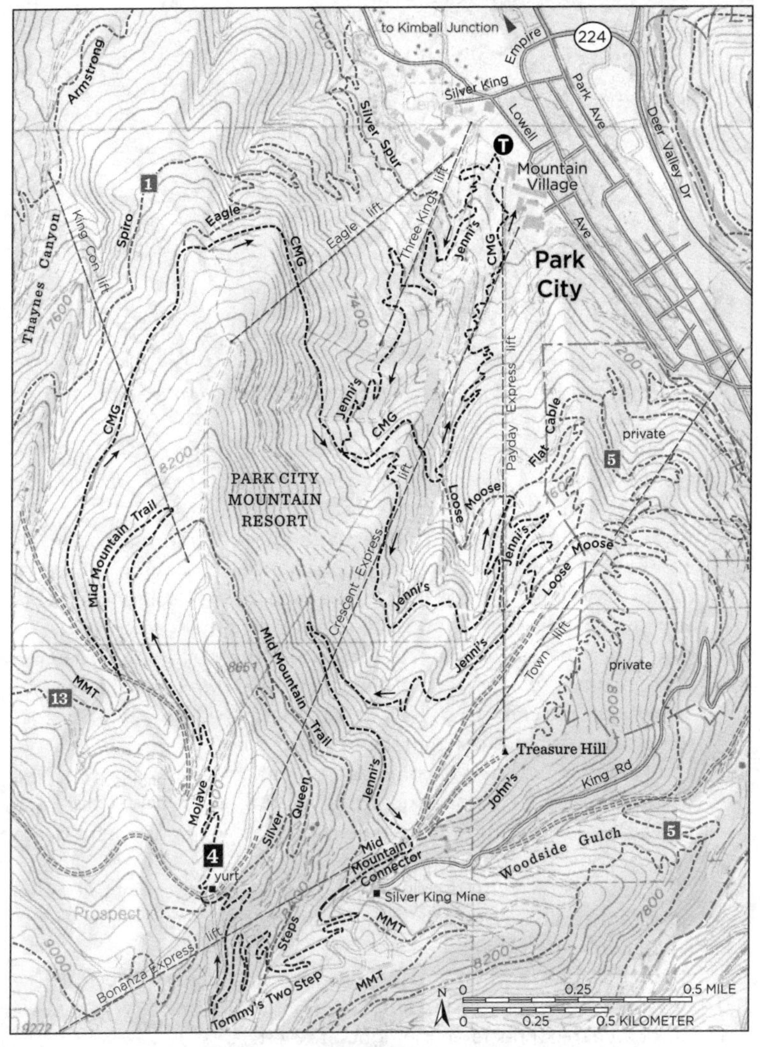
to Kimball Junction
224
Empire
Silver King
Lowell
Armstrong
Thaynes Canyon
King Con lift
Spiro
1
Eagle
CMG
Eagle lift
Silver Spur
Three King's lift
Jenni's
CMG
Mountain Village
Park Ave
Ave
Deer Valley Dr
Park City
7600
7400
8200
Jenni's
CMG
lift
Crescent Express
CMG
PARK CITY MOUNTAIN RESORT
Mid Mountain Trail
Payday Express lift
Loose Moose
Flat Cable
7600
200
private
5
Jenni's
Jenni's
Loose Moose
8000
MMT
13
8661
Mid Mountain Trail
Jenni's
Town lift
private
Mojave
Silver Queen
Jenni's
Treasure Hill
John's
King Rd
4
yurt
Mid Mountain Connector
Silver King Mine
Woodside Gulch
5
7600
7800
Prospect
8500
Steps
MMT
8200
9000
Bonanza Express lift
9222
Tommy's Two Step
MMT
N
0   0.25   0.5 MILE
0   0.25   0.5 KILOMETER

A thrilling descent on Mojave just before it connects with the Mid Mountain Trail

1.5   At the four-way intersection, keep going straight on Jenni's. The cross-trail is CMG. Soon after this point Jenni's crosses a doubletrack and descends for a short while before climbing again.

2.6   After going under the Payday Express chairlift, you reach a major intersection that is a bit confusing. You'll want to stay on Jenni's by taking a hard right (going straight takes you to Flat Cable and left puts you on Loose Moose). From here Jenni's climbs more steeply.

3.2   At the intersection with Loose Moose, keep going straight on Jenni's.

4.5   Jenni's comes to a dirt road at the top of the Town Lift. Take the first singletrack you come to on the right. This is the Mid Mountain Connector. It soon becomes doubletrack as you ascend.

4.7   Mid Mountain Trail (MMT) comes in on the right. Stay straight on the doubletrack as it continues uphill. At the top of this climb, the track curves around and becomes singletrack again where it enters dense woods. You are now on the MMT.

4.9   MMT intersects with Tommy's Two Step. This is designated as an uphill-only trail. Go right on Tommy's as the trail switchbacks up into a beautiful aspen grove.

5.4   Steps Trail intersects on the right. Stay left on Tommy's Two Step.

6.0   Keystone Trail enters on the left. Stay right on Tommy's Two Step.

6.3   Silver Queen connects on the right. Stay left.

6.4   Tommy's Two Step ends at a dirt road. Go left on this road for a short climb to a yurt. This is a great place to rest and have a bite to eat. To continue, go around to the back of the yurt on the road. Here you will find the start of the Mojave Trail on the right. Mojave is a downhill-only trail, which is good, because it's perfect for hitting corners at speed without having to worry about uphill traffic. This fun descent has large berms and fast straightaways.

7.7 Mojave ends at the Mid Mountain Trail. Go left on MMT while following the signs to CMG. The trail goes underneath the King Con lift at the next switchback.

8.0 Mid Mountain crosses a dirt road. Instead, take a hard right onto CMG. This part of your descent is much different than Mojave. Instead of berms and flow, you'll experience a more rough-and-tumble trail that is equal parts fast and rough. There are few corners as CMG traverses much of Park City Mountain's ski runs.

9.0 At a fork, stay right on CMG (left is Eagle). Soon after this intersection CMG goes under the Eagle chairlift.

9.7 You're back at the intersection with Jenni's that you encountered on the way up. Go straight and stay on CMG. From here CMG is downhill only, so open 'er up and enjoy the ride.

10.2 CMG intersects with Loose Moose on the right. Stay left and continue downhill on CMG. Near the bottom there is a series of very fun berms with nice flow. It's a great way to end the loop.

10.8 At the bottom of CMG, get off your bike and walk it through the Park City Mountain Village base area, a requirement per resort operations. Once you've cleared the roller coasters and throngs of children, ride your bike down to the parking lot.

OPTIONS

To avoid the climbs, you can take the Crescent Express high-speed quad from the base. It whisks riders almost to the yurt where the Mojave downhill begins. A short 0.2-mile ride up a dirt road gets you from the lift's top station to the yurt and Mojave. From here, follow the downhill section described in this route.

To include another fun downhill section, at mile 6.3 take the Silver Queen Trail that connects with Tommy's Two Step. This newer, downhill-only trail is super fun, with flow and berms. It connects at the bottom with Mid Mountain Trail, so you can do laps on a loop with Tommy's Two Step— highly recommended as a destination ride or to add mileage to this route.

5 OLD TOWN LOOP

LOOP

Trail Type: 83% singletrack, 12% doubletrack, 5% paved	**Season:** Summer–fall
Distance: 8 miles	**Maps:** Mountain Trails Foundation Summer Map; Adventure Maps Salt Lake City, Park City, and the Wasatch; USGS 7.5-minute Park City West, Park City East
Elevation Gain/Loss: 1445/1445 feet	
High Point: 8196 feet	
Ride Time: 2–3 hours	
Technical Difficulty: Advanced	**GPS:** 40°38'47.09"N, 111°30'05.41"W
Fitness Intensity: Moderate	**Land Manager:** Park City Mountain

OVERVIEW

As the name suggests, the Old Town Loop takes mountain bikers on a tour of Park City's mining history. The ride begins above historical Old Town and switchbacks up the mountainside on classic, hand-cut singletrack. In fact, many of the trails on this loop, such as Sweeny's Switchbacks and John's, are among the first built in the area. As you ride up steep, narrow, winding trails on Treasure Hill, you'll pass several mining relics. The most obvious are the Silver King tramway towers that long ago were part of the system used to haul ore down from the mountain.

You can link trails in many ways to create an "Old Town Loop." My variation utilizes the not-so-old Jenni's Trail to get to the top of the Town Lift and avoid any boring ascents on dirt road. From there, a twisting, root-filled, technical descent down John's is the highlight. Some parts of the trail are so narrow that modern, wide handlebars barely fit between the trees.

At the bottom of John's, a traverse on 4:20 trail, then down Gravedigger, lands riders into the bottom of Daly Canyon. This is where you can check out even more relics of Park City's mining heyday. A fast coast on dirt road and a bit more trail above town completes the loop.

GETTING THERE

From the intersection of Park Avenue and Kearns Boulevard in Park City, drive south on Park Avenue for 0.3 mile. Turn right onto Empire Avenue while following the signs to Park City Mountain. Empire Avenue curves back south for 0.1 mile to Silver King Drive. Turn right. After only a few hundred feet, turn left on Lowell Avenue and continue for 0.7 mile until the street makes a left turn. Park here along the southwest side of the road in one of the few pullouts. The Treasure Hill Trailhead is just on the other side of the metal gate that goes across a dirt road.

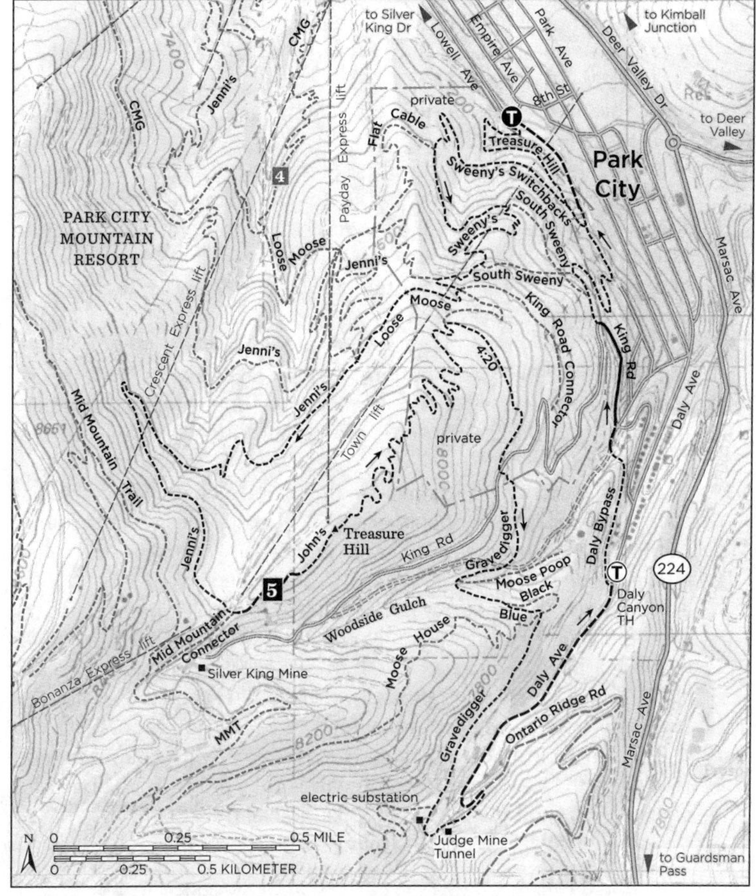

If there are no spaces, park at the Park City Mountain base area back at the corner of Lowell Avenue and Silver King Drive, and pedal to the trailhead.

MILEAGE LOG

0.0   Ride up the dirt road at the center of where Lowell Avenue curves, and go around the gate. Then go right up the Treasure Hill singletrack.

0.5   Treasure Hill ends at Sweeny's Switchbacks. Go right at the intersection. This bit of uphill is rocky, root-filled, and a reminder of what it's like to pedal up old, hand-cut trail. Stop and take a breather to check out the Silver King tramway towers.

1.0   Flat Cable Trail enters on the right. This is an optional ascent route. Stay left on Sweeny's Switchbacks.

1.2   At the intersection with the bottom of South Sweeny's on the left, stay right on Sweeny's Switchbacks. The trail gets even rockier, where good line choice is essential, especially on the tight, obstacle-filled switchbacks. Don't be ashamed to hike your bike if needed.

1.6   At the intersection with the top of South Sweeny's, stay right on Sweeny's Switchbacks.

1.7   You'll meet the top of Flat Cable on the right (you'll end up here if you choose the Flat Cable option). Stay left on Sweeny's Switchbacks. Immediately after this you come to a four-way intersection with John's Trail and King Road Connector on the left. Stay right on Sweeny's Switchbacks.

1.9   Sweeny's Switchbacks connects with Loose Moose where the trail exits the forest into an open ski run. Take Loose Moose on the right.

2.0   At the three-way intersection, go left on Jenni's. From here it's a nice, moderate climb.

3.3   Jenni's comes to an open area at the Town Lift top station. Pedal to the lift and follow the signs to John's Trail up a doubletrack that climbs a hillside—a steep and loose climb that passes mining relics. At the top, John's Trail is on the right. Head down into the trees on the singletrack. This is among the wildest descents in Park City, not because it's fast and thrilling, but because it's narrow and tight, with countless turns through a thick aspen forest. Numerous root drops, handlebar-wide squeezes through parallel tree trunks, and all those turns make this a slow, technical descent that is, in my opinion, very fun.

Relics of Park City's silver-mining past abound on the Old Town Loop.

4.6 Leave John's Trail and go right onto 4:20 Trail. This trail may be unmarked, so reference the map. 4:20 switchbacks south down the mountainside and also features tight corners.

5.0 4:20 ends at the paved King Road. Cross the road and find the Gravedigger singletrack on the other side.

5.3 Gravedigger exits onto an overgrown dirt road. Go right and up the rocky, steep grade. Luckily, it's only about 50 yards before the singletrack continues and goes down on the left. Right after this, at a bend in the trail, Moose Poop connects on the left. Stay on Gravedigger and cross on flat rocks over a dry creek.

5.5 At a fork, stay right. A sign indicates right is "blue" and left is "black." Both options are Gravedigger, and both take you to the same place. Pick your poison, but I prefer the blue line.

5.7 Gravedigger tops out on a ridge where there is a four-way intersection with Moose House on the right and the "black" Gravedigger on the left. Stay straight on Gravedigger as it descends the other side of the ridge.

6.1 Gravedigger ends at the dirt Ontario Ridge Road next to an electric substation. Ride down the road past abandoned mine buildings, such as the Judge Mine Tunnel. Stay left as the road curves past the buildings.

6.3 Leave Ontario Ridge Road and go left onto Daly Avenue. Signs indicate the way to Park City. Continue going down this road as it passes even more left-behind mining history.

6.9 Just before a metal gate at the Daly Canyon Trailhead, leave the road and go left onto the Daly Bypass singletrack.

7.2 At a dirt road, go right down to a gate at the paved King Road. Go around the gate and left on King Road. Pedal up the steep hill through a neighborhood.

7.5 When King Road curves left, leave the pavement and get on the South Sweeny access trail. Right after this, you intersect with South Sweeny proper. Take the right fork and go down.

7.8 Sweeny's Switchbacks connects on the left. Stay right and down on a road grade.

8.0 The road grade ends at Lowell Avenue and the Treasure Hill Trailhead. You've reached the end of the ride.

OPTIONS

There are numerous options in this trail network. Use the Mountain Trails Foundation Summer Map to design your own loops. One obvious option is to use John's or Flat Cable as an ascent route. For the descent, you can link together John's 99, Speedbag, Empire Link, Moose House, and more to choose your own adventure.

6 LOST PROSPECTOR LOOP

LOOP

Trail Type: 85% singletrack, 15% paved trail

Distance: 7.1 miles

Elevation Gain/Loss: 665/665 feet

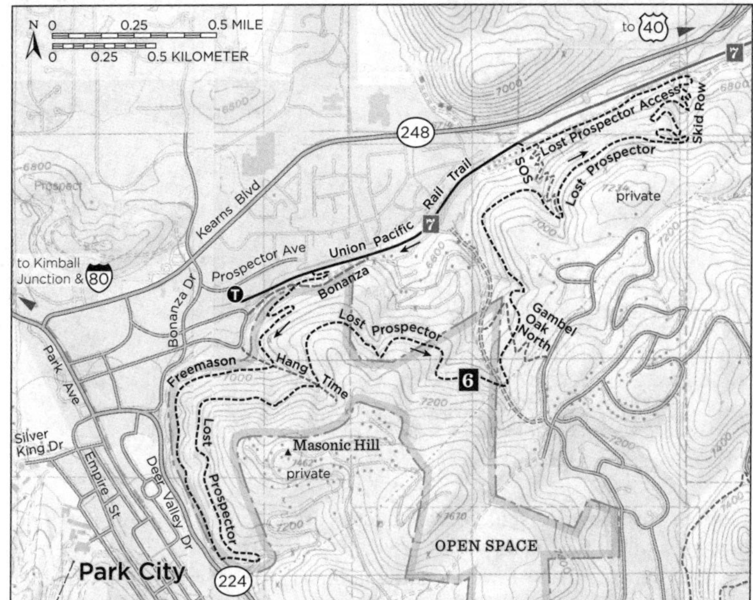

High Point: 7147 feet

Ride Time: 45 minutes to 1.5 hours

Technical Difficulty: Intermediate

Fitness Intensity: Easy

Season: Spring–fall

GPS: 40°39'40.93"N, 111°29'53.71"W

Maps: Mountain Trails Foundation Summer Map; Adventure Maps Salt Lake City, Park City, and the Wasatch; USGS 7.5-minute Park City East

Land Manager: Park City Municipal Corporation

OVERVIEW

This Park City classic is right in the middle of town on the Masonic Hill/April Mountain open space. For years the trail required mountain bikers to ride on city streets to create a loop. But in 2017, with the completion of the Freemason Trail, this ever-popular route became even better. Now mountain bikers can put together a 7.1-mile loop on mostly singletrack with just a little paved bike trail necessary for access.

The loop I've designed links several trails. You begin on the Union Pacific Rail Trail to the Freemason Trail and then enjoy a nice climb to

Lost Prospector is a good springtime ride when snow lingers higher up.

connect with Lost Prospector, which loops around to a fun descent on Skid Row back to the Rail Trail.

The route involves a few rock gardens, but all of the terrain is easy enough for intermediate riders or beginners looking for their first singletrack experience. This scenic ride with views of Park City proper can be done in about an hour, making it a great lunchtime loop or quick ride if you're short on time. This route can be ridden in either direction, but the counterclockwise option maximizes the fun with a more thrilling descent.

GETTING THERE

From the intersection of Park Avenue and Kearns Boulevard in Park City, drive northeast on Kearns Boulevard for 0.5 mile. Turn right on Bonanza Drive and keep your eyes peeled for the "Rail Trail" sign. Turn left onto Prospector Avenue, then right into the parking lot for the Rail Trail. Locate the trail entrance at the south end of the parking lot.

MILEAGE LOG

0.0 Follow the dirt trail a short distance uphill to the paved Rail Trail. Go left (northeast) while keeping an eye out for the Freemason singletrack trail on your right.

0.25 Freemason joins Rail Trail on the right. Take it and ride up into an aspen forest on a very enjoyable and easy ascent, with bermed corners and a low climbing grade. When the trail exits the forest, you'll see nice views of Park City and the ski resort above town.

0.3 At a fork with a footpath, stay right on Freemason. Immediately after, you'll come to a fork with a doubletrack called Bonanza. This time stay left on Freemason.

0.9 At the intersection with Hang Time, stay left on Freemason.

1.7 At the intersection with Masonic, take a hard left onto the Lost Prospector Trail. This is the old, classic trail. It traverses back around Masonic Hill and above the way you came in on Freemason.

1.9 Masonic meets up with Lost Prospector again. This trail intersects Lost Prospector several times in the next few miles. Ignore them all and stay on Lost Prospector. Each intersection is well signed, and you'll know you're on the right path because Masonic is narrower and much more overgrown. Because Masonic parallels and intersects Lost Prospector so much, I've left it off the map to avoid confusion.

2.6 At the intersection with Hang Time, stay straight on Lost Prospector.

3.5 Cross the doubletrack and continue straight on Lost Prospector.

3.6 You'll come to an Intersection with Gambel Oak North. Continue straight on Lost Prospector.

4.4 The SOS Trail comes in from the left. Stay straight on Lost Prospector.

4.8 Lost Prospector Trail runs into the middle of the Skid Row Trail. Go left and down on Skid Row. This descent is fast, fun, and full of flow. But it is bi-directional, so keep your speed down, as you will likely encounter uphill riders or hikers.

5.6 When you reach the bottom of Skid Row, instead of getting on the paved Rail Trail, take a hard left on the singletrack marked as Lost Prospector Access.

6.2 Rejoin Rail Trail and go left.

7.1 End your ride back at the Rail Trail parking area.

OPTIONS

You can always ride the loop clockwise by ascending Skid Row and descending Freemason. For longer loops on Masonic Hill, you can explore a few other, less maintained trails that connect to Lost Prospector, but they are often narrow and better suited for hiking than mountain biking.

7 UNION PACIFIC RAIL TRAIL

SHUTTLE OR OUT-AND-BACK

Trail Type: 90% doubletrack, 10% paved
Distance: 28 miles
Elevation Gain/Loss: 180/1520 feet
High Point: 6804 feet
Ride Time: 2–3 hours
Technical Difficulty: Beginner
Fitness Intensity: Strenuous

Season: Spring–fall
Maps: Mountain Trails Foundation Summer Map; Adventure Maps Salt Lake City, Park City, and the Wasatch; USGS 7.5-minute Park City East, Wanship, Coalville
GPS: 40°39'40.80"N, 111°29'53.72"W
Land Manager: Utah State Parks

OVERVIEW

Are you getting on a mountain bike for the first time ever? Or maybe you're an expert looking for a leisurely workout that covers a ton of miles? Then the Union Pacific Rail Trail is just the ride for you.

The Rail Trail follows an old rail line that begins in Park City and heads north through Tollgate Canyon for 28 miles to the far side of Echo Reservoir near the town of Coalville. Union Pacific abandoned the line in 1989. In 1992, the Utah Division of Parks and Recreation transformed the rail corridor into a nonmotorized recreational trail.

The entire trail is either paved or easy doubletrack, and riding it from south to north is a breezy pedal as the trail drops more than 1518 feet over those 28 miles. Still, riding the whole thing is a big effort, so be prepared with plenty of food and water, plus legs that can keep pedaling the entire way.

For a shorter ride, you can use any of seven trailheads along the route to create smaller shuttles or out-and-back options. However you decide to mountain bike the Rail Trail, you'll be treated to plenty of scenery, including wetlands, farms, mountains, canyons, rivers, and blue-water reservoirs. Along the way, you'll also find informational plaques highlighting local history.

GETTING THERE

To begin, you'll need to leave a shuttle vehicle at Echo Reservoir. From the intersection of Park Avenue and Kearns Boulevard in Park City, drive

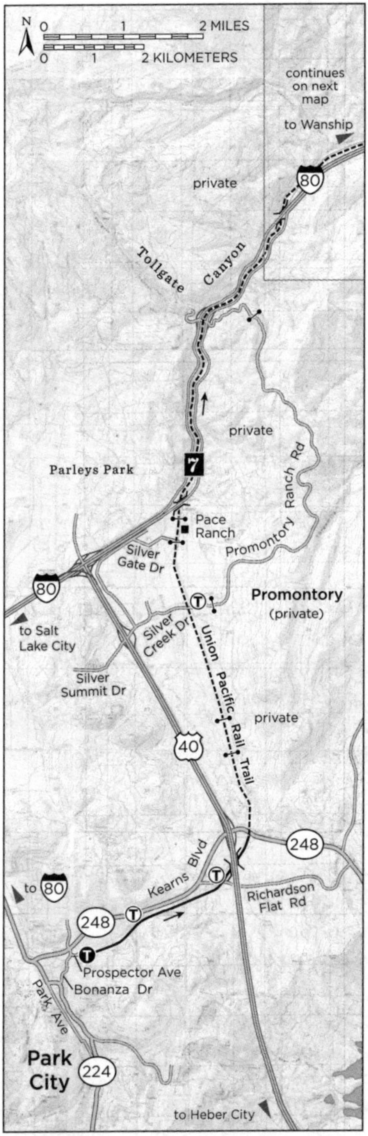

Left map

N

0   1   2 MILES
0   1   2 KILOMETERS

continues
on next
map

to Wanship

private

80

Tollgate Canyon

private

7

Parleys Park

private

Pace
Ranch

Promontory Ranch Rd

Silver
Gate Dr

80

Promontory
(private)

to Salt
Lake City

Silver
Creek Dr

Union Pacific Rail Trail

Silver
Summit Dr

private

40

to 80

248

Kearns Blvd

Richardson
Flat Rd

248

Prospector Ave
Bonanza Dr

Park
Ave

Park
City

224

to Heber City

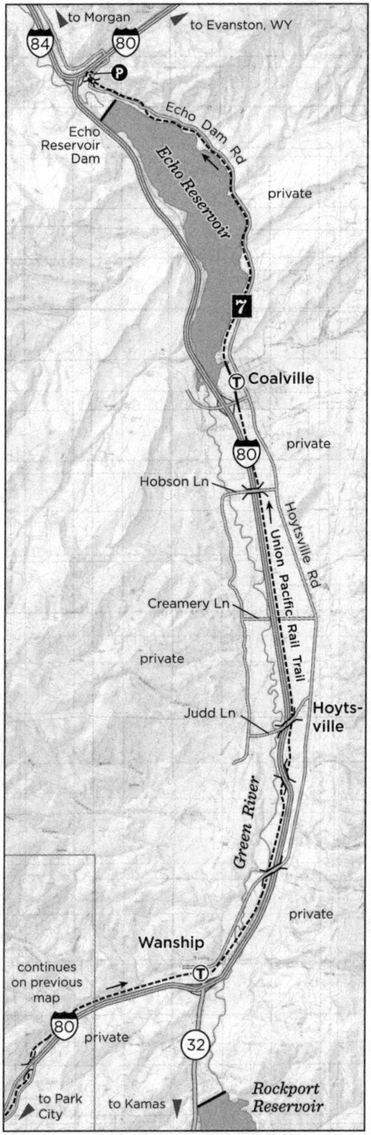

Right map

84

to Morgan

to Evanston, WY

80

P

Echo
Reservoir
Dam

Echo Dam Rd

Echo Reservoir

private

7

Coalville

80

private

Hobson Ln

Hoytsville Rd

Creamery Ln

Union Pacific Rail Trail

private

Judd Ln

Hoyts-
ville

Green River

private

Wanship

continues
on previous
map

80

private

32

to Park
City

to Kamas

Rockport
Reservoir

northeast on Kearns Boulevard for 3.7 miles, then turn left to merge onto US 40. In 3 miles, get on I-80 and go northeast for 21 miles. Then take exit 169. Turn right. Just before you reach the Echo Reservoir Dam, park your shuttle car in a pullout on the west side of the road.

To return to Park City, go back the way you came by way of I-80 and US 40. After leaving US 40 at the Kearns Boulevard exit, go right and drive southwest back toward Park City on Kearns Boulevard for 2.6 miles to Bonanza Drive. Turn left on Bonanza Drive and keep your eyes peeled for the "Rail Trail" sign. Turn left onto Prospector Avenue, then right into the parking lot for the Rail Trail. Locate the trail entrance at the south end of the parking lot.

MILEAGE LOG

0.0 At the southern corner of the parking lot, ride up a ramp to the paved Rail Trail. Go left (northeast). This section of the Rail Trail is the most popular and can get very crowded, so stay in your lane and go slow when pedestrians and other cyclists are around.

2.0 Cross Richardson Flat Road and continue on the other side. There is an alternate parking area and trailhead near this intersection.

2.8 Cross SR 248. Use the crossing signal. On the other side, the pavement ends, and the Rail Trail becomes dirt. At this point the trail goes through private property, but the public is allowed through an easement. Stay on the trail. Soon after crossing the road, you come to a cattle gate. Go through it and be sure to close it behind you so the cows don't escape—this is a working ranch.

5.7 Cross Promontory Ranch Rd., the location of the Promontory Rail Trail Trailhead and an alternate start or endpoint.

6.5 At the next intersection, cross dirt Silver Gate Drive and continue on the Rail Trail.

7.0 Near the entrance to Pace Ranch, go through a wildlife gate and close it behind you. You'll soon be underneath an I-80 overpass. This is where you enter Tollgate Canyon and the most scenic portion of the Rail Trail. Enjoy the view of rock formations and canyon walls as the trail parallels the interstate.

14.0 Enter the town of Wanship. Here, the Rail Trail temporarily returns to pavement. Continue following the trail through town. At the north end of town, the trail becomes dirt once more. There is a Rail Trail trailhead near the corner of SR 32 and Hoytsville Rd.

Wood bridges cross Silver Creek and Weber River on the Union Pacific Rail Trail.

18.2 The trail crosses Creamery Lane. Continue on the other side.

21.5 Reach the town of Coalville. Cross the street off the I-80 exit ramp and continue going north on the other side. The trail becomes pavement and skirts around the edge of town.

22.0 The Coalville Rail Trail Trailhead is on the right.

22.7 The pavement ends on the edge of town and becomes dirt. From here the trail wraps around the east side of Echo Reservoir and parallels Echo Dam Road. You can enjoy excellent views of the water or even stop and take a break on the shoreline. There are parking areas and pullouts along this stretch that you can use for alternate ride starts and/or endings.

27.0 Cross a bridge covered in a half-dome, chain-link fence. On the other side, go right and follow the trail down to Echo Dam Road below. When you hit the road, go left.

28.0 You are back at the dirt pullout on the side of the road where you left a shuttle vehicle.

OPTIONS

Tailor the Rail Trail ride to your liking by starting and stopping at any of the alternate trailheads. Or, for a really epic day, do the whole thing as an out-and-back for a ride totaling 56 miles.

DEER VALLEY

Deer Valley is home to the largest lift-served bike park in Utah. Snowy ski runs in the winter transform in the summer to the domain of gravity mountain bikers wearing body armor and full-face helmets. The downhill-only trails that spill from the summit of Bald Mountain and the 1000 vertical feet between the Silver Lake Village and Snow Park Lodge are world class. Flowing singletrack with massive berms, tabletop jumps, and wood features were built by Gravity Logic, the company responsible for the world's number one bike park in Whistler, British Columbia. Deer Valley Bike Park (Route 12) is the epicenter of downhill mountain biking in the entire state.

But Deer Valley offers more than getting rad without earning your adrenaline on the up. Routes like the Bowhunter Loop (Route 10), Lower Empire Canyon (Route 11), and Spin Cycle (Route 15) offer good workouts as well as a rollicking good time on the down. You can also ride the classic Tour des Suds (Route 8), an annual race all about the up. You can start a point-to-point ride on the ever-popular Mid Mountain Trail (Route 13) from Deer Valley. The resort constantly cuts new trails and expands their bike park offerings, so check www.deervalley.com for the latest updates.

8 TOUR DES SUDS

SHUTTLE OR OUT-AND-BACK

Trail Type: 83% singletrack, 17% doubletrack
Distance: 6 miles one-way
Elevation Gain/Loss: 1700/215 feet
High Point: 8496 feet

Maps: Mountain Trails Foundation Summer Map; Adventure Maps Salt Lake City, Park City, and the Wasatch; USGS 7.5-minute Brighton, Heber City, Park City West, Park City East

Opposite: *More than just berms and bike parks, Deer Valley also features old-school, classic singletrack.*

Ride Time: 1.5–2 hours one-way
Season: Summer–fall
Technical Difficulty: Intermediate

Fitness Intensity: Moderate
GPS: 40°37′57.85″N, 111°29′50.83″W
Land Manager: Deer Valley Resort

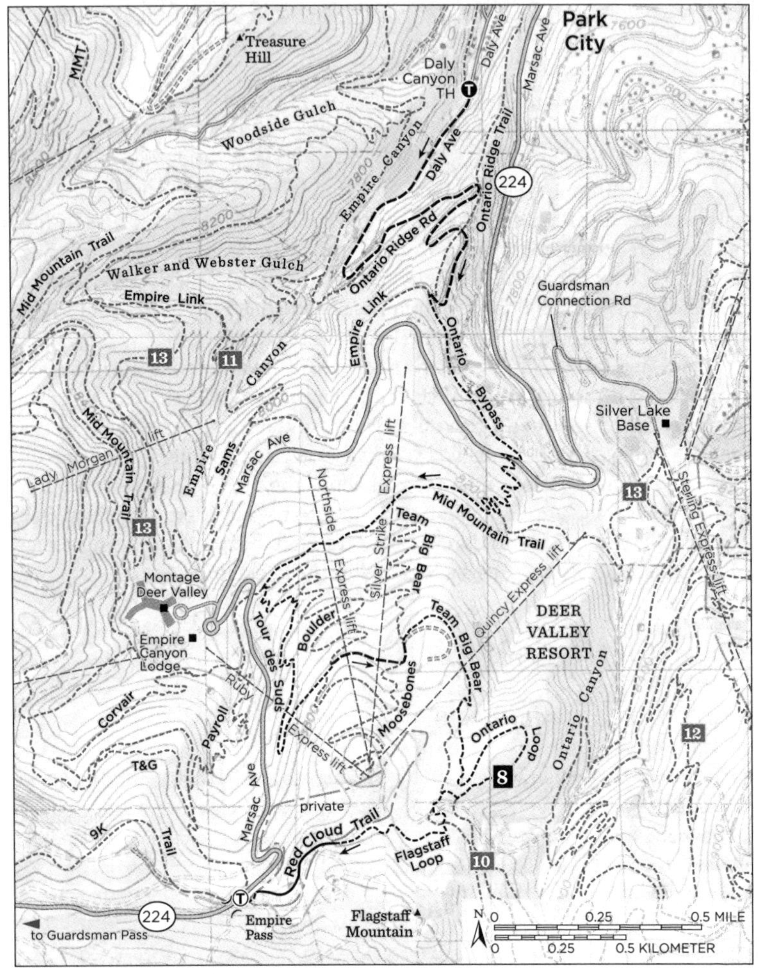

OVERVIEW

Tour des Suds is a classic Park City mountain bike race and tradition that dates back to 1983. Each fall, to mark the end of biking season, hundreds of riders dress up in costumes and pedal from town up a series of trails, through Deer Valley, to Empire Pass. At the pass, the participants consume the "suds" and then ride back down.

But you don't have to slip on a superhero cape or lederhosen to enjoy Tour des Suds on race day. The course is a fun and aerobic ascent where, from Empire Pass, you can choose any number of routes to descend. The official racecourse begins in the middle of town at City Park. But for this route I cut out all paved streets and start the ride on dirt at the mouth of Empire Canyon. A short mile of dirt road and doubletrack transitions to some of the most enjoyable singletrack climbing in Park City—no costume required.

GETTING THERE

From the intersection of Park Avenue and Kearns Boulevard in Park City, drive south on Park Avenue for 0.3 mile. Turn left onto Deer Valley Drive while following the signs to Deer Valley Resort. In 1.1 miles, you'll come to a traffic circle. Follow it to the opposite side and continue straight, leaving the circle on Marsac Avenue. In 0.4 mile, turn right onto Prospect Avenue, then continue straight on Hillside Avenue as it goes downhill. At the bottom of the hill, turn left on Daly Avenue. Follow it through a neighborhood in the canyon for 0.5 mile until the road ends at a gate, right when pavement turns to dirt. Park at a pullout on the left.

MILEAGE LOG

0.0 Go around the gate and pedal up the Daly Avenue dirt road.

0.5 Right after the road makes a hairpin turn, it intersects Ontario Ridge Road. Go left onto Ontario Ridge Road.

0.9 Leave Ontario Ridge Road by going right onto the Ontario Bypass doubletrack. Ignore the Ontario Ridge singletrack on the left.

1.1 After rounding a corner, go left onto Ontario Bypass. Signs indicate that this is the Tour des Suds route.

1.2 At a second intersection with Ontario Ridge, stay straight on Ontario Bypass.

Route-finding on Tour des Suds can be confusing, but thankfully signs show the way.

1.5 At a large four-way intersection with Ontario Ridge on right and Empire Link ahead, go left on Ontario Bypass as it steeply rises into an aspen grove.

1.9 Cross Marsac Avenue and continue on Ontario Bypass on the other side.

2.3 Ontario Bypass ends at the Mid Mountain Trail (MMT) in Deer Valley Resort. Go right on MMT.

2.7 Team Big Bear connects on the left. Stay straight on Mid Mountain Trail.

3.0 Leave Mid Mountain Trail and go left onto Tour des Suds going uphill. Immediately after, there is a fork. Left is Boulder. Stay right on Tour des Suds.

3.6 At a dirt road, go left and pedal up the road.

3.8 Pass the Boulder Trail and stay on the road.

4.1 Pass the Moosebones Trail on the right and stay on the road as it curves around left. Just when the road turns right and climbs up a hill, leave the road by getting on the right fork of Team Big Bear, which is found on the left side of the road.

4.5 At the next intersection, go left onto Ontario Loop where signs show the way to Flagstaff Loop.

5.1   Leave Ontario Loop by going right onto Flagstaff Loop.

5.3   Cross a dirt road and pick up the singletrack on the other side. Immediately after going into the trees, go right on Flagstaff Loop. Right after this at a four-way, stay straight on Flagstaff.

5.7   Flagstaff ends at a paved road called Red Cloud Trail. Go left and up the road.

6.0   Red Cloud Trail connects with SR 224 at the top of Empire Pass. This is the finish line for the Tour des Suds race. From here, choose your own adventure to get back down to your vehicle. Going back the way you came is not a bad option for a 12-mile out-and-back ride.

OPTIONS

There are several ways to descend after completing the Tour des Suds, especially via the numerous trails in Deer Valley Resort. But I suggest you head north and coast down (right) on SR 224 a few switchbacks to the T&G Trailhead on the left. Follow this down to Payroll and descend to Mid Mountain Trail (MMT). Once there, go right on MMT and retrace your ascent route back to the bottom of Empire Canyon.

Alternatively, you can get on the new 9K Trail (Route 16) at Empire Pass and traverse above Daly Bowl to the Black Forest Trail (see Route 16). This descent is an advanced, steep, rooty, twisty downhill that also connects with Mid Mountain Trail. Same deal—go right on MMT to return to Ontario Bypass. Or, go left on MMT to Empire Link and take that to go down Speedbag. That also gets you to Empire Canyon, where your car awaits.

 CORVAIR TO PAYROLL

LARIAT LOOP

Trail Type: 100% singletrack

Distance: 2.3 miles

Elevation Gain/Loss: 345/345 feet

High Point: 8726 feet

Ride Time: 30 minutes to 1 hour

Technical Difficulty: Advanced

Fitness Intensity: Easy

Season: Summer–fall

Maps: Mountain Trails Foundation Summer Map; Adventure Maps, Salt Lake City, Park City, and the Wasatch; USGS 7.5-minute Brighton

GPS: 40°36′58.31″N, 111°30′26.48″W

Land Manager: Deer Valley Resort

Swinging around a big berm on Payroll, before dropping into a technical gully

OVERVIEW

For a short loop that packs a punch, climb up Corvair and head down Payroll. The best downhill-only trail at Deer Valley outside the bike park, Payroll has advanced technical features like rock gardens, jumps, and a few big drops. It ends with a flowing ride through a gully where the singletrack swoops up and down the canyon walls like a bobsled course.

Start at the roadside parking area on Marsac Avenue and take a short ride west on the ever-popular Mid Mountain Trail (MMT) to just above Deer Valley's Empire Canyon Lodge. From there, pedal up Corvair, a great trail with wide open corners and mostly smooth dirt (also a fun trail to ride

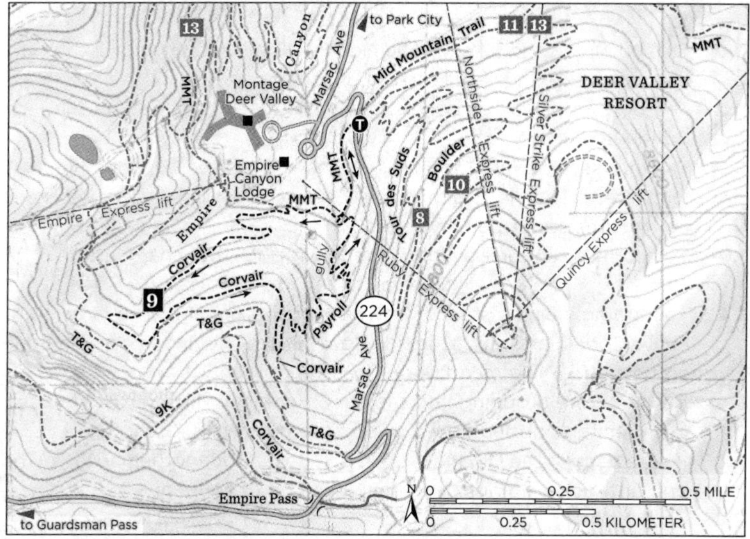

down as well). With less than 350 vertical feet of climbing, you can be at the top of Payroll in under a half hour.

This loop makes a great option if you're short on time. It's also super easy to lap over and over again to practice your bike skills on the rollicking descent.

GETTING THERE

From the intersection of Park Avenue and Kearns Boulevard in Park City, drive south on Park Avenue for 0.3 mile. Turn left onto Deer Valley Drive while following the signs to Deer Valley Resort. In 1.1 miles, you'll come to a traffic circle. Follow it to the opposite side and continue straight, leaving the circle on Marsac Avenue. Follow this road as it winds up through a canyon and into the mountains for 3.6 miles to a traffic circle at Deer Valley's Empire Canyon Lodge. Take the circle all the way around and continue up Marsac where it bends in a tight switchback. Just after this bend, you'll see a large parking area on the left. This Mid Mountain Trail trailhead marks the start of the ride.

MILEAGE LOG

0.0 Cross the road and take the Mid Mountain Trail west and down through the aspen forest toward Empire Canyon Lodge.

0.2 The bottom of Payroll connects with Mid Mountain Trail on the left. Continue on MMT.

0.3 The intersection with Corvair is on the left. Leave Mid Mountain Trail and ascend Corvair. This technically easy climb will get your heart rate up on some steep, punchy sections.

1.0 You come to a four-way intersection with T&G. Stay hard left on Corvair. A right on T&G will take you to the top of Payroll.

1.4 You are now at the start of Payroll, which is marked by a large sign. Leave Corvair and enjoy the ride down. Payroll begins steep with tight corners and a few mandatory rock drops. Then it transitions to wide berms before dropping into the gully. Here you will find rock gardens between the bobsled-style turns on the gully walls. Great fun.

2.0 You're back at the Mid Mountain Trail. Go left for another lap. If you're one-and-done, go right and head back up to your car.

2.3 End of ride.

OPTIONS

T&G is another option to get to Payroll, though it's better suited for downhill. Access it from higher up on Marsac Avenue just below Empire Pass and ride it down to Corvair near the top of Payroll.

10 BOWHUNTER LOOP

LOOP

Trail Type: 95% singletrack, 5% doubletrack
Distance: 7.7 miles
Elevation Gain/Loss: 1037/1037 feet
High Point: 9057 feet
Ride Time: 2–3 hours
Technical Difficulty: Intermediate
Fitness Intensity: Moderate

Season: Summer–fall
Maps: Mountain Trails Foundation Summer Map; Adventure Maps Salt Lake City, Park City, and the Wasatch; USGS 7.5-minute Brighton, Heber City
GPS: 40°36'58.31"N, 111°30'26.48"W
Land Manager: Deer Valley Resort

OVERVIEW

The Bowhunter Loop is one of my favorite ways to mountain bike at Deer Valley. To connect to the Bowhunter Trail, a short loop at the upper elevation of this ride, you link several other classic bits of singletrack. Despite the number of other trails included in this route, I call it the Bowhunter Loop for simplicity.

This ride is for anyone who wants to explore the trails on the Bald Mountain area of Deer Valley without using the lifts or dive-bombing down gravity trails. The ascent climbs easily with a little routefinding to nearly the start of the downhill-only trails. Pedaling up offers a pleasant meander through evergreen and aspen forests. On Bowhunter Trail, a gorgeous view of Jordanelle Reservoir in the valley below rewards your climbing effort.

You'll find many options to descend back to the trailhead, and you really can't go wrong whichever way you choose. The route I describe offers a combination of fast downhill sections and tight, technical spots that will test your low-speed bike handling skills. But overall this loop makes for a solid intermediate ride.

GETTING THERE

From the intersection of Park Avenue and Kearns Boulevard in Park City, drive south on Park Avenue for 0.3 mile. Turn left onto Deer Valley Drive while following the signs to Deer Valley Resort. In 1.1 miles, you'll come to a traffic circle. Follow it to the opposite side and continue straight, leaving the circle on Marsac Avenue. Follow this road as it winds up through a canyon and into the mountains for 3.6 miles to a traffic circle at Deer Valley's Empire Canyon Lodge. Take the circle all the way around and continue up Marsac where it bends in a tight switchback. Just after this bend, you'll see a large parking area on the left. There is a Mid Mountain Trail trailhead here, which marks the start of the ride.

MILEAGE LOG

0.0 At the lowest part of the parking pullout on the east side of the road, go right onto the Mid Mountain Trail. Almost immediately after, turn right onto Tour des Suds. Then immediately turn left at a fork onto the Boulder Trail and start climbing. I find Boulder to be a nice ascent on a mellow grade over several large switchbacks. You can also pedal up

Views of Jordanelle Reservoir and the Kamas Valley beyond are your reward for climbing to the Bowhunter Loop.

Tour des Suds if you'd rather test your mettle with rocks, roots, and tighter turns.

1.1 Boulder crosses a wide, dirt road. Instead of continuing on Boulder, go left on the road. Pedal on the mostly flat surface while keeping an eye out for a trail marked "Team Big Bear."

1.2 Pass the intersections for Moosebones and Red Cloud and continue on the road.

1.3 The road makes a sharp right turn. At this point you'll see Team Big Bear on your left. Get off the road and take the right fork at Team Big Bear, which goes northeast.

1.7 At the intersection with Ontario Loop, follow the signs that lead the way to Flagstaff Loop by taking the left fork.

2.4 At the next intersection, stay left onto Flagstaf for a rocky, somewhat technical descent.

2.5   At fork, go right (uphill) on Road to Ruby. Left is the continuation of Flagstaff. Both trails will get you to Bowhunter, but I prefer the climb on Road to Ruby.

3.0   Road to Ruby turns left where it becomes downhill-only near a dirt road. Go straight and then turn left to get on that road. Pedal up the road.

3.1   Where the road splits at a fork, stay left on the mellower grade.

3.3   Leave the road by turning right onto an unmarked singletrack that goes into the sagebrush, the start of the Bowhunter Trail. Take this trail as it loops around a small mountain (Point 9363).

3.7   The singletrack runs into a doubletrack road. Go left on the road for just a few yards and pick up the Bowhunter singletrack again on the left. From here, Bowhunter is less traveled and narrow, sometimes

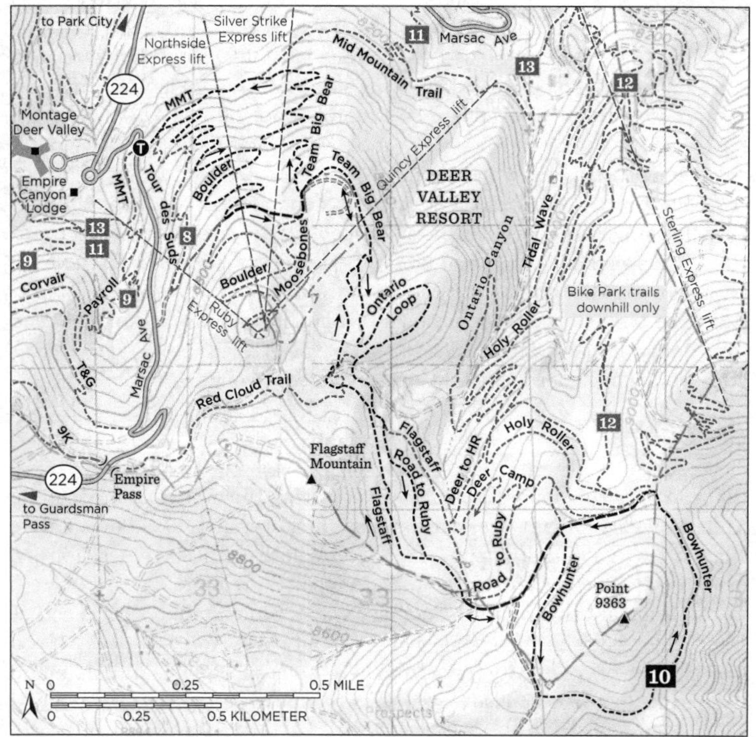

even overgrown. On the far side, the hillside steepens, revealing a jaw-dropping view of Jordanelle Reservoir to the east.

4.5 After making the loop around the mountain, Bowhunter ends at a doubletrack near the many downhill-only trails of the Deer Valley bike park. Go left on the road, following signs to Flagstaff Loop. You'll pass the start of Holy Roller and Deer Camp along the way.

4.8 The doubletrack splits into a fork. Stay right and ride downhill into a beautiful alpine meadow.

5.1 Leave the doubletrack and go right onto a singletrack four-way intersection. Take the left option onto Road to Ruby.

5.2 At the fork with Flagstaff, go left onto it (although staying on Road to Ruby takes you to the same destination).

5.7 At another four-way intersection in a stand of thick pine trees, stay straight on Flagstaff. You may also go right. Both end up on the same dirt road. Across the road, locate the Flagstaff/Road to Ruby trail and follow it. Immediately after, where Road to Ruby/Flagstaff makes a hard right, stay left and go on Ontario Loop.

5.9 Back at the three-way intersection with Ontario Loop and Team Big Bear, continue downhill on Team Big Bear.

6.3 Back on the lower dirt road, cross it, continuing down Team Big Bear. From here the slow, technical descent has rock obstacles and roots. The switchbacks can also be tight. It's challenging but still doable for intermediate riders.

7.2 The trail intersects with the Mid Mountain Trail. Go left on MMT and follow it back to the trailhead.

7.7 You're back at the parking area on Marsac Avenue.

OPTIONS

You can vary this loop in several ways. During the ascent you can climb Tour de Suds or Team Big Bear to reach the lower dirt road. Beyond that, Flagstaff is a good alternate to Road to Ruby, both uphill and down. You can also ride the Bowhunter portion in the opposite direction.

Additionally, this route is a popular way for mountain bikers to access Deer Valley's downhill-only bike park without paying for a lift ticket. If you descend one of the gravity trails from here, you can take the Mid Mountain Trail from Snow Park Lodge to get back to your car.

11 LOWER EMPIRE CANYON

LOOP

Trail Type: 95% singletrack, 5% doubletrack
Distance: 5.6 miles
Elevation Gain/Loss: 875/875 feet
High Point: 9057 feet
Ride Time: 1–2 hours
Technical Difficulty: Intermediate
Fitness Intensity: Easy

Season: Summer–fall
Maps: Mountain Trails Foundation Summer Map; Adventure Maps Salt Lake City, Park City, and the Wasatch; USGS 7.5-minute Brighton, Heber City, Park City West
GPS: 40°36'58.31"N, 111°30'26.48"W
Land Manager: Deer Valley Resort

OVERVIEW

There's something deflating about finishing a nice ride with an uphill grind to the car, but I will make an exception if the downhill portion of the ride is awesome. And this loop delivers.

The descent you're earning up front is on the Empire Link Trail. It has well-worn berms, smooth (but small) jumps and rollers, and some scary-fast straightaways. The Mid Mountain Trail (MMT) provides the trade route to access this downhill fun. At the bottom, that aforementioned climb comes courtesy of Ontario Bypass on Ontario Ridge. In truth, it's a pretty easy climb back to the car and worth the price of admission.

But if you're like me and really insist on ending your loop on a downhill, you can make the loop longer by climbing up Tour des Suds and then descending Boulder back to the car.

GETTING THERE

From the intersection of Park Avenue and Kearns Boulevard in Park City, drive south on Park Avenue for 0.3 mile. Turn left onto Deer Valley Drive while following the signs to Deer Valley Resort. In 1.1 miles, you'll come to a traffic circle. Follow it to the opposite side and continue straight, leaving the circle on Marsac Avenue. Follow this road as it winds up through a canyon and into the mountains for 3.6 miles to a traffic circle at Deer Valley's Empire

The massive complex of Montage Deer Valley dominates the landscape in Lower Empire Canyon.

Canyon Lodge. Take the circle all the way around and continue up Marsac where it bends in a tight switchback. Just after this bend, you'll see a large parking area on the left. This Mid Mountain Trail trailhead marks the start of the ride.

MILEAGE LOG

0.0 From the parking area, go west across Marsac Avenue to the Mid Mountain Trail (MMT) on the other side. The singletrack descends into Empire Canyon through an aspen grove. There are a few exposed roots to negotiate here, but nothing too difficult. For the next half mile, stay right on MMT while ignoring Payroll and Corvair Trails that all intersect on the left.

0.7 After riding above the massive Montage Deer Valley hotel, stay left on MMT where it intersects with Little Chief on the right. This next section of trail is nice, as it traverses ski runs between the forests, offering excellent views.

1.5 At the intersection with T&G, stay straight on MMT. Immediately after this, MMT intersects with the Link Trail. Again, stay on MMT.

2.1 After a series of berms that switchback down through an aspen grove, leave MMT and make a hard right on Empire Link (Mid Mountain continues on the left, ascending into Park City Mountain). This is where the fun begins. Enjoy the descent but be careful of uphill travelers. The grass can get long in late summer, so that will also dictate your speed due to a lack of trail visibility.

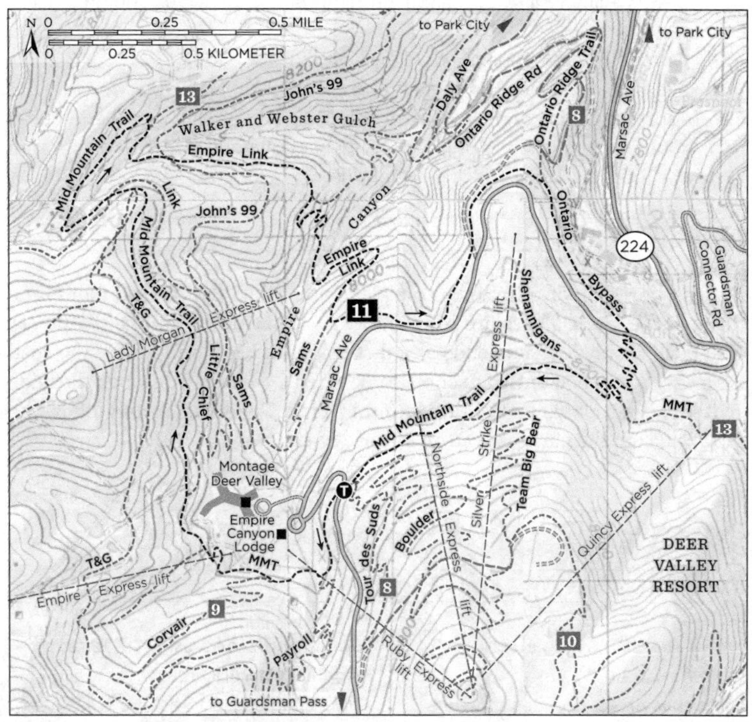

2.3 At the intersection with John's 99, stay straight on Empire Link.

3.0 Empire Link drops into the bottom of Empire Canyon with a series of tight switchbacks below the bottom station of the Lady Morgan Express chairlift. Cross a doubletrack road and a bridge over a creek that is usually dry to continue on Empire Link. From here, however, you begin climbing.

3.5 At the intersection with Sam's, which enters on the right, stay straight on Empire Link. If you'd like to have another go at Empire Link, however, take Sam's, as it climbs up to Little Chief, which you can use to return to the MMT and repeat as above.

4.1 At the four-way intersection, take a hard right turn onto Ontario Bypass.

4.5 The trail comes out onto the paved road, Marsac Avenue. Cross the road while angling uphill to find the singletrack continuing on the other side.

4.9 Ontario Bypass ends at the Mid Mountain Trail. Go right onto MMT.

5.3 Pass Team Big Bear on the left and continue on MMT.

5.6 Tour des Suds connects on the left. Stay on the MMT for the featured route back to the parking area on Marsec Avenue. To extend your ride via Tour des Suds, check out Options.

OPTIONS

For that longer loop, climb up Tour des Suds for a 334-vertical foot climb through the trees. There are some rocky sections but nothing too difficult. When the Tour des Suds ends at a dirt road, turn left and follow the road for a short distance until you come to Boulder. Go left and descend the wide switchbacks back down to Mid Mountain Trail. Go left again and follow the MMT back to the parking area on Marsac Avenue.

12 DEER VALLEY BIKE PARK

NETWORK

Trail Type: 100% singletrack and wide flow trail

Distance: Up to 27 miles of downhill-only trails

Elevation Gain/Loss: 0/2200 feet

High Point: 9400 feet

Ride Time: As long as you want from open to close, 10 AM–5 PM daily

Technical Difficulty: Intermediate to Expert
Fitness Intensity: Easy to Strenuous
Season: Summer–fall
GPS: 40°38'18.94"N, 111°28'40.79"W
Land Manager: Deer Valley Resort

Maps: Mountain Trails Foundation Summer Map; Adventure Maps, Salt Lake City, Park City, and the Wasatch; Deer Valley Summer Trail Map; USGS 7.5-minute Park City East

OVERVIEW

The best lift-served mountain biking in Park City is at the Deer Valley Bike Park. Boasting up to 27 miles of flow and pro trails between three lifts, there is no better place to maximize downhill vertical in a single day. The park is a mix of hand-dug tech and machine-built fun with huge berms, rollers, table-tops, gap jumps, wood features, rock drops, steep lines, and everything in between. Deer Valley applies a rating system of difficulty from green to red, with green being "easier" and red being "extreme." But even the so-called easier trails are not for beginners. It is recommended that you are, at minimum, an advanced intermediate rider before tackling these flow trails.

To ride the Deer Valley Bike Park, it's best to start at the Snow Park base area (which has tons of parking) where you purchase your lift ticket and sign a waiver. You then ride the Silver Lake Express lift to Silver Lake Village. From there, the Sterling Express lift takes you to the top of Bald Mountain where the bulk of the downhill-only trails begin. The Homestake Express lift gets riders from Silver Lake back to the top of the Snow Park area where more flow trails descend to the parking lot.

The season generally begins in mid-June, with daily operations lasting through Labor Day. After that date, riding is restricted to weekends through the end of September. Lift hours are from 10 AM to 5 PM. On Tuesdays, check out the Twilight Ride Series, where you can bike from 4 PM to 8 PM on the Silver Lake and Sterling Express lifts. Bike rentals are available at Snow Park Lodge.

Bikers must wear a helmet to ride the lifts. It's also a good idea to ride a full-suspension bike with at least 5 inches of travel and disc brakes. Body armor or knee and elbow pads and a full-face helmet aren't a bad idea either, especially if you're riding any of the black- or red-labeled trails.

While you can access all of Deer Valley's trails from the lifts, I've only listed the downhill directional trails below. They're separated by area (Snow Park and Silver Lake), then by difficulty. To get the big picture of

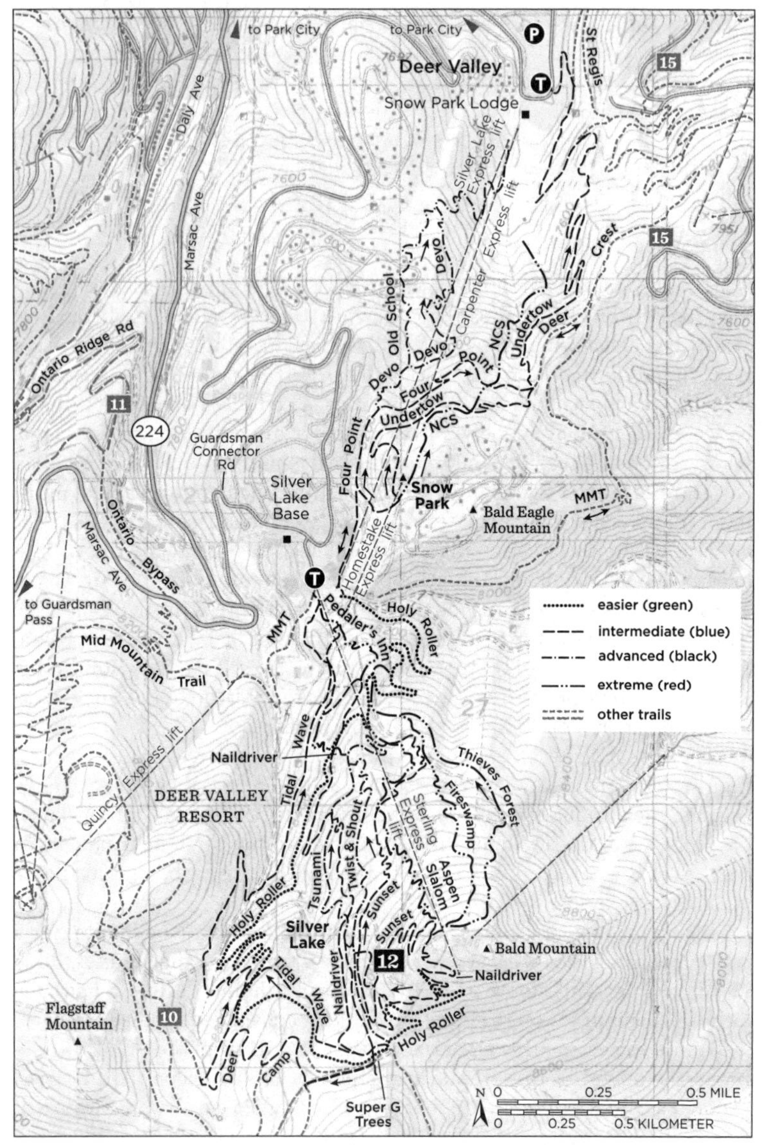
to Park City
to Park City
P
Deer Valley
T
Snow Park Lodge
St Regis
15
15
7600
7951
Silver Lake Express lift
Carpenter Express lift
Devo
Devo Old School
Devo
Four Point
Undertow
NCS
Undertow
Deer
Crest
NCS
Daly Ave
Marsac Ave
7600
7800
Ontario Ridge Rd
11
224
Guardsman Connector Rd
Silver Lake Base
Four Point
Snow Park
Bald Eagle Mountain
MMT
Ontario Bypass
Marsac Ave
Homestake Express lift
to Guardsman Pass
Mid Mountain Trail
MMT
Pedaler's Inn
T
Holy Roller
8000
easier (green)
intermediate (blue)
advanced (black)
extreme (red)
other trails
27
Quincy Express lift
DEER VALLEY RESORT
Naildriver
Wave
Tidal
Thieves Forest
Fireswamp
Sterling Express lift
Aspen
Slalom
Twist & Shout
Sunset
Sunset
8400
Holy Roller
Tsunami
Silver Lake
Bald Mountain
12
Naildriver
Tidal
Wave
Naildriver
Holy Roller
Flagstaff Mountain
10
Super G
Trees
Deer
Camp
N
0   0.25   0.5 MILE
0   0.25   0.5 KILOMETER

the bike park, or for current updates and lift ticket rates, visit www.deer valley.com.

GETTING THERE

From the intersection of Park Avenue and Kearns Boulevard in Park City, drive south on Park Avenue for 0.3 mile. Turn left onto Deer Valley Drive while following the signs to Deer Valley Resort. In 1.1 miles, you'll come to a traffic circle. Take the second exit and stay on Deer Valley Drive. Follow this road for 1.2 miles to the Snow Park Lodge. Park in the uppermost large parking lot.

MILEAGE LOG

SILVER LAKE

EASIER "GREEN" TRAIL

Holy Roller The easiest downhill-only option of all the trails in this network, this 4.2-mile trail features wide berms, smooth rollers, and small jumps. It starts at the top of Bald Mountain and goes all the way to Silver Lake Village.

INTERMEDIATE "BLUE" TRAILS

Tidal Wave 3.0 miles. The next level up from Holy Roller, Tidal Wave's berms and jumps get bigger and badder. It features more than fifty jumps, most of which are of the tabletop variety. Tidal Wave also starts at the top of Bald Mountain and ends at Silver Lake Village.

Naildriver 2.5 miles. Naildriver gives a more old-school vibe on a narrower trail. You'll find less in the way of jumps, but the trail still has large berms. Naildriver is a personal favorite. It starts near the top of Holy Roller and ends at Silver Lake Village.

Sunset 1.5 miles. Another traditional singletrack with tighter turns and a few techy sections, Sunset begins near the top of Naildriver and reconnects with Naildriver near the bottom.

Deer Camp 1.0 mile. This short option starts at the large meadow on upper Holy Roller. It's a nice flow trail with big views and a fun section through an aspen forest. It reconnects with Holy Roller farther down.

Super G Trees 0.4 mile. Super G Trees offers a short variation from Naildriver—a nice jaunt through the aspen trees.

ADVANCED "BLACK" TRAILS

Tsunami 1.5 miles. One of the most popular trails here, Tsunami is a roller coaster of the park's biggest jumps, berms, and wood features. One thing's for sure—this trail is fast! It starts at the meadow below Bald Mountain summit. Ride Tidal Wave to get there.

Twist and Shout 1.2 miles. Old-school tech with super tight corners through a dense aspen forest are some of the features of Twist and Shout. To add to the thrill, this trail is very steep. Access is from Tidal Wave. The trail ends when it connects with Naildriver near Silver Lake Village.

Everything at Deer Valley Bike Park is big—trails, berms, jumps, and views. (Photo by Lexi Dowdall)

Pedaler's Inn 0.3 mile. Pedaler's Inn offers a short hit with wood bridges, ramps and other technical features. The trail connects lower Naildriver with Silver Lake Village.

EXPERT "RED" TRAILS

Fireswamp 1.5 miles. One of the most technical trails at Deer Valley, Fireswamp was once a State Championship Downhill course. The trail is loose with a lot of big rocks and drops. Deer Valley recommends you wear pads and have a downhill bike. Fireswamp starts at the Bald Mountain Summit and ends at Silver Lake Village.

Thieves Forest 1.0 mile. You'll find Thieves Forest a bit easier than Fireswamp, but still loaded with natural features like massive rocks, roots, and big drops. The trail starts atop Bald Mountain and connects with lower Fireswamp.

Aspen Slalom 1.0 mile. Tight and steep singletrack through an aspen forest with natural drops, Aspen Slalom is best known for the insane amount of tight turns. Aspen Slalom starts near the top of Bald Mountain on Tidal Wave and connects with Sunset just above Silver Lake Village.

SNOW PARK

INTERMEDIATE "BLUE" TRAILS

Undertow 3.5 miles. One of the newer additions to the bike park, Undertow is now the most fun way to ride back down to Snow Park from Silver Lake. This fast flow trail has large berms, rollers, and mini jumps. Undertow begins at the top of the Homestake Express lift and ends at Snow Park.

Four Point 1.0 mile. A good option if you're not into berms and rollers, this trail is more traditional singletrack. Four Point starts at the top of Homestake Express and connects with the bi-directional Deer Crest and Mid Mountain Trail lower down.

ADVANCED "BLACK" TRAILS

Devo 1.1 miles. Devo boasts a steep and tight trail that also was once a National Championship Series Sport Downhill course complete with a lot of turns with steep root drops. Access it from upper Four Point. It ends at Snow Park.

Old School 0.5 mile. Old School is a short but fast variation on Devo that features a large bridge drop. Connects with the bi-directional Tour de Homes at the bottom.

EXPERT "RED" TRAIL

NCS 1.5 miles. NCS is an acronym for "National Championship Series." NCS was purpose-built for this professional downhill race, so you know it's gotta be tough. In fact, Deer Valley claims that NCS is one of the most difficult downhill courses in the country. The trail features huge rock gardens, big drops, and rock faces. Ride at your own risk! It begins at the top of Homestake Express and ends at Snow Park.

13 MID MOUNTAIN TRAIL

SHUTTLE

Trail Type: 95% singletrack, 5% doubletrack

Distance: 26.2 miles

Elevation Gain/Loss: 2470/4040 feet

High Point: 8270 feet

Ride Time: 4–6 hours

Technical Difficulty: Intermediate

Fitness Intensity: Very Strenuous

Season: Summer–fall

Maps: Mountain Trails Foundation Summer Map; Adventure Maps Salt Lake City, Park City, and the Wasatch; USGS 7.5-minute Heber City, Brighton, Park City West

GPS: 40°3'16.54"N, 111°29'19.90"W

Land Manager: Deer Valley Resort, Park City Mountain, Utah Olympic Legacy Foundation

OVERVIEW

This Park City classic is one of the longest continuous trails in the Wasatch, stretching from Deer Valley Resort to the Canyons side of Park City Mountain over the course of 20 miles. Mountain bikers mostly use Mid Mountain Trail (MMT) as a connector or segment in a loop, as it can be accessed from numerous locations and trailheads. Others may ride the trail out and back in short sections. But the intrepid and in-shape rider will want to pedal the entire length from end to end for an epic day in the mountains.

The MMT generally follows the 8000-foot elevation contour line with a lot of short climbs and descents through open meadows and ski runs, alternating with aspen and evergreen forests. The occasional overlook allows for sweeping views of the Park City area.

The route I describe here includes the entire length of the MMT starting at the Silver Lake Base Area in Deer Valley and ending with a descent

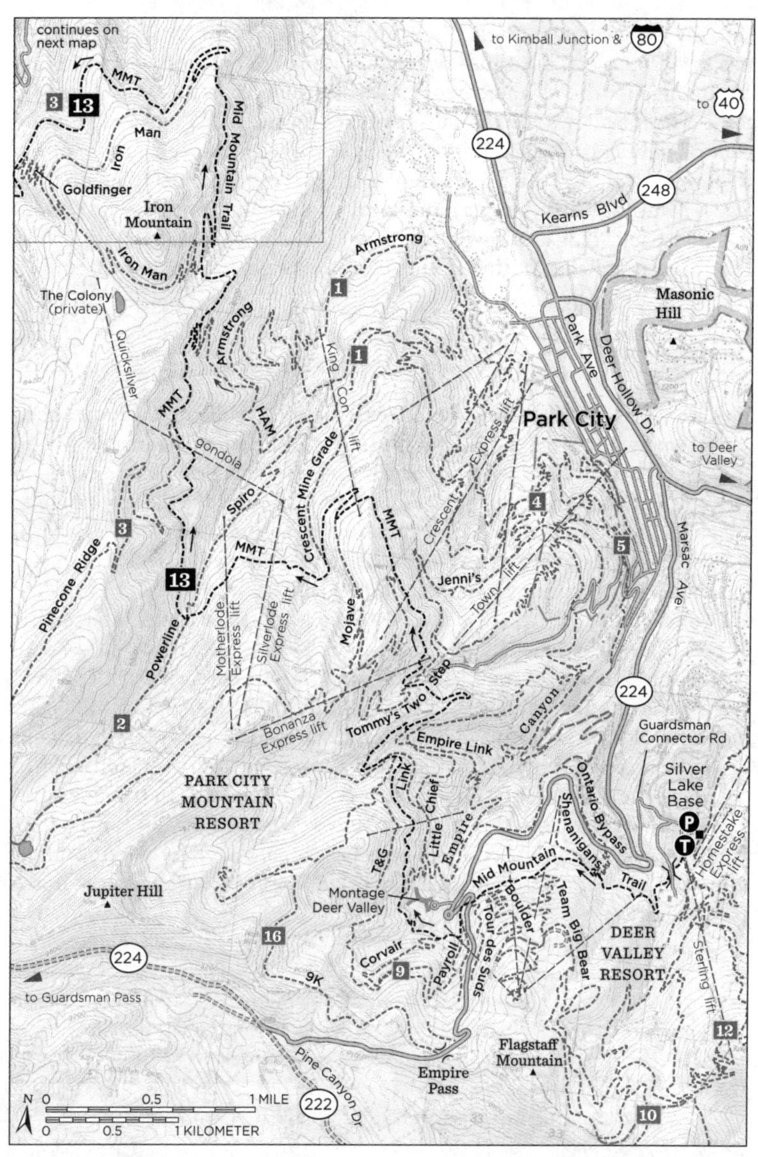

continues on next map
MMT
3
13
Iron Man
Goldfinger
Iron Mountain
Mid Mountain Trail
Iron Man
The Colony (private)
Quicksilver
Armstrong
MMT
HAM
gondola
Spiro
MMT
Powerline
Motherlode Express lift
Silverlode Express lift
Pinecone Ridge
3
13
2
Armstrong
1
1
King Con lift
Crescent Mine Grade
MMT
Mojave
Crescent
Express lift
Jenni's
Town lift
Tommy's Two Step
Bonanza Express lift
Empire Link
Link
Little Chief
Empire
T&G
PARK CITY MOUNTAIN RESORT
Jupiter Hill
16
9K
Corvair
9
Payroll
Montage Deer Valley
Canyon
Ontario Bypass
Shenanigans
Mid Mountain
Boulder
Tour des Suds
Team Big Bear
Trail
Mid Mountain Trail
to Kimball Junction &
80
to 40
224
248
Kearns Blvd
Masonic Hill
Park Ave
Deer Hollow Dr
Park City
to Deer Valley
4
5
Marsac Ave
224
Guardsman Connector Rd
Silver Lake Base
P
T
Homestake Express lift
Sterling lift
DEER VALLEY RESORT
12
Flagstaff Mountain
Empire Pass
224
to Guardsman Pass
Pine Canyon Dr
222
10
N
0   0.5   1 MILE
0   0.5   1 KILOMETER

into the Utah Olympic Park. The Hunter's Trail of Mid Mountain continues into Pinecrest, but those descent options are open only to residents of the neighborhood homeowner's association. Therefore, the Olympic Park descent allows for the most mileage on the MMT possible for the general public. Do it as a shuttle ride by leaving a car at the bottom of the RTS trail system at the Millennium Trail parking lot, located behind the Tanger Outlets. Or if you're a glutton for punishment, you can ride it as an out-and-back. This ride may be mostly nontechnical and somewhat flat, but the long mileage of undulating elevation gain/loss makes this ride a worthy challenge.

GETTING THERE

To begin, you'll need to leave a shuttle vehicle at the Millennium Trailhead at the RTS network. From the intersection of Park Avenue and Kearns Boulevard in Park City, drive northwest on Park Avenue for 5.1 miles, then turn left on Olympic Parkway. In 0.1 mile, you enter a roundabout. Take the first exit onto N. Landmark Drive. Follow it for 0.1 mile and turn left on Tech Center Road. In 0.5 mile, you'll see parking for the Millennium Trailhead (also called the Overland Trailhead). Leave your shuttle vehicle here.

To reach the start of the ride at Deer Valley, go back to the intersection of Park Avenue and Kearns Boulevard in Park City. From there, drive south on Park Avenue for 0.3 mile. Turn left onto Deer Valley Drive while following the signs to Deer Valley Resort. In 1.1 miles, you'll come to a traffic circle. Follow it to the opposite side and continue straight onto Marsac Avenue. Follow this road as it winds up through a canyon and into the mountains for 1.9 miles, then turn left on Guardsman Connection Road. In 0.3 mile, after a few switchbacks into the land of condos, turn right on Royal Street. As you approach Deer Valley's Silver Lake base area, search for parking on the street. Otherwise, in 0.3 mile, turn right on Sterling Court and park in the parking garage.

MILEAGE LOG

0.0 At Silver Lake Village, next to the bottom of the Sterling chairlift, go right on a gravel road as it goes underneath a bridge. Right after, leave the road by going left onto the MMT singletrack.

0.7 The Ontario Bypass Trail enters on the right. Soon after, Shenanigans connects on the right. Stay straight on MMT.

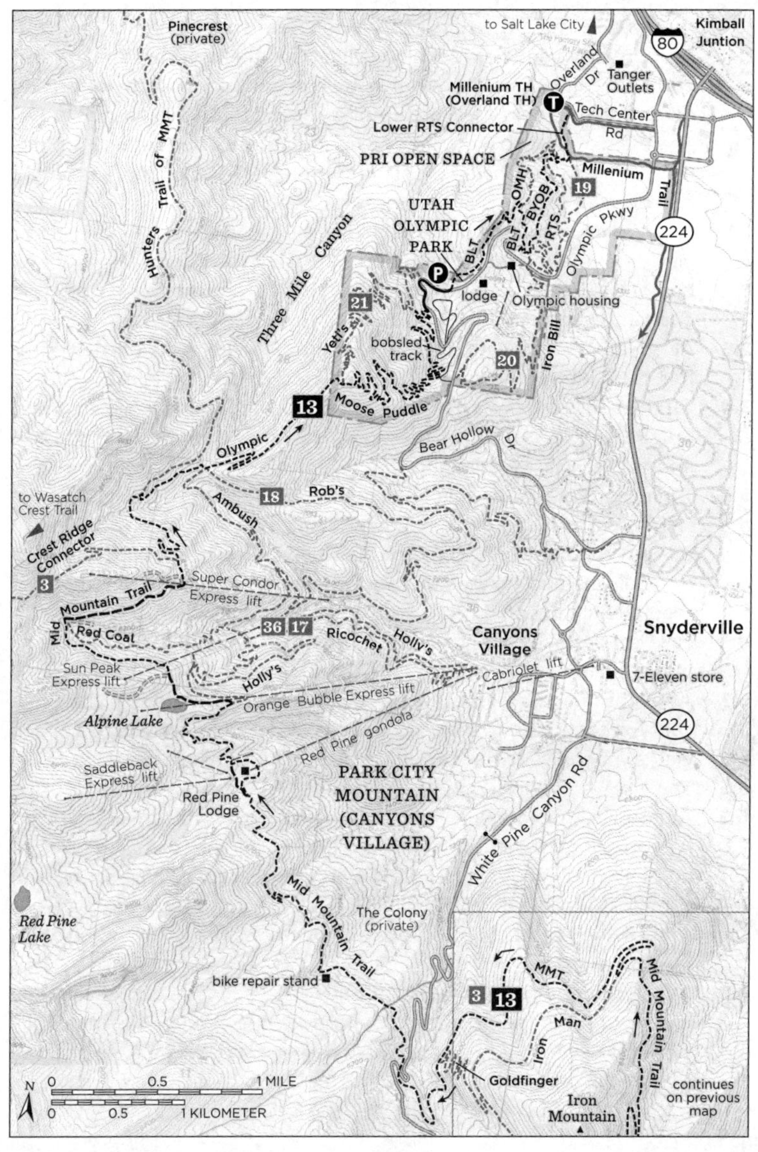
Pinecrest (private)
to Salt Lake City
Kimball Juntion
80
The Hungry S
Overland Dr
Tanger Outlets
Millenium TH (Overland TH)
T
Tech Center Rd
Lower RTS Connector
PRI OPEN SPACE
OMH
BLT
BYOB
RTS
Millenium
19
Olympic Pkwy
224
Hunters Trail of MMT
UTAH OLYMPIC PARK
P
BLT
21
lodge
Olympic housing
Iron Bill
Three Mile Canyon
Yeti's
bobsled track
20
13
Moose Puddle
Olympic
Bear Hollow Dr
to Wasatch Crest Trail
18
Rob's
Ambush
Crest Ridge Connector
3
Super Condor Express lift
Mid Mountain Trail
Snyderville
Red Coal
36 17
Ricochet
Holly's
Canyons Village
Cabriolet lift
7-Eleven store
Sun Peak Express lift
Holly's
Orange Bubble Express lift
224
Alpine Lake
Red Pine gondola
Saddleback Express lift
PARK CITY MOUNTAIN (CANYONS VILLAGE)
Red Pine Lodge
White Pine Canyon Rd
Red Pine Lake
The Colony (private)
Mid Mountain Trail
bike repair stand
3 13
MMT
Iron Man
Mid Mountain Trail
Goldfinger
continues on previous map
Iron Mountain
N
0   0.5   1 MILE
0   0.5   1 KILOMETER

1.1 Here you come to the start of Team Big Bear on the left. Stay on MMT.

1.4 Tour des Suds and Boulder also connect on the left. Stay straight and cross the paved Marsac Avenue to continue on singletrack on the other side as it descends into Empire Canyon through an aspen grove. There are a few exposed roots to negotiate here, but nothing too difficult. For the next half mile, stay right on MMT while ignoring Drifter, Payroll, and Corvair that all intersect on the left.

2.1 After riding above the massive Montage Deer Valley hotel, stay left on MMT where it intersects with Little Chief on the right. This next section of trail is nice as it traverses ski runs between the forests, offering excellent views.

2.8 At an intersection with T&G, stay straight on MMT. Immediately after this, MMT intersects with the Link Trail. Again, stay on MMT.

3.4 After a series of berms that switchback down through an aspen grove, Empire Link connects on the right. Continue straight on MMT as it enters Park City Mountain Resort.

3.9 Tommy's Two Step connects on the left. Stay straight on MMT.

4.1 MMT crosses a ski run then curves right onto a doubletrack. Follow this dirt road downhill. Look for the well-marked continuation of MMT on your left and take it. After a switchback, go left on another dirt road and climb uphill.

4.3 MMT singletrack continues on the right. Leave the road here and continue on MMT.

5.2 After the trail crosses a few ski runs and goes underneath the Crescent Express chairlift, a bit of a short, rocky climb takes you to a bench with a magnificent view, a very popular spot to take a break.

5.5 The Mojave downhill-only trail enters on the left. Stay right on MMT.

6.2 At a fork, Crescent Mine Grade goes right. Go left to stay on MMT.

7.1 At a major intersection with Spiro and Powerline, continue straight on MMT as it begins to climb. From this point you have to ride an 11-mile stretch with no downhill exits until you reach the Canyons side of the resort. So be prepared, because this is the point of no return.

8.3 At the top of a short climb, Pinecone Ridge connects on the left. You can go up this trail to access the Wasatch Crest. For this ride, stay straight on MMT. At this point you'll descend, but take it slow because this area is very crowded with other mountain bikers.

8.9   At a switchback the Armstrong Trail (uphill only) connects on the right. Stay left on MMT. From this point, MMT gets more technical. While it never gets steep, there are numerous rock gardens with stones big enough that many riders dismount here and walk their bikes. But these sections are short.

9.4   At a fork, Iron Man connects on the left. Stay right on MMT. Iron Man circumnavigates Iron Mountain and reconnects with MMT on the other side. This is an option if you want to add a little 300-vertical foot up-and-down to your ride.

10.8   MMT makes a hard right turn where the other end of Iron Man joins in. Take that hard right and continue on MMT.

12.7   Where Goldfinger enters in on the left, stay right on MMT. Goldfinger switchbacks up to Iron Man, so is another option to change up this route. At this point you enter The Colony—an exclusive, mansion-filled neighborhood. You must stay on the trail as you are now surrounded by private property. You're not even allowed to ride on the neighborhood streets. You will cross several paved roads. Mid Mountain Trail is easy to pick back up on the other side of each road crossing.

14.0   Just before the second street crossing, there is a bike repair stand with tools next to a concrete building. Use this if you have to make any fixes to your bike as, again, you have to stay on Mid Mountain Trail and are not allowed to venture off the path.

15.5   Cross a bridge that takes you to the base terminals of the Saddleback Express and High Meadow Express chairlifts next to the Red Pine Lodge. The lodge is open in the summer and is a great place to stop and refuel. Here you'll also find the top terminal of the Red Pine gondola, which provides lift-served mountain biking. If you need to get back to town, you can ride the gondola down to Canyons Village. Mid Mountain Trail becomes doubletrack as it passes in front of the Red Pine Lodge and the gondola. But as of this writing, a singletrack detour goes around the back side of the lodge because of construction. Ride either way depending on what is open—both will end up at the same place on the other side.

15.8   On the opposite side of the lodge and gondola, MMT becomes singletrack again underneath a couple of zip lines.

16.5   At a dirt road, after going under the Orange Bubble Express chairlift, go left on the road but then immediately head right to continue on MMT.

Traversing Deer Valley and Park City Mountain ski resorts on the MMT is a classic.

16.8 At the Alpine Lake catch-and-release fishing pond, go right onto a dirt road. Immediately after, pick up the singletrack on the right that parallels the road.

17.4 After going underneath the Sun Peak Express chairlift, the MMT comes to another dirt road. Stay left and go up the road. Almost immediately after, leave the road where MMT singletrack begins again on the right.

18.1 Soon after going beneath the Super Condor Express chairlift, you'll come to the intersection with Crest Ridge Connector, which comes in on the left. This is another access trail to the MMT. Stay straight on MMT.

19.1 The main Mid Mountain Trail terminates at the Hunters Trail of MMT. You can continue down Hunters Trail, but it enters the Pinebrook neighborhood trail system, where only residents are allowed to ride. So, you can continue your MMT ride if you want to add an out-and-back that adds more mileage. But when you reach Pinebrook, you must turn around and come back to this spot. At this intersection, go right on Ambush.

19.5 Ambush intersects with Rob's Trail (uphill only) and Olympic Trail. Take the left-most option on Olympic. It switchbacks uphill a few times until it tops out on a ridge that offers a dizzying traverse. Soon after, the trail enters a tight stand of trees.

20.6 Olympic intersects Moose Puddle, which is part of the Utah Olympic Park trail system. Go right (downhill). Left is the uphill-only Yeti's Trail. Enjoy a fast descent punctuated with tight switchbacks down Moose Puddle. Watch your speed, as hikers abound.

23.6 Moose Puddle ends at the paved Bear Hollow Drive in the Utah Olympic Park. Go left and head downhill on the road.

23.9 BLT Trail starts on the northeast end of a parking lot. Ride this as it climbs then descends into the RTS Loop.

25.0 BLT ends at the RTS Loop. Go left on RTS. Almost immediately after you make this turn, go left onto the BYOB downhill-only trail, a fun descent with some berms. Note that there are some difficult options on this downhill section, including a rock slab feature. Stay left for an easier way down.

25.7 Now at the bottom of BYOB as it intersects with the RTS Loop, go left on RTS.

25.9 Turn left onto the paved Millennium Trail bike path, and climb about 100 yards to the RTS Connector Trail on the right. Take this singletrack.

26.2 The singletrack ends at another paved bike trail. Go left until the paved trail ends at the Lower RTS/ Millennium Trail parking lot where you left a shuttle car.

OPTIONS

So many trails intersect the Mid Mountain Trail that the options seem limitless. But to ride the longest stretch of the trail, this route is the way to go, especially if you add the Hunters Trail of MMT out-and-back to the ride.

14 SNOWTOP TO SOLAMERE LOOP

LOOP

Trail Type: 75% singletrack, 25% paved trail/road

Distance: 4 miles

Elevation Gain/Loss: 870/870 feet

High Point: 7621 feet

Ride Time: 45 minutes to 1.5 hours

Maps: Mountain Trails Foundation Summer Map; Adventure Maps Salt Lake City, Park City, and the Wasatch; USGS 7.5-minute Park City East

GPS: 40°38'33.51"N, 111°28'40.66"W

Technical Difficulty: Intermediate

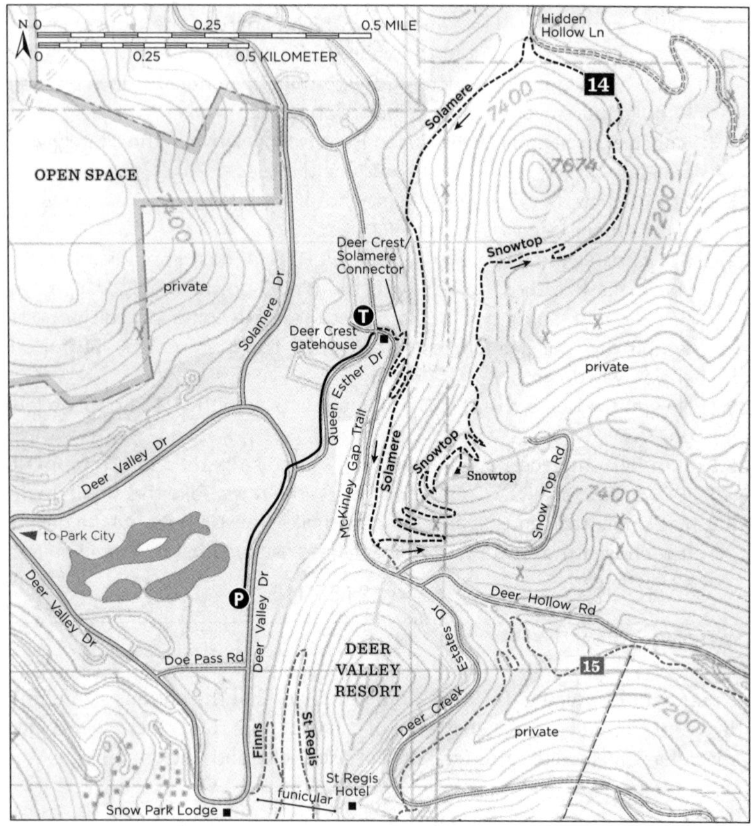

Fitness Intensity: Moderate
Season: Spring–fall

Land Manager: Private (managed by Mountain Trails Foundation)

OVERVIEW

The trails at Deer Valley generally aren't rideable until early summer after the snow melts, but the Snowtop–Solamere loop is an exception. Despite the name, Snowtop does not get much snow. Low-elevation, sun-exposed slopes mean the snow disappears fast, just in time for mid-to-late spring mountain biking. As a result, this loop is among the first to open for the season in Park City.

The loop can be done in both directions, but going counterclockwise (as described here) means ascending the Snowtop Trail and descending Solamere. Climbing up Snowtop is steep, with dozens of tight switchbacks. But thankfully the ascent is short with only 870 feet of elevation gain. Going the other direction with an ascent up Solamere means a less steep climb but a not-so-fun descent on Snowtop with all those tight switchbacks. But really, it's personal preference.

The sun-exposed, lower elevation trails on Snowtop are among the first to become rideable in spring.

This loop is entirely on private property with a public easement on the trails. As a result, you must stay on the trail at all times.

GETTING THERE

From the intersection of Park Avenue and Kearns Boulevard in Park City, drive south on Park Avenue for 0.3 mile. Turn left onto Deer Valley Drive while following the signs to Deer Valley Resort. In 1.1 miles, you'll come to a traffic circle. Take the second exit and stay on Deer Valley Drive. Follow this road for 1.2 miles to the Snow Park Lodge. Continue past the lodge as the road loops back to the north and passes the large parking lots. Go to the lowest lot and park. Locate the paved bike trail at the northeast corner of the lot and begin the ride here.

MILEAGE LOG

0.0 Ride north on the paved bike trail as it curves around the ponds. The trail parallels Deer Valley Drive.

0.2 Leave the paved trail and go right, crossing Deer Valley Drive onto Queen Esther Drive. Stay on this street as it goes northeast into a neighborhood of condos and huge homes.

0.5 On your right you'll see the private Deer Crest gate house. To the left of this drive is a singletrack trailhead. The sign here marks the Deer Crest Trails and is one of the possible starts to enter this network. The trail is marked as private property, but the public is allowed to ride here as long as they stay on designated trails. Climb up this Deer Crest/Solamere Connector Trail as it switchbacks up through a beautiful aspen grove.

0.8 At the end of the connector trail, go right at the intersection and continue on Solamere. The sign here points the way to Snowtop. The trail traverses south on a bench above ritzy condos and townhomes.

1.0 At a fork, hang a left onto the Snowtop Trail (right goes to Snow Top Road). Here the trail climbs with dozens of tight switchbacks and a few steep, punchy sections. It's a good workout, but thankfully the climb is relatively short.

1.6 The ascent tops out near the summit of Snowtop. To reach the true top, take a 150-foot spur trail on the right for a great view of Deer Valley Resort and Jordanelle Reservoir. This is a nice spot to take a breather and have a snack. When finished with your break, continue on Snowtop as it now descends down the other side of the mountain. This fun downhill has a few bermed turns and fast straightaways.

2.7   The Snowtop Trail ends at a paved road, Hidden Hollow Lane. Stay left and get on the Solamere Trail on the other side. After a very short climb, the singletrack slightly descends southwest on a long straightaway where you can pick up some more speed.

3.0   At this fork, ignore the trail on the right labeled Solamere. This is another access trail for Solamere Connector located on the other side of a neighborhood below. Instead, go left on Solamere where the sign directs riders to Snowtop.

3.3   Rejoin the intersection with the Deer Crest/Solamere Connector that you rode up at the beginning of the ride. Go right and return down to the gate house.

3.6   Back at the gate house, you can retrace your route on Queen Ester Drive and Deer Valley Drive back to the Snow Park lot.

4.0   You've reached the end of the ride and are back at the lower parking lot.

OPTIONS

For a mellower climb up Solamere followed by a steeper, slower, tighter descent on Snowtop, ride this loop clockwise.

15 SPIN CYCLE

LOOP

Trail Type: 85% singletrack, 15% doubletrack or paved road

Distance: 6 miles

Elevation Gain/Loss: 1355/1355 feet

High Point: 7642 feet

Ride Time: 1.5–2.5 hours

Technical Difficulty: Advanced

Fitness Intensity: Moderate

Season: Summer–fall

Maps: Mountain Trails Foundation Summer Map; Adventure Maps Salt Lake City, Park City, and the Wasatch; USGS 7.5-minute Park City East

GPS: 40°38'18.94"N, 111°28'40.79"W

Land Manager: Deer Valley Resort

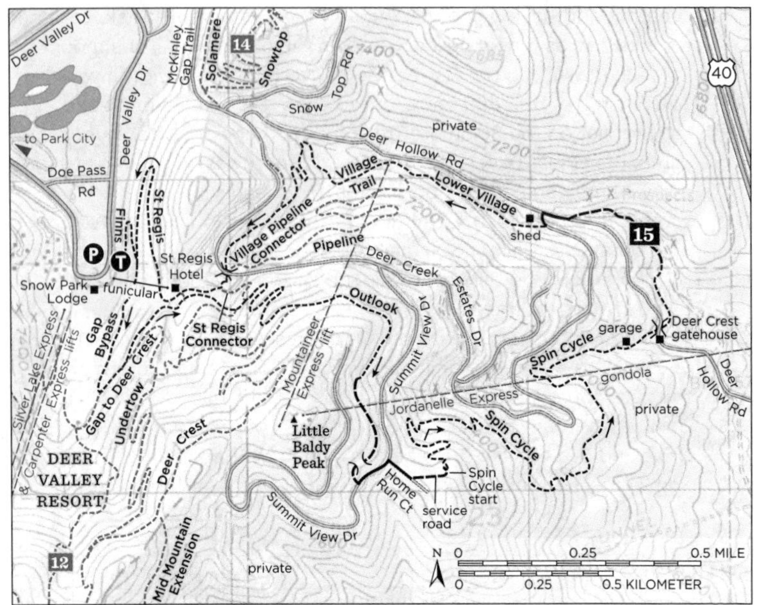

OVERVIEW

Spin Cycle represents classic Deer Valley downhill. But unlike the newer gravity trails in the resort's bike park, riders will find this descent a bit more old school. The trail begins in open meadows along wide switchbacks that crisscross ski runs. It then enters a large aspen grove before entering a natural half-pipe in a tight gully. Seemingly never-ending turns and curves get tighter and tighter as the trail crisscrosses a tiny stream. Just when you can't take much more of the fun, Spin Cycle spits you out at a garage with a neighboring rusty washing machine—the inspiration for the trail's name.

Another old-school aspect of riding Spin Cycle is that you can't get there with the help of a chairlift. Instead, you have to climb on your bike. Plus, finding the entrance to Spin Cycle is not easy. There are a few ways to access it, but I prefer the option that begins at Deer Valley's Snow Park Lodge. The ascent utilizes multiple trails, including Finns, Gap to Deer Crest, Pipeline, and, finally, Outlook to get to the top. A short ride down paved roads in the

All smiles on Spin Cycle, arguably the most fun downhill ride at Deer Valley outside the bike park.

Deer Crest neighborhood gets you to the top of Spin Cycle. At the bottom, Village Trail provides a climb back to the resort and a return to Snow Park for a 6-mile loop.

Getting to and exiting from Spin Cycle may be a bit of work for a mere 2 miles and 800 vertical feet of downhill. But this joyride is so fun that you won't mind the navigation and a little exercise to experience it.

GETTING THERE

From the intersection of Park Avenue and Kearns Boulevard in Park City, drive south on Park Avenue for 0.3 mile. Turn left onto Deer Valley Drive while following the signs to Deer Valley Resort. In 1.1 miles, you'll come to a traffic circle. Take the second exit and stay on Deer Valley Drive. Follow this road for 1.2 miles to Snow Park Lodge. Park in the uppermost large parking lot.

MILEAGE LOG

0.0 From the upper lot, ride east toward the St. Regis Hotel funicular on the other side of the street. You'll see the start of Finns Trail on your left. Start climbing the singletrack. Almost immediately after, stay right at an intersection (left goes to a different trailhead for Finns). Continue climbing on Finns.

0.2 Go right on Gap Bypass as it goes underneath the funicular track.

0.4 At an intersection, stay left on Gap Bypass (right simply descends to a ski run).

0.5 Go left as the trail curves uphill. This is the start of the Gap to Deer Crest Trail. The intersecting network of trails here is confusing, but a sign pointing the way to Deer Crest helps with orientation.

0.9 After traversing alongside the St. Regis Hotel, Gap to Deer Crest intersects the Pipeline Trail. Go right on Pipeline and follow up in a series of switchbacks. Signs mark the way to Spin Cycle.

1.3 Pipeline intersects the Outlook Trail. Go left on Outlook. Signs continue to show the way to Spin Cycle. Outlook traverses around the north side of Deer Valley Resort. It goes beneath the Mountaineer Express chairlift and alternates between forest and bare ski runs. Enjoy the view of Jordanelle Reservoir glistening far below.

1.7 Outlook ends at a dirt road. At this point you leave the Deer Valley Resort boundary and enter the private Deer Crest neighborhood.

The public is allowed to travel on the trail here under an easement. Go left and follow the road down into a neighborhood of mansions. On the way you'll ride beneath the Jordanelle Express gondola and go through a tunnel.

1.9 Turn left onto the paved Summit View Drive, then go right on Home Run Court. As you ride through the Deer Crest neighborhood, look for the small signs that direct the way to Spin Cycle.

2.0 Watch for a dirt service road on your left as you ride down Home Run Court. Go down this road. Just where the road makes a sharp left turn is the start of Spin Cycle. Drop your seatpost and crack your braking fingers for the big, bobsled-style descent.

3.5 The trail exits the trees at a garage. Catch your breath then ride around the building where the Spin Cycle singletrack continues.

3.6 Near the Deer Crest gatehouse, go under the bridge. There may be snowcats parked underneath this bridge for summer storage. On the other side, the trail ends at a doubletrack road. Go left onto this road as it climbs steeply.

4.0 The doubletrack ends at Deer Hollow Road. Go right on the paved street.

4.1 Turn left on Deer Crest Estates Drive. Immediately after making this turn, you'll see a singletrack trail next to the snow gun storage and a large rock wall. Go right on this trail, which is called Lower Village.

4.5 At the base of the Mountaineer Express chairlift, stay right (straight) on Village Trail. If you want to ride Spin Cycle again, go left here on Pipeline and follow it to Outlook for another round.

5.0 At a fork, Village Trail continues on the right. Instead, go left on Village Pipeline Connector. Go under a bridge, then go right on Pipeline.

5.2 After a few switchbacks, go right on the unmarked St. Regis Connector Trail. This trail goes directly to the lower level of the hotel.

5.3 After riding past the swimming pool, go right on the St. Regis Trail. It soon goes under the funicular track. Beyond that, stay left at a minor intersection.

5.6 Turn left onto Gap Bypass.

5.8 Go right, then immediately left on Finns to get back to the Snow Park parking lot.

6.0 End of the ride.

OPTIONS

There are a few other ways to approach Spin Cycle. You can start at the resort's Silver Lake base area and ride the Mid Mountain Extension to the Deer Crest Trail, which connects to Outlook. Second, you can ride the Solamere Trail from Snow Park. When you reach the gatehouse on Deer Hollow Road, ride the paved streets, keeping right onto Deer Crest Estates Drive until you see Village Trail on the right. Take it to Village Pipeline Connector, which leads to Pipeline. Continue to Spin Cycle as described above. Finally, if you are a Deer Crest resident and you (or your friends) have vehicle access to this exclusive, mansion-filled neighborhood, you can arrange for a shuttle on this trail.

16 9K TRAIL TO BLACK FOREST

SHUTTLE

Trail Type: 87% singletrack
13% doubletrack
Distance: 5.3 miles
Elevation Gain/Loss: 290/1830 feet
High Point: 9843 feet
Ride Time: 1–2 hours
Technical Difficulty: Advanced
Fitness Intensity: Easy
Season: Summer–fall

Maps: Mountain Trails Foundation Summer Map; Adventure Maps Salt Lake City, Park City, and the Wasatch; USGS 7.5-minute Brighton, Park City West, Park City East
GPS: 40°36'22.53"N, 111°30'31.86"W
Land Manager: Deer Valley Resort, Park City Mountain

OVERVIEW

It's hard to imagine Park City's Trail system improving, but then Mountain Trails Foundation went and did just that with the new 9K Trail. Much like the famous Mid Mountain Trail following the 8000-foot contour line from Deer Valley to the far side of Canyons Village, the 9K Trail meanders on the 9000-foot contour line. The 9K Trail begins at Empire Pass above Deer Valley. From there it heads generally northwest along the ridge above the Daly Chutes and Empire Bowl. The views are impressive the entire way as the path crosses open ski runs and winds through aspen and evergreen forest. Soon after passing under the Empire Express chairlift, the 9K Trail

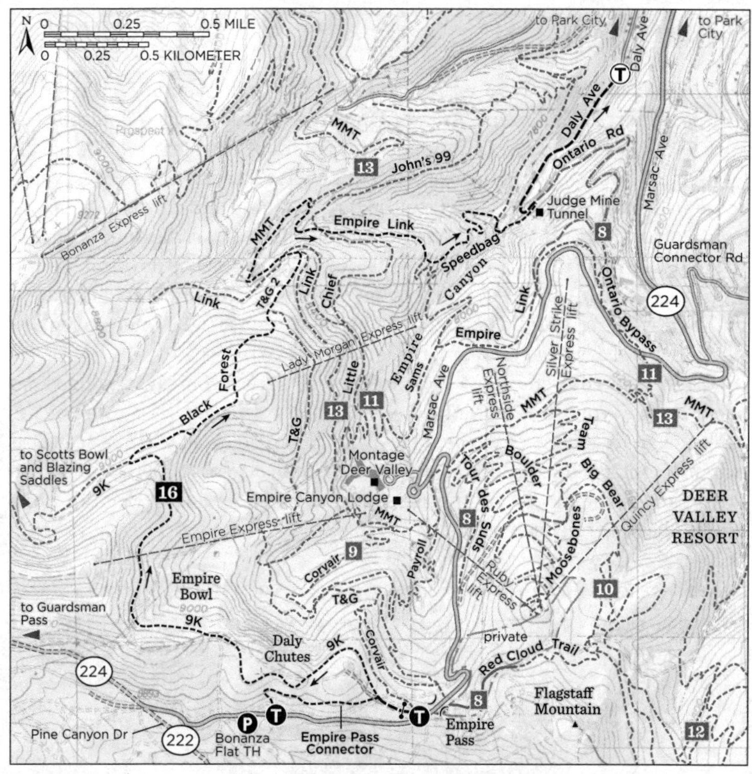

intersects the Black Forest Trail. Intermediate riders should continue on the 9K Trail and ride it as an 11-mile out-and-back, because Black Forest is a very steep, advanced downhill with innumerable root drops, rutted loose dirt, and tight switchbacks in a thick forest.

Beyond Black Forest, the 9K Trail goes to Shadow Lake and Scott's Bowl where it connects to the Blazing Saddles Trail. It's a great ride, but for this route, Black Forest is the most challenging way down to Mid Mountain Trail. I like to ride it as a shuttle, how it is described here.

If the parking lot at Empire Pass is full, use the new Bonanza Flat trailhead, 0.5 mile down the road on the west side of the pass. Then climb the Empire Pass Connector to the start of 9K.

GETTING THERE

First, you'll want to leave a return vehicle at the Daly Avenue Trailhead. To get there start at the intersection of Park Avenue and Kearns Boulevard in Park City. Drive south on Park Avenue for 0.3 mile. Turn left onto Deer Valley Drive while following the signs to Deer Valley Resort. In 1.1 miles, you'll come to a traffic circle. Follow it to the opposite side and continue straight, leaving the circle on Marsac Avenue. In 0.4 mile, turn right onto Prospect Avenue, then continue straight on Hillside Avenue as it goes downhill. At the bottom of the hill, turn left on Daly Avenue. Follow it through a neighborhood in the canyon for 0.5 mile until the road ends at a gate, right when pavement turns to dirt. Park at a pullout on the left.

Then take your shuttle vehicle to Empire Pass. From the trailhead, go back the way you came to Marsac Avenue and turn right. Take Marsac for 3.2 miles to the traffic circle near the Empire Canyon Lodge. Take the third exit and continue up. In 1.2 miles after the traffic circle, you'll reach Empire Pass. Park in the dirt lot on the right where there is a Forest Service bathroom. The 9K Trail begins here.

Due to its high elevation, the 9K Trail has some of the best vistas in Park City.

MILEAGE LOG

0.0 From the parking area, walk your bike around the metal gate and pedal up a doubletrack road, passing Corvair Trail on the right.

0.4 Leave the dirt road and get onto the 9K Trail singletrack on the right. The trail traverses above the Daly Chutes (double-black diamond runs at Deer Valley) and has excellent views of the valleys below.

1.3 The trail passes under the Empire Express chairlift and goes in and out of stands of forest, both aspen and pine.

1.8 The 9K Trail intersects the Black Forest Trail. Black Forest is recommended for advanced-level riders only because it is steep, narrow, loose, and rowdy. If you're not at that sort of skill level, you should complete an out-and-back ride on the full 9K Trail. Otherwise, go right and descend the thrill ride that is Black Forest.

2.4 The bottom of Black Forest intersects with the T&G 2 Trail. Stay left and continue down T&G 2. This is still advanced riding that's very similar to what you've already descended on Black Forest.

2.7 T&G 2 ends at the Mid Mountain Trail. You have many descent options here, but I suggest going left on MMT. You'll immediately pass the Link Trail on your left. Stay on MMT.

3.3 At the intersection, go right onto Empire Link.

3.5 At the intersection with John's 99 Trail, stay straight (down) on Empire Link.

4.0 You come to an intersection with Speedbag. Take a hard left to go down this advanced-level trail. As you descend, take a moment to appreciate the manmade wood turns built into the steep mountainside.

4.3 Speedbag ends at a doubletrack road. Go right and down to the historical Judge Mine Tunnel. Follow the road past the mine until you're on the dirt Ontario Road. Continue straight.

4.7 Leave Ontario Road and go left on Daly Avenue. Follow this down, back to the Daly Avenue Trailhead where you left a shuttle vehicle.

5.3 End of ride.

OPTIONS

If you're not comfortable with navigating the advanced-level Black Forest Trail, the 9K Trail is an easy-intermediate out-and-back. The 9K Trail is already a popular classic to Scotts Bowl above Shadow Lake. Riders can use the 9K Trail to access a few other descents at points in between.

CANYONS VILLAGE & UTAH OLYMPIC PARK

Canyons Village is nestled in the western base area of Park City Mountain ski resort. Prior to 2015, the resort operated as a separate ski area called The Canyons with a downhill bike park that rivaled Deer Valley's trails. But when Vail Resorts bought Park City Mountain Resort and The Canyons, they combined the two mountains into the largest ski area in the United States. Unfortunately, the new ownership wanted little to do with gravity-fed mountain biking and dismantled the bike park. Many of the trails were closed and left to return to a natural state. But some trails remain at Canyons Village, and lift-served mountain biking still exists (Route 17). In addition to the former bike park, other trails within the resort boundary are maintained by Basin Recreation, like the Rob's to Ambush Loop (Route 18), which trends toward more classic mountain bike fare.

Connected to the trails at Canyons Village is the Utah Olympic Park (UOP), the venue for the bobsled, skeleton, luge, ski jumping, and Nordic combined events in the 2002 Winter Olympics. Today, future Olympic athletes use it as a training facility. The public can visit and enjoy a free museum, plus adventure activities like zip lines, tubing, ropes courses, and of course, bobsled rides. The venue is also home to a decent trail network. The UOP Bobsled loop (Route 21) climbs and descends the mountain that looms over the park. It's a great choice for intermediate riders. For beginners, the RTS network (Route 19) offers short, mellow loops with no obstacles and little elevation gain. Although Canyons Village lacks the mountain biking energy of its former self, a dedicated group of riders and volunteers

Pedaling beneath a chairlift at Canyons Village (Route 17)

have kept the network alive. It's still great fun and often sees fewer crowds than Park City proper.

17 CANYONS VILLAGE DOWNHILL TRAILS

NETWORK

Trail Type: 100% singletrack

Distance: Up to 10 miles

Elevation Gain/Loss: 300/1385 feet

High Point: 8371 feet

Ride Time: As long as you want from open to close, hours vary

Technical Difficulty: Intermediate to Advanced

Fitness Intensity: Moderate

Season: Summer–fall

Maps: Mountain Trails Foundation Summer Map; Adventure Maps Salt Lake City, Park City, and the Wasatch; USGS 7.5-minute Park City West

GPS: 40°41'9.38"N, 111°33'23.99"W

Land Manager: Park City Mountain

OVERVIEW

From 2012 to 2017, the downhill bike park at Canyons Resort was among the most well-known in the country. Featuring dozens of gravity trails complete with huge wooden features, jumps, gaps, and drops, the park was a gathering place for riders to test their bravery and skills on a bike.

But soon after Vail Resorts bought Canyons, they shut down and closed the bike park in 2018. All manmade features were dismantled, and the trails were blocked off to become overgrown and returned to a natural state. Despite these closures, Park City Mountain continued to provide lift-served bike haul on the Canyons Village side via the Red Pine gondola. While the current trails at Canyons Village lack the scale of the bike park's former glory, there is still fun singletrack to flow down, including Red Coat, Insurgent, Ricochet, and Holly's. All these trails are accessed from the Mid Mountain Trail starting at the Red Pine gondola top station and end back at the Canyons Village base area.

If you don't want to pay for a lift ticket, you can pedal up the bi-directional Holly's Trail to access Mid Mountain Trail at the Red Pine area. Holly's is also a fun descent, but the trail sees a lot of uphill traffic and hikers.

The bike haul lift season generally begins in mid-June, with daily operations lasting through the end of September. In late summer, the lifts

Cruising down Ricochet across a Canyons Village ski run in summer

run only Thursdays through Sundays. Check www.parkcitymountain.com for current hours and pricing. Bike rentals are available at Canyon Mountain Rentals in Canyons Village.

GETTING THERE

From the intersection of Park Avenue and Kearns Boulevard in Park City, drive north on Park Avenue (SR 224) for 2.8 miles to Canyons Resort Drive. Turn left and park your car in the lot adjacent to the Cabriolet lift, behind the 7-Eleven store. Ride the free Cabriolet lift with your bike to the Canyons Village base area. Purchase your lift ticket here, then ride the Red Pine gondola to the top, where you will find the Mid Mountain Trail.

MILEAGE LOG

Below I've listed a few different options to ride your bike down to Canyons Village from the Red Pine gondola top station. Each ride is categorized based on difficulty.

INTERMEDIATE DESCENTS

MID MOUNTAIN TRAIL TO HOLLY'S: 4.6 MILES

0.0 Ride Mid Mountain Trail (MMT) north away from the Red Pine area.

0.8 Mid Mountain Trail makes a sharp left turn where it ends up on a dirt road. Leave MMT and go right on Holly's. The intersections are a bit

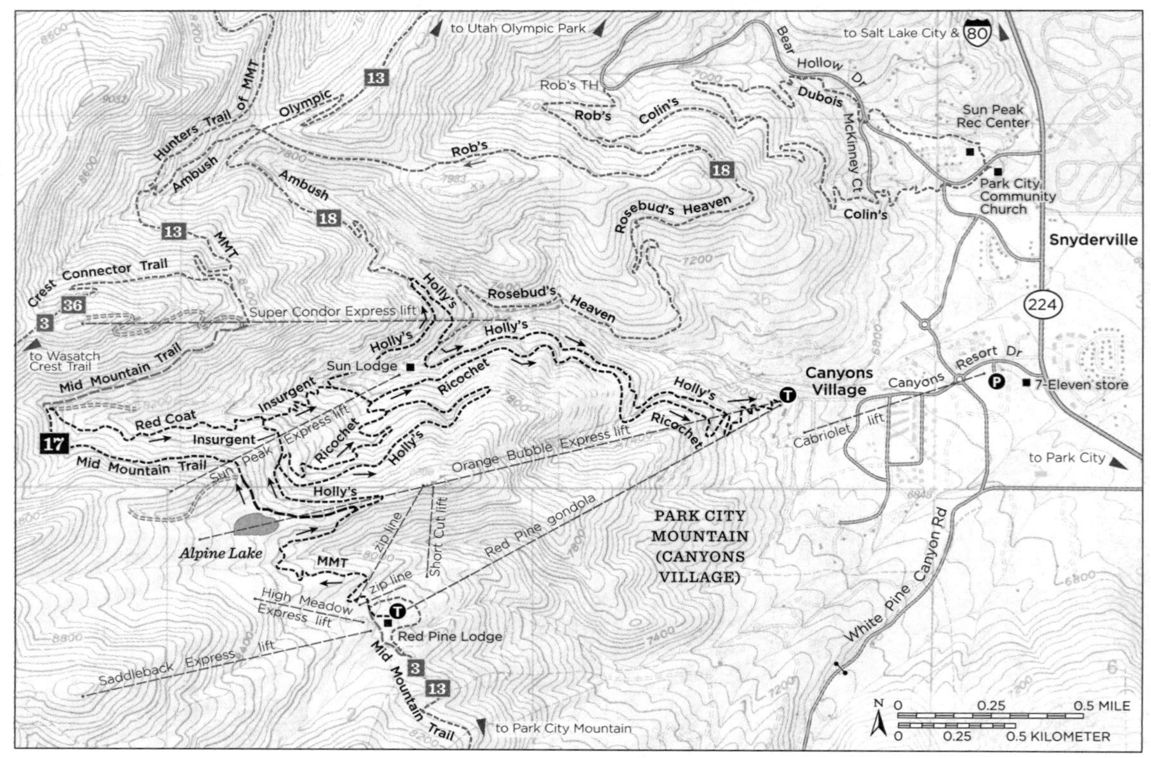

to Utah Olympic Park
to Salt Lake City & 80
Bear Hollow Dr
Rob's TH
Dubois
McKinney Ct
Sun Peak Rec Center
Hunters Trail of MMT
Olympic
13
Rob's
Colin's
Park City Community Church
Ambush
Rob's
18
Ambush
18
Rosebud's Heaven
Colin's
Snyderville
13
MMT
224
Crest Connector Trail
Rosebud's
Heaven
36
3
Super Condor Express lift
Holly's
Resort Dr
to Wasatch Crest Trail
Mid Mountain Trail
Holly's
Sun Lodge
Holly's
Ricochet
Canyons Village
Canyons
P
7-Eleven store
Red Coat
Insurgent
Insurgent
Express lift
Ricochet
Holly's
Ricochet
Holly's
T
17
Mid Mountain Trail
Sun Peak Express lift
Holly's
Orange Bubble Express lift
Cabriolet lift
to Park City
Alpine Lake
MMT
zip line
Short Cut lift
Red Pine gondola
PARK CITY MOUNTAIN (CANYONS VILLAGE)
High Meadow Express lift
zip line
T
Red Pine Lodge
3
Saddleback Express lift
13
Mid Mountain Trail
White Pine Canyon Rd
to Park City Mountain
N
0   0.25   0.5 MILE
0   0.25   0.5 KILOMETER

confusing here; when in doubt, follow the signs pointing the way to Holly's and Ricochet.

1.2   You reach a three-way intersection. To the left is Insurgent, an advanced, downhill-only trail. The middle is Ricochet, a moderate, downhill trail with fun rollers, jumps, and berms. To the right is the continuation of Holly's. For this option, take Holly's.

2.3   Holly's intersects Ricochet near the Sun Lodge. Stay straight and continue on Holly's. Soon after the intersection, you'll pass the end of Insurgent where it connects on the left. Stay right on Holly's.

2.9   Ambush connects on the left. Stay right on Holly's.

3.1   Rosebud's Heaven connects on the left. Stay right on Holly's.

4.6   Holly's ends at the Canyons Village base.

MID MOUNTAIN TRAIL TO HOLLY'S TO RICOCHET: 3.7 MILES

0.0   Ride Mid Mountain Trail north away from the Red Pine area.

0.8   MMT makes a sharp left turn where it ends up on a dirt road. Leave MMT and go right on Holly's. The intersections are a bit confusing here; when in doubt, follow the signs pointing the way to Holly's and Ricochet.

1.2   You reach a three-way intersection. To the left is Insurgent, an advanced, downhill-only trail. The middle is Ricochet, a moderate, downhill trail with fun rollers, jumps, and berms. To the right is the continuation of Holly's. For this intermediate option, take Ricochet.

3.7   Ricochet ends back at the Canyons Village base.

ADVANCED DESCENT

MMT TO RED COAT TO INSURGENT TO RICOCHET: 4.7 MILES

0.0   Ride Mid Mountain Trail north, away from the Red Pine area.

0.8   Mid Mountain Trail makes a sharp left turn where it ends up on a dirt road. You'll see the turnoff for Holly's on the right. Stay left on MMT.

1.0   MMT runs into a dirt road near a fishing pond called Alpine Lake beneath the Orange Bubble Express chairlift. Stay right on the MMT singletrack.

1.8   When MMT intersects Red Coat, turn right. This intermediate downhill-only, hand-cut trail is used less frequently and can be loose. It is steep, tight, and has a few manmade rock features.

2.5   Red Coat ends where it intersects Insurgent. Go left on Insurgent, an advanced-level, very steep downhill trail with tight corners, jumps, and drops. A few wood features smooth things out, but overall, it's a rough-and-tumble descent.

2.9   Insurgent ends where it intersects Holly's. Go right on Holly's. Only a few dozen yards later, Holly's comes to Ricochet. Go left down Ricochet and follow it all the way to the bottom at Canyons Village.

4.7   Ride ends at the Canyons Village base.

OPTIONS

If you choose to pedal up Holly's to reach the top of the downhill-only trails, the ascent is steep and a bit of a slog. Riding the Red Pine gondola allows you to make multiple laps.

18 ROB'S TO AMBUSH LOOP

LOOP

Trail Type: 95% singletrack, 5% paved
Distance: 8.7 miles
Elevation Gain/Loss: 1860/1860 feet
High Point: 7986 feet
Ride Time: 2–3 hours
Technical Difficulty: Intermediate
Fitness Intensity: Moderate
Season: Summer–fall

Maps: Mountain Trails Foundation Summer Map; Adventure Maps Salt Lake City, Park City, and the Wasatch; USGS 7.5-minute Park City West
GPS: 40°41'45.49"N, 111°32'47.32"W
Land Manager: Park City Mountain, a private company (managed by Basin Recreation)

OVERVIEW

The uphill-only Rob's Trail offers a main thoroughfare to access the Mid Mountain Trail on the Canyons Village side of Park City Mountain. Three trailheads provide access: Colin's, Dubois, and Rob's. This section of single-track used to be bi-directional, but Basin Recreation recently changed its designation to uphill only, which drastically changed the way mountain bikers make loops on this side of the ski resort.

Holly's and Ricochet to the south are options, but those trails technically exist as part of the Canyon's pay-to-play bike park. Basin Recreation suggests riders descend either Olympic to the Utah Olympic Park, or Ambush

Rob's to Ambush has smooth, buttery singletrack—a mountain biker's dream.

to Rosebud's Heaven. For this loop, I chose the latter because it allows riders to start and end the ride at the same trailhead (either Colin's or Dubois) and avoid a shuttle.

For simplicity's sake, I suggest parking at the Park City Community Church and riding up Dubois to Colin's and then Rob's. At the top, a return on Ambush, Rosebud's Heaven, and Colin's gets you back to the church. This is a quick and moderate ride that showcases most trails between the Utah Olympic Park and Canyons Village. Due to the wishes of private property owners, the upper section of Rob's is open only between May 15 and November 1.

GETTING THERE

From the intersection of Park Avenue and Kearns Boulevard in Park City, drive north on Park Avenue (SR 224) 3.4 miles to Bear Hollow Drive. Turn left. Right after making this turn, you'll see the Park City Community Church on your left. Trail users are allowed to park in the church's lot any time except for Sundays between 8 AM and noon. The ascent up Dubois begins on the other side of Bear Hollow Drive.

MILEAGE LOG

0.0 Exit the parking lot from the main entrance and ride across Bear Hollow Drive to the Sun Peak Recreation Center. On the right, a dirt path has a sign pointing the way to Dubois. Go up it, and in 300 feet cross a bridge and then go up a steep incline. At the top, turn left on Sun Creek Trail. The trail winds up through a neighborhood before dipping down into a shady creek bottom.

0.4   Cross Bear Hollow Drive and immediately after that, cross McKinney Court. When you regain the singletrack on the other side, ascend up Dubois as it now actively switchbacks up the mountainside.

1.3   Dubois ends at Colin's. Go right onto Colin's and continue uphill.

1.9   Colin's ends at Rob's. If you go right, you'll end up at the Rob's Trailhead on Bear Hollow Drive. Instead turn left on Rob's and keep going up the mountainside.

2.2   An intersection with Rosebud's Heaven is on the left. Stay right on Rob's. From this point on, Rob's is uphill-only for mountain bikers and signs make this point very clear.

2.6   A large sign nailed to a tree reads, "Trail closed Nov. 1–May 15. Private property beyond this point." Heed this warning and do not trespass if you arrive here between those dates.

3.0   At a small meadow you'll see a bench in remembrance of Sam Jackenthal, a Park City freeskier who died after a crash in Australia. This is a good spot to rest and reflect.

3.4   Here is a major intersection with Ambush to the left and straight ahead and Olympic on the right. If you go straight and continue uphill, you'll get to the Mid Mountain Trail. Right on Olympic takes you down to the Utah Olympic Park by way of Moose Puddle. For this loop, go left on Ambush to descend to Rosebud's Heaven.

4.4   Ambush ends at Holly's. Go left (downhill) on Holly's.

4.6   Rosebud's Heaven enters on the left. Take this fork. Rosebud's Heaven goes down a short way, then climbs up in a series of switchbacks. This trail is a bit narrow and underutilized.

6.4   On the left is another memorial bench that is a good resting spot with a nice view. This bench is engraved with the words, "Pedal, Pete. Pedal." Right after, you come back to the intersection with Rob's. Take the right fork and head down.

6.9   Rob's intersects with Colin's. Go right and continue down Colin's.

7.4   The top of Dubois comes in on the left. Stay right on Colin's and enjoy the downhill ride. At this point Colin's gets a bit more technical with rock gardens and tight corners. It's still a solidly intermediate descent though.

8.5   At the Colin's Trailhead on Sun Peak Drive, go left on the street then go right onto Bear Hollow Drive and follow it back to the church where you parked your vehicle.

8.7   You've reached the end of the ride.

OPTIONS

You can do this same loop but start instead at either the Colin's or Rob's Trailheads. Colin's offers a great option but presents a more technical climb than Dubois, with more rocks and tighter switchbacks. The Rob's Trailhead starts a lot farther up Bear Hollow Drive, so you get less singletrack and need to pedal up a lot of paved street to make a complete loop.

As stated above, Rob's provides a great way to get to Mid Mountain Trail via Ambush. Or you can descend Olympic, Moose Puddle, and Iron Bill to the RTS network for either a shuttle ride option or a paved pedal on the Millennium bike path back to the Park City Community Church.

19 RTS NETWORK

NETWORK

Trail Type: 100% singletrack
Distance: Up to 3 miles

Elevation Gain/Loss: Up to 505/505 feet
High Point: 6819 feet

Ride Time: Up to 45 minutes
Technical Difficulty: Beginner to Intermediate
Fitness Intensity: Easy
Season: Spring–fall
GPS: 40°42'96.57"N, 111°33'25.33"W

Land Manager: PRI Open Space (managed by Basin Recreation)
Maps: Mountain Trails Foundation Summer Map; Adventure Maps, Salt Lake City, Park City, and the Wasatch; USGS 7.5-minute Park City West

OVERVIEW

The RTS network offers one of the most beginner-friendly areas in Park City. This trail system is below the Utah Olympic Park within PRI Open Space. The RTS Loop is the easiest ride in this small network, which features non-technical family-friendly singetrack. The dirt is smooth, the corners are wide, and the trail is never steep. Still, this short loop has plenty of twists and turns through aspen forests and sagebrush meadows to keep the ride interesting. You can pedal in either direction—both are fun—but this featured loop goes clockwise. If you're a first-time mountain biker, out of shape, or a Park City newbie, the RTS Loop is a great place to get some singletrack experience.

More advanced riders can find fast and technically challenging descents on the BYOB and OMH downhill-only trails. BYOB starts at the upper end of the RTS loop, while OMH begins midway up BLT. I describe the easier RTS loop with mileage below and add the downhill trails at the end.

GETTING THERE

From Park City, drive north on SR 224 toward Kimball Junction. After about 5.5 miles, turn left onto Olympic Parkway. At the roundabout, go three-quarters of the way around the circle to continue south on Olympic Parkway. From here, the road climbs toward the Utah Olympic Park. About 0.5 mile from the roundabout, turn right into the gravel parking area where you will find the RTS Trailhead.

The RTS Loop is great for beginners.

MILEAGE LOG

RTS Loop

First-timers and kids can practice mountain biking skills on this easy, non-technical, wide singletrack loop. The mileage log focuses on this ride, with options described below.

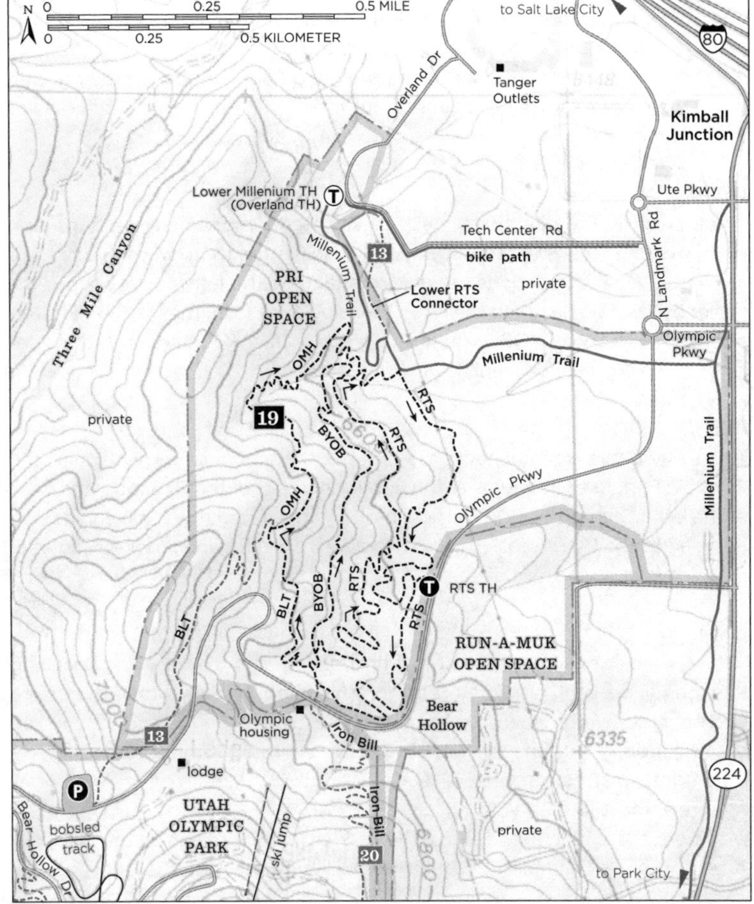

0.0   Go through the break in the fence and head left (south) onto the RTS Loop. Ride uphill through sagebrush and into a large stand of aspens.

0.5   At the UOP (Iron Bill) and BLT Trail intersection, stay right on RTS.

0.6   At an intersection with the BYOB downhill-only trail, stay right to remain on RTS.

1.5   Here you meet up with the BYOB Trail exit. Stay right. Immediately after this intersection, keep right again on the main trail, ignoring the few short trails on the left that end at the paved Millennium Trail.

2.1   Avoid the shortcut back to the trailhead on the left, and stay right on the main RTS Trail to squeeze out more mileage.

2.4   The ride ends by looping back to the trailhead.

BYOB

This downhill-only directional trail has sculpted jumps, rocky sections, and berms. In one technical section you can choose from three ways of descending a rock face with various degrees of difficulty. The left-most option is the easier bypass. While riding the RTS Loop clockwise from the trailhead, go left after 0.6 mile onto BYOB Trail. At the bottom, take RTS back to the top for laps on the 0.6-mile descent.

BLT

This easy, 1-mile trail connects the Lower UOP trail network with the Utah Olympic Park itself. It begins at the uppermost part of the RTS loop and ends at the Utah Olympic Park's overflow parking area. From there you can ride up the road to the UOP Bobsled Loop (Route 21) on Yeti's and Moose Puddle for that ride and other trails beyond.

OMH

"Oh My Heck" is the newest-cut downhill-only trail in the network. Reaching this longer descent requires a bit more climbing, but it's worth the effort. OMH is flowy, with dozens upon dozens of sculpted berms and rollers. You might get dizzy with the amount of twists and turns. But those turns can be a little tight, so although OMH is technically intermediate in difficulty, it does require some bike-handling skills.

To get there, ride to the top of the RTS loop and turn left on the BLT Trail. After 0.3 mile of climbing on BLT, the OMH entrance is on the right.

OPTIONS

Add a bit more trail by parking at Overland Trailhead on Overland Drive, behind the Tanger Outlets. From there you can access the RTS loop by taking the Lower RTS Connector Trail, a 0.2-mile singletrack and useful alternative if the main trailhead parking is full, or to make laps on BYOB and OMH, since those downhill-only trails end near the Overland Trailhead. You can also connect RTS to the Utah Olympic Park trails by climbing up Iron Bill or BLT.

20 IRON BILL AND LEGACY LOOP

LARIAT LOOP

Trail Type: 95% singletrack, 5% doubletrack
Distance: 6 miles
Elevation Gain/Loss: 1030 feet
High Point: 7417 feet
Ride Time: 1–2 hours
Technical Difficulty: Advanced
Fitness Intensity: Moderate

Season: Spring–fall
Maps: Mountain Trails Foundation Summer Map; Adventure Maps, Salt Lake City, Park City, and the Wasatch; USGS 7.5-minute Park City West
GPS: 40°42'58.03"N, 111°33'14.04"W
Land Manager: Utah Olympic Legacy Foundation

OVERVIEW

Iron Bill and the Legacy Loop Trails are part of the Utah Olympic Park's trail network. Access both from the top of the RTS Loop. While RTS is one of the most beginner-friendly trails in Park City, Iron Bill definitely is not. As a climb, it's steep and rocky, has a lot of sun exposure, and requires solid bike-handling skills to clear technical switchbacks. But Iron Bill offers nice views of Snyderville Basin on your climb to the Legacy Loop atop the mountain.

As for that Legacy Loop, it's a short, less-than-a-mile jaunt around the summit of the mountain. Another trail, called Legacy Ridge, splits down the middle of the loop for another ride option. Both Legacy trails are mostly flat and easy in difficulty, though they can be overgrown at times. The ride I describe here takes RTS to the Iron Bill climb, then circumnavigates the full

Legacy Loop before doing yet another loop with Legacy Ridge, finally coming back down Iron Bill and back to RTS for a lariat-style loop.

GETTING THERE

From the intersection of Park Avenue and Kearns Boulevard in Park City, drive north on Park Avenue (SR 224) to Kimball Junction. After about 5.5 miles, turn left onto Olympic Parkway. At the roundabout, go three-quarters of the way around to continue south on Olympic Parkway. From here, the road climbs toward the Utah Olympic Park. About 0.5 mile from the roundabout, turn right into the gravel parking area for the RTS Trailhead.

MILEAGE LOG

0.0 At the trailhead, go through the break in the fence and head left (south) onto the RTS Loop. Ride uphill through sagebrush and into a large stand of aspens.

0.5 You'll come to an intersection at the start of Iron Bill on the left. Leave RTS and climb up Iron Bill. Right after making this turn, cross Olympic Parkway and regain the singletrack on the other side below the large Olympic housing building. Soon after, it becomes a doubletrack road-grade for a few yards before the singletrack begins again on the right.

0.8 Cross another road grade and find the singletrack on the other side. Avoid the temptation of following the road grade up because it does looks like the continuation of the trail. Instead follow the singletrack on the right. From here Iron Bill gets steeper and a lot rockier as it switchbacks up through scrub oak and brush.

1.9 At its highest point, Iron Bill connects with the UOP Trail on the right. If you stay on Iron Bill, it connects with Bear Hollow Drive and the start of Rob's Trail in the Canyons Village side of Park City Mountain. For this ride, go right on UOP where signs direct you to the Legacy Loop.

2.2 At a fork in the trail, go right on UOP (left is Legacy Loop). It is best to ride this loop in a counterclockwise direction because there is a short section that is best ridden downhill.

2.3 Legacy Ridge comes in on the left. You will take this left on your second time around, but for now stay right on UOP to do the full Legacy Loop.

2.4 The singletrack crosses a gravel trail used by park-goers who hike to the top of the zip line tour. At this point you are now on the Legacy

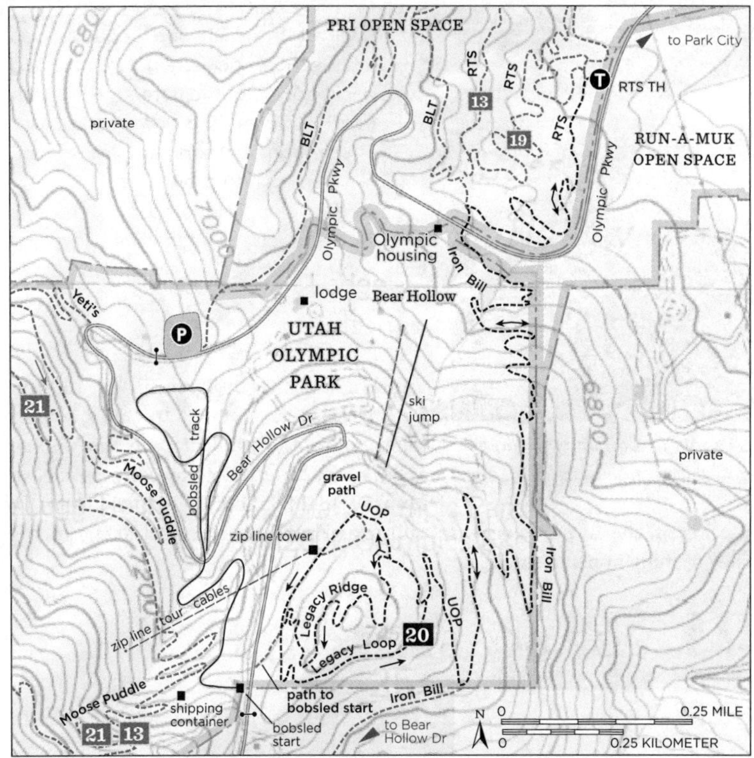

Loop. Soon after crossing the hiking trail, you come to a zip line starting tower. Keep on the singletrack and ride past it.

2.5 You arrive at an intersection with a trail that goes down to the top of
the Olympic bobsled track on the right. On the left is the exit point of
the Legacy Ridge Trail. Stay straight on Legacy Loop downhill as the
trail traverses back around to the other side of the mountain.

2.9 Rejoin the intersection with UOP and Legacy Loop. To ride Legacy
Ridge, go left on UOP.

3.0 Go left on Legacy Ridge. This trail goes over the top of the mountain.
It's an easy ride but can get overgrown.

3.4 You're back at Legacy Loop. Go left and enjoy the short downhill once
again.

Swooping around on the short downhill section of Legacy Loop

3.7 Back at the UOP and Legacy Loop intersection, go straight and head back down to the intersection with Iron Bill. Go left and down on Iron Bill. Those tight corners and rocks you climbed up add a bit of technical fun on the down. Follow it back to the RTS loop and retrace your route.

6.0 End the ride back at the parking lot.

OPTIONS

You can continue on Iron Bill beyond the Legacy Loop to connect to Rob's, which takes you to the trails at Canyons Village at Park City Mountain. You can also access Moose Puddle on the UOP Bobsled loop by getting off the Legacy Loop and riding across the parking lot at the top of the Olympic bobsled track.

21 UOP BOBSLED

LOOP

Trail Type: 95% singletrack, 5% paved
Distance: 6 miles
Elevation Gain/Loss: 1130/1130 feet
High Point: 7975 feet
Ride Time: 1–1.5 hours
Technical Difficulty: Intermediate
Fitness Intensity: Moderate
Season: Summer–fall

Maps: Mountain Trails Foundation Summer Map; Adventure Maps Salt Lake City, Park City, and the Wasatch; USGS 7.5-minute Park City West
GPS: 40°42'40.20"N, 111°33'52.06"W
Land Manager: Utah Olympic Legacy Foundation

OVERVIEW

Say "mountain biking the bobsled" and riders immediately think of the Bobsled downhill trail in the foothills of Salt Lake City. But the UOP Bobsled is located at the Utah Olympic Park in Park City. No, you don't ride your bike down the actual Olympic bobsled track—though how crazy would that be? But the UOP Bobsled's 6-mile loop resembles a bobsled course because it is very much switchback city.

Two trails—Yeti's and Moose Puddle—make up the loop. Yeti's is uphill-only for mountain bikers, while Moose Puddle is bi-directional. As a result, you have two options: Either do Moose Puddle as an out-and-back or as a loop going up Yeti's and down Moose Puddle. I'll describe the strongly preferred loop route here.

The loop starts off climbing through forests of scrub oak and threadbare aspens. It makes a few switchbacks as it rises above the actual bobsled and luge track used in the 2002 Winter Games. In what seems like hundreds of switchbacks, many of which are pretty tight, the trail gains a bunch of elevation. Vegetation transitions into old-growth evergreens that provide nice shade. As you near the top, the trees thin out, allowing for spectacular views of the entire Park City area.

At the top of the mountain, after climbing over 1000 vertical feet, the trail loops around to the other side for the descent. Both trails are almost identical, with a lot of of tight switchbacks. There are a few buff straight sections

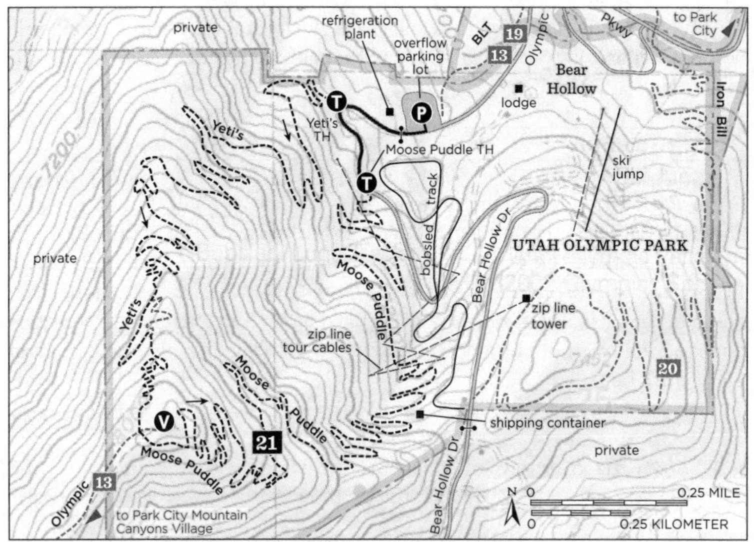

Where Yeti's rises above the aspen forest, riders are treated to mountain views that stretch to the horizon.

for going fast, but that speed is quickly scrubbed when you hit the next of many tight corners. The ride doesn't provide much for the gravity rider (or anyone who appreciates "flow" on their descents). But if you're looking for a good workout on steep trails with amazing views, then the UOP Bobsled is worth your saddle time.

The Utah Olympic Park entrance gate closes at 8 PM, so finish your ride before then or your car will be trapped there until the park reopens the next morning.

GETTING THERE

From Park City, drive north on SR 224 toward Kimball Junction. After about 5.5 miles, turn left onto Olympic Parkway. At the roundabout, go three-quarters of the way around to continue south on Olympic Parkway. From here, the road climbs toward the Utah Olympic Park. In 1.6 miles you come to the park. Drive past the main parking lot and entrance to continue down to the overflow lot, located next to the bobsled track's refrigeration plant. Park here.

MILEAGE LOG

0.0   From the overflow lot, ride past the lift gate that goes across the paved Bear Hollow Drive. Pedal up the road.

0.2   On your right, you'll see the Yeti's Trailhead. It is well signed, with a large map detailing the area and required directions of travel. Leave the road and pedal up Yeti's. You'll first be ascending through a scrub oak forest that soon transitions to aspen groves.

1.5   After around ten moderately steep switchbacks, the trail leaves the aspens, revealing a stunning view of the valley below. At this point the path alternates between forest and open views to the top.

2.2   Yeti's splits two ways. Either choice is fine. If you go left, you'll find it to be steeper with five tight switchbacks. I prefer the right fork, as it climbs less steeply, with only one switchback. Both options rejoin in less than a quarter mile.

2.7   After climbing many more tight switchbacks, you finally make it to a three-way intersection at the top. Moose Puddle is straight, while the Olympic Trail enters on the right. You can take Olympic to access Ambush and the Mid Mountain Trail at the Canyons Village of Park City Mountain. You may also drop your bike here and hike a few hundred feet to the mountain summit for a 360-degree view. But to continue the UOP Bobsled loop, go straight and head down Moose Puddle. This descent is a smooth ride with multiple tight corners. There are so many corners, in fact, that once you get some decent speed, you have to slow down for the next corner. It's probably for the best, as there are always hikers on this trail as well as other mountain bikers climbing up. It's still a fun ride down though.

4.6   After entering a heavily wooded forest, you come to a metal shipping container on the right, located just off a switchback. This is the top station of the Olympic bobsled track. Stay left on Moose Puddle. From here you will pass underneath several cables and a few towers from the park's zip line tour.

5.7   Moose Puddle exits at Bear Hollow Drive. Go left and follow it back down to the overflow parking lot.

6.0   You've reached the end of the ride and your car.

OPTIONS

You can ride Moose Puddle as an out-and-back, but it's a steeper climb than Yeti's. You can also make the ride longer by linking the UOP Bobsled Loop with the RTS Trails via the BLT Trail.

PARLEYS CANYON TO KIMBALL JUNCTION

This region encompasses mountain biking routes that extend from Kimball Junction north of Park City and west to Mountain Dell Reservoir in Parleys Canyon. The area is split by Interstate 80, the main thoroughfare between Park City and Salt Lake City. These trails cut through and above the outlying neighborhoods of Jeremy Ranch, Summit Park, and Silver Summit.

To the north of the interstate, the trails in the Glenwild area are among the first to be rideable in the spring, as the slopes are generally south facing and the trailheads are at lower elevations. Two classic rides here, the Glenwild Loop (Route 22) and Flying Dog (Route 23), are both loved by locals for their stout climbs and exciting, fast descents. Another route of note is Bob's Basin (Route 24). This small network features four downhill-only trails of varying difficulty, making it one of the best spots in Park City to learn and practice downhill mountain biking skills.

South of Interstate 80, there are two routes: Road to Arcylon (Route 26) and Road to WOS (Route 27). The former is an advanced-level, single-loop bike park with massive jumps, drops, and manmade features. The latter is a mellow loop of buff singletrack that meanders through forests of fir and pine. Due to their north-facing aspect, these rides tend to open later in spring.

Opposite: *Descending through aspen groves on the north end of the much-loved Flying Dog Loop (Route 23)*

Rock fins are a cool landmark on the lower part of Glenwild Loop.

I've also included the Mormon Pioneer Trail (Route 28), located about halfway between Park City and Salt Lake City. This out-and-back (or shuttle) takes riders on the path of Mormon pioneers as they trekked into the Salt Lake Valley in 1847. Along with the history lesson, mountain bikers can expect one of the fastest descents in this book.

22 GLENWILD LOOP

LOOP

Trail Type: 100% singletrack
Distance: 8.3 miles
Elevation Gain/Loss: 1310/1310 feet
High Point: 7138 feet
Ride Time: 1–2.5 hours
Technical Difficulty: Intermediate
Fitness Intensity: Moderate
Season: Spring–fall

Maps: Mountain Trails Foundation Summer Map; Adventure Maps, Salt Lake City, Park City, and the Wasatch; USGS 7.5-minute Big Dutch Hollow, Park City West
GPS: 40°43'40.95"N, 111°32'10.45"W
Land Manager: Private (managed by Basin Recreation)

OVERVIEW

The Glenwild Loop, a shorter ride in this trail system, can be connected to longer excursions on Flying Dog and others, but it's also fun on its own.

Glenwild has a lot of southern exposure, so it is one of the first loops to melt out in the spring (usually by April), making it a great early-season option.

At around eight miles and just over 1300 feet of elevation gain, this loop tests beginners and some intermediate riders, but it does not have any overly technical features. A few tight switchbacks and one rocky section present a challenge, but overall it is pretty mellow. You can ride in either direction, but I recommend clockwise as described below. Riding counterclockwise makes for a steeper climb to the top, but really you can't go wrong either way. Be aware, however, you will likely encounter many other mountain bikers and hikers on this very popular trail.

The southernmost portion of this loop is within Swaner Preserve, but the majority lies within private neighborhoods, including Glenwild and The Preserve, and is available to riders through a public easement. Stay on the trail at all times to respect private property and this privilege.

GETTING THERE

From Park City, drive north on SR 224 toward I-80. Cross over I-80 on the overpass at the Kimball Junction interchange, then turn right (east) onto Rasmussen Road. Drive 0.25 mile (the road becomes Bitner Road) and turn left on Glenwild Drive. Park here at the Spring Creek Trailhead parking lot where there is a trail map kiosk and public bathroom.

MILEAGE LOG

0.0 From the parking lot, ride up the road toward a neighborhood entrance. Just after crossing the bridge, turn right onto the Stealth Trail. This section is flat and traverses above East Canyon Creek before ascending a series of switchbacks.

1.2 After several switchbacks, stay right on Stealth Trail (left is the Blackhawk Trail). Just after the next switchback, you'll hit the Glenwild intersection. Go left on Glenwild for the clockwise version. Cross the paved road (Glenwild Drive) and continue on the singletrack on the other side.

1.7 Here you'll come across a cool rock spine. Where the trail intersects this geologic feature there is also a bench where you can sit and take in the view. Immediately after this, you hit the intersection with Blackhawk. Stay right on Glenwild.

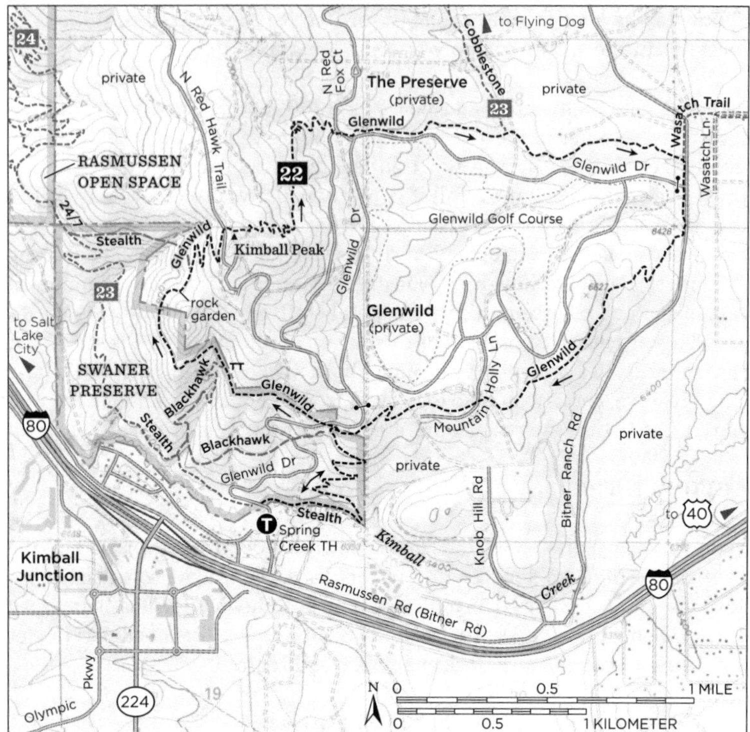

2.2   This chunky rock garden is the most technical section of the loop. While it may be difficult for beginner and intermediate riders to clear, it is blessedly short. At the top of the rock garden there is an old dirt road that leads to the Stealth Trail on the left. Cross the road and continue on Glenwild.

2.8   Cross a paved road, Red Hawk Trail, and continue on Glenwild on the other side.

3.0   This is the top of the climb. Kimball summit is home to a few communications towers. This is a sweet place to take a breather. On the other side of the hill, Glenwild Trail descends into a forest of Gambel oak. This is the longest section of downhill and it's a fast and sometimes steep descent. Watch your speed through tight, blind corners, as this trail is bi-directional and popular with riders coming up.

3.9 At the bottom of the descent, you'll come to a three-way, paved intersection. Cross the street (North Red Fox Court) and then continue on Glenwild on the other side. The trail keeps descending here but is much less steep.

4.5 At the intersection with Cobblestone, stay right on Glenwild.

5.2 At the minor fork with Wasatch Trail, stay right on Glenwild. Here the trail ascends at a low grade through sagebrush meadows.

6.5 Cross Mountain Holly Lane, another paved road.

7.0 At this fork, you've returned to the start of the Glenwild Loop. Go left on Stealth and descend through the switchbacks to the Spring Creek Trailhead.

8.3 Arrive back at Spring Creek Trailhead.

OPTIONS

In addition to riding this loop in the opposite direction (counterclockwise), you can change it up by adding the Blackhawk spur. You can also go left on Stealth at mile 2.2 and use it to return to the Spring Creek Trailhead. But if you want to add serious mileage, connect to the Flying Dog Loop at the Cobblestone Trail.

23 FLYING DOG LOOP

LOOP

Trail Type: 100% singletrack

Distance: 16.5 miles

Elevation Gain/Loss: 1935 feet/ 1935 feet

High Point: 7770 feet

Ride Time: 3–4 hours

Technical Difficulty: Intermediate

Fitness Intensity: Strenuous

Season: Late spring–fall

Maps: Mountain Trails Foundation Summer Map; Adventure Maps Salt Lake City, Park City, and the Wasatch; USGS 7.5-minute Big Dutch Hollow, Park City West

GPS: 40°43'40.95"N, 111°32'10.45"W

Land Manager: Private (managed by Basin Recreation)

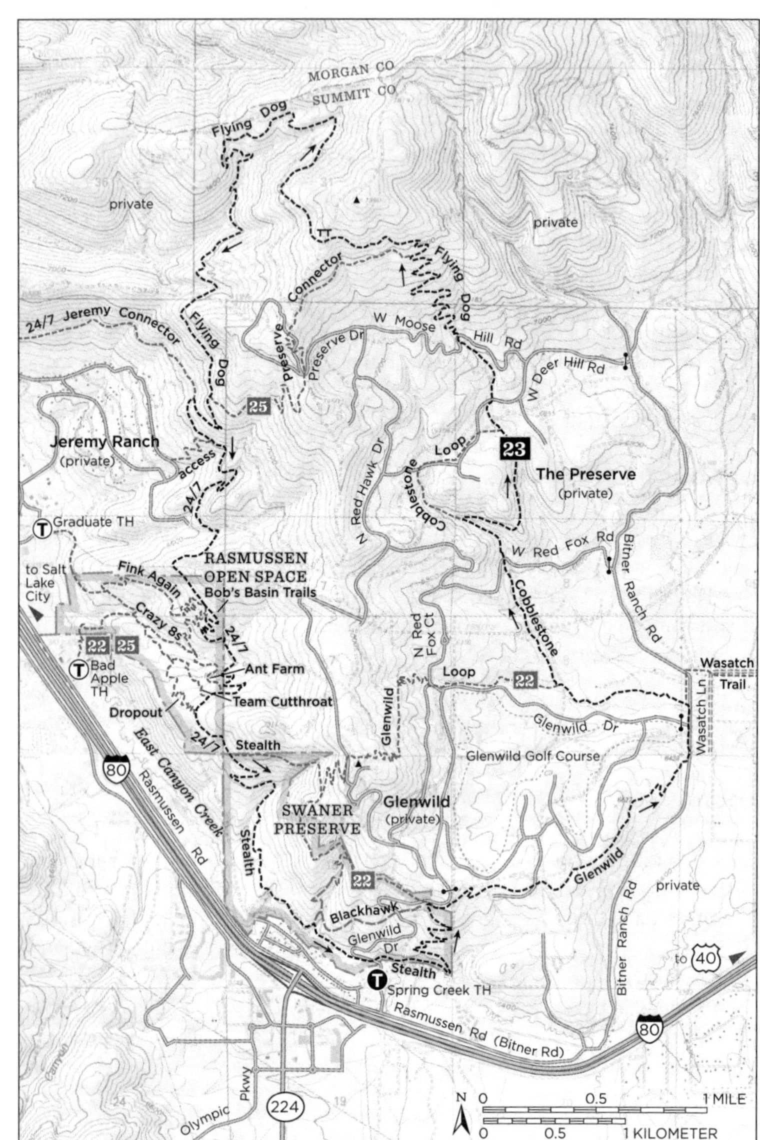
MORGAN CO
SUMMIT CO
Flying Dog
private
private
TT
Connector
Flying Dog
W Moose Hill Rd
Preserve Dr
W Deer Hill Rd
24/7 Jeremy Connector
Flying Dog
Preserve
25
Loop
23
The Preserve
(private)
Jeremy Ranch
(private)
access
24/7
N Red Hawk Dr
Cobblestone
W Red Fox Rd
Graduate TH
Bitner Ranch Rd
to Salt
Lake
City
Fink Again
RASMUSSEN
OPEN SPACE
Bob's Basin Trails
Cobblestone
Crazy 8s
24/7
N Red Fox Ct
22 25
Loop
Bad
Apple
TH
Ant Farm
22
Wasatch
Trail
Dropout
Team Cutthroat
Glenwild
Glenwild Dr
Wasatch Ln
East Canyon Creek
24/7
Stealth
Glenwild Golf Course
80
Rasmussen Rd
Stealth
SWANER
PRESERVE
Glenwild
(private)
Glenwild
private
22
Blackhawk
Glenwild
Dr
Bitner Ranch Rd
to 40
Stealth
Spring Creek TH
Rasmussen Rd (Bitner Rd)
80
Olympic Pkwy
224
N 0   0.5   1 MILE
0   0.5   1 KILOMETER

OVERVIEW

Flying Dog is the "Big Dog" of mountain bike trails in the Glenwild system, and it has never been more popular, perhaps because it's a nontechnical ride with few rocks, roots, or scary drop-offs. This long ride does have a few stout climbs to earn a rollicking fun descent. Both intermediate and expert mountain bikers can enjoy swooping down super-fast, buffed-out dirt.

This loop features a diversity of ecosystems, as riders begin in the sagebrush flats, climb to Gambel oak groves, and finally reach shady aspen forests before screaming back down to the trailhead. While some of the trail goes through the Swaner Preserve and Rasmussen Open Space, the vast majority of the ride is within private neighborhoods: Glenwild, The Preserve, and Jeremy Ranch. A public easement allows access. Stay on the trail at all times to avoid trespassing.

There are several ways to ascend to the Flying Dog Trail with longer or shorter mileages and degrees of difficulty. The loop described here is the classic, 16.5-mile, counterclockwise variation that begins at the Spring Creek Trailhead in Kimball Junction. The route then ascends the Stealth, Glenwild, Cobblestone, and Flying Dog Trails before the joyous Flying Dog downhill. Above the Jeremy Ranch neighborhood, the 24/7 and Stealth Trails finish the loop. There is much debate as to which direction is best to ride Flying Dog—clockwise or counterclockwise. I prefer counterclockwise by far because the downhill side has more flow and is therefore more fun.

GETTING THERE

From Park City, drive north on SR 224 toward I-80. Cross over I-80 on the overpass at the Kimball Junction interchange, then turn right (east) onto Rasmussen Road. Drive 0.25 mile (the road becomes Bitner Road) and turn left on Glenwild Drive. Park here at the trailhead parking lot where there is a trail map kiosk and public bathroom.

MILEAGE LOG

0.0 From the parking lot, ride up the road toward a neighborhood entrance. Just after crossing the bridge, turn right onto the Stealth Trail. This section is flat before you reach a series of switchbacks.

1.2 After several switchbacks, stay right on Stealth Trail (left is the Blackhawk Trail). Just after the next switchback, you'll hit the Glenwild intersection. Stay right on Glenwild, following the sign that directs you to the Cobblestone Trail. Continue up to the top, where the trail then descends on twisting singletrack through fields of sagebrush.

1.9 Cross a paved road and pick up the singletrack on the other side.

3.1 Cross another paved road and pass around metal, speed-scrubbing gates on the other side. Cross a wood boardwalk.

3.2 Go left at the fork, staying on Glenwild Loop Trail (right is the Wasatch Trail). Follow the sign directions for Cobblestone Trail. At this point the path levels out at a large meadow.

3.8 At the fork, go right onto the Cobblestone Trail, following the sign directions for Flying Dog (left is the continuation of the Glenwild Loop).

4.4 Cross a paved road and continue on singletrack on the other side. The trail enters a small, tree-filled canyon before aggressively going uphill.

4.8 At the fork, go right. This is the start of the Cobblestone Loop for both directions of riding. You may do this short loop to add a mile to your ride. Otherwise, follow the sign that directs you to Flying Dog.

5.6 At the fork, go right onto Flying Dog Trail. This is the official start of the Flying Dog Loop (left continues the Cobblestone Loop). Immediately

Soaring down the flowy descent of Flying Dog is an absolute treat.

after this intersection, cross a paved road and pick up the trail on the other side.

6.0 Cross another road. This is the start of a long series of switchbacks up the mountainside.

7.4 At an intersection, continue on Flying Dog by going right (left is the Preserve Connector Trail).

8.1 Reach the top of the climb and highest point of the loop. This open area is a good spot to take a break on the wooden bench. From here, the descent begins on the other side of the meadow. It is mostly smooth and flowing as it meanders through an aspen forest.

11.4 At a fork, stay right on Flying Dog (left is the Preserve Connector Trail).

11.8 This intersection is the end of the Flying Dog Trail. Go left on the 24/7 Trail (right is the 24/7 Jeremy Connector Trail). From here the trail traverses above the Jeremy Ranch neighborhood.

12.9 Cross a paved road where the trail climbs once more for a short distance before descending again.

13.5 At the intersection with the first of the Bob's Basin Trails, stay left on 24/7, as the trail on the right travels down Fink Again. Immediately after this turn, you'll come to the downhill-only Crazy 8s Trail on your right. Keep left as the 24/7 Trail switchbacks downhill in a fun, berm-filled descent. At the bottom, the trail climbs again with a series of switchbacks.

14.6 At the intersection with two more of Bob's Basin downhill trails, Ant Farm and Team Cutthroat, stay left on 24/7. Immediately after this is the turnoff for The Dropout downhill trail. Again, stay left.

15.0 At the intersection with Stealth Trail, go right on Stealth, following the signs for Spring Creek Trailhead.

16.0 Red Hawk connects on the left. Stay right on Stealth to get to Spring Creek Trailhead.

16.5 Stay right at the Swaner Preserve Kiosk. Cross the wooden bridge to end your ride at the Spring Creek Trailhead parking lot.

OPTIONS

For a longer figure-eight loop, go west from the Spring Creek Trailhead on Stealth. When you reach the Flying Dog/Preserve Connector intersection, turn right onto Preserve Connector. Ascend this trail to the top and descend Flying Dog counterclockwise. Then go right back up the Preserve Connector and descend Flying Dog clockwise to the Cobblestone Loop and return to the trailhead via Glenwild Trail.

You can also add Glenwild, Blackhawk, Jeremy Connector, and the Bob's Basin downhill trails to create multiple variations on the classic Flying Dog Loop.

24 BOB'S BASIN

NETWORK

Trail Type: 100% singletrack
Distance: Up to 12.4 miles
Elevation Gain/Loss: 300/300 feet
High Point: 6727 feet
Ride Time: 0.5 to 3 hours
Technical Difficulty: Intermediate to advanced
Fitness Intensity: Easy to Moderate
Season: Spring–fall

Maps: Mountain Trails Foundation Summer Map; Adventure Maps Salt Lake City, Park City, and the Wasatch; USGS 7.5-minute Park City West, Big Dutch Hollow
GPS: 40°44'50.05"N, 111°33'42.75"W
Land Manager: Rasmussen Open Space (managed by Basin Recreation)

OVERVIEW

The downhill trails at Bob's Basin are short quick hitters that pack in a lot of fun. Conveniently located just off I-80 in Jeremy Ranch, this small network exists within the Rasmussen Open Space. Access them from the Bad Apple Trailhead. Bob's Basin can be ridden as a series of loops, or connect it to the rest of the Glenwild trail system for bigger rides.

Because of its location, elevation, and south-facing exposure, Bob's Basin boasts one of the longest seasons of all the Park City trails. As a result, you will find many other riders here in early spring and late fall when the upper trails are muddy or covered with snow.

A short, 1-mile ascent on Fink Again gets you to the 24/7 Trail, where four unique, downhill-only trails line up. Each has various levels of technical difficulty and are well maintained with wood features, smooth berms, drops, and rock faces. All four trails terminate at Fink Again, so you can lap them all to make a 12.4-mile ride or do just one if you're short on time. These downhill

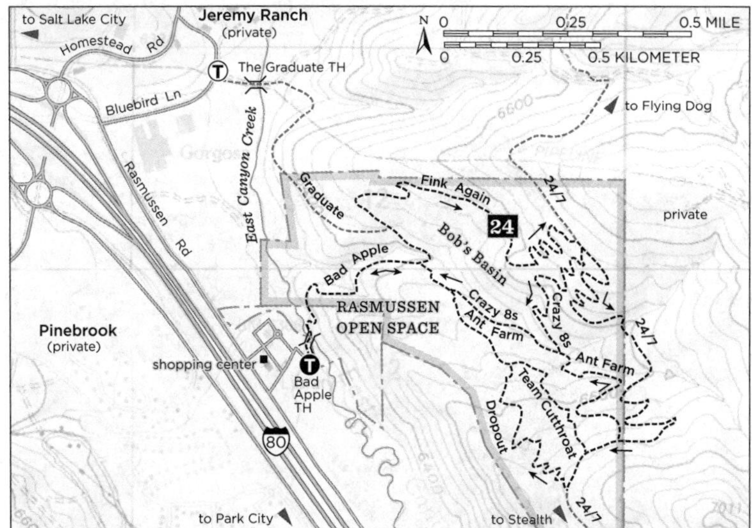

trails are also a fun way to end longer rides in the Glenwild system if you park at the Bad Apple Trailhead.

GETTING THERE

From the intersection of Park Avenue and Kearns Boulevard in Park City, drive north on Park Avenue (SR 224) to Kimball Junction. In 5.5 miles continue on the overpass crossing above I-80. North of the interstate, turn left on Rasmussen Road. Drive northwest 1.7 miles until you see a shopping center on the right. Turn right at the first entrance and make your way through to the far northeast corner above East Canyon Creek. The Bad Apple Trailhead is located here with a parking area and signage. The trail starts at the east end of the parking lot.

MILEAGE LOG

0.0   Get on the Bad Apple Trail and ride down to East Canyon Creek. After crossing a bridge, the trail ascends with a few switchbacks into Bob's Basin.

0.5   At the intersection with the end of The Dropout downhill-only trail, stay left on Bad Apple.

0.6   At this fork, keep going straight (right) onto Fink Again. Left is the Graduate Trail, which is another option for accessing Bob's Basin from the Graduate Trailhead. Fink Again gradually climbs for about a mile through sagebrush meadows and terminates after several switchbacks near the top.

1.5   Fink Again ends where it meets the 24/7 Trail. Go right on 24/7. At this point you get to choose your own adventure between four different downhill trails, each with varying difficulty and features.

End   All four downhill trails rejoin Fink Again. Ride back up to make multiple laps and loops in this cool little network.

Crazy 8s

The first downhill trail you'll come to is only a few hundred feet from the top of Fink Again. Crazy 8s is a moderately difficult descent with fun berms. After 0.5 mile from the start, it joins Ant Farm for 0.3 mile, ending with a 0.1-mile finish on The Dropout for a 0.9-mile total descent.

Ant Farm

Ant Farm is 1.2 miles from the top of Fink Again. To get to Ant Farm, stay on 24/7 where you get a bonus, very fun downhill section featuring corners and small jumps. At the bottom of the basin, 24/7 climbs back up with a few switchbacks to the start of Ant Farm off to the right. This is an advanced descent with small rock drops and wooden features. In 0.5 mile it merges with Crazy 8s and then The Dropout for a 0.9-mile descent.

Team Cutthroat

Immediately after the start of Ant Farm is Team Cutthroat. This is the most advanced and technical trail in Bob's Basin—for experts only. Be ready for natural obstacles, rock drops, and overgrown sections. In 0.4 mile, Team Cutthroat joins The Dropout for another 0.3 mile to the bottom.

The Dropout

The Dropout, 1.3 miles from the top of Fink Again, is perhaps the most popular descent in Bob's Basin, and many consider it the easiest way down. The

Opposite: *It's fun to launch from small wood jumps in Bob's Basin.*

Dropout is moderately difficult, with smooth, well-crafted berms. Wood drops and jumps keep the heart racing but are easily avoided with ride-arounds. The descent is 0.8 mile and 311 vertical feet. To access it from the top, stay on 24/7 from where it descends from Fink Again, then turn right on The Dropout.

25 FLYING DOG VIA PRESERVE CONNECTOR

LOOP

Trail Type: 100% singletrack

Distance: 12.7 miles

Elevation Gain/Loss: 1770/1770 feet

High Point: 7770 feet

Ride Time: 1.5–2.5 hours

Technical Difficulty: Intermediate

Fitness Intensity: Moderate

Season: Spring–fall

Maps: Mountain Trails Foundation Summer Map; Adventure Maps, Salt Lake City, Park City, and the Wasatch; USGS 7.5-minute Big Dutch Hollow, Park City West

GPS: 40°44'50.05"N, 111°33'42.75"W

Land Manager: Rasmussen Open Space, private (managed by Basin Recreation)

OVERVIEW

If you want to ride the famed Flying Dog Trail but don't have time for the full loop, then Preserve Connector is the ticket. This option shaves nearly four miles and 170 vertical feet from the full loop. Many locals prefer this ascent for riding counterclockwise on Flying Dog. I agree—Preserve Connector is a much more enjoyable ascent. I prefer to start at the Bad Apple Trailhead and ascend Fink Again and 24/7 Connector Trails to Preserve Connector, then continue on up the mountainside.

The grade is steady, without any of the tedious switchback squiggles of the original Flying Dog uphill. You'll ride through sagebrush meadows and aspen forests, all the while enjoying views of the Wasatch Mountains to the south. When Preserve Connector connects (hence the name) with Flying Dog, a short bit of uphill puts you atop the Flying Dog downhill. From here, lower your seatpost for a "flying" 5-mile descent that loops back to 24/7 Connector and the trailhead.

GETTING THERE

From the intersection of Park Avenue and Kearns Boulevard in Park City, drive north on Park Avenue (SR 224) to Kimball Junction. In 5.5 miles continue on the overpass crossing above I-80. North of the interstate, turn left on Rasmussen Road. Drive northwest 1.7 miles until you see a shopping center on the right.

Turn right at the first entrance and make your way to the far northeast corner above East Canyon Creek. The Bad Apple Trailhead is located here with a parking area and signage. The trail starts at the east end of the parking lot.

MILEAGE LOG

0.0 Get on the trail and ride it down to the creek. Cross the bridge and proceed up the Bad Apple Trail as it ascends into Bob's Basin.

0.5 At the intersection of the bottom of the Bob's Basin downhill trails, stay left on Bad Apple.

0.6 At the intersection with the Graduate Trail on the left, go right onto Fink Again Trail. The left fork leads to the Graduate Trailhead, which is an alternate start for this ride. Fink Again Trail switchbacks up through a large meadow. There is a lot of traffic on this ascent, as it's the primary access to the Bob's Basin downhills.

1.5 At the top of Fink Again, go left on 24/7 Connector, which traverses west toward Jeremy Ranch.

2.1 Cross a paved road and continue on the other side.

2.9 A trail comes in on the left. This is access for residents of the Jeremy Ranch Owner's Association. Stay right on 24/7.

3.1 At this point 24/7 intersects with the end of Flying Dog. There are a bench and map located here. 24/7 continues on the left as it traverses west into Jeremy Ranch. Instead, go right and climb up Flying Dog for just a couple switchbacks.

3.5 Intersect here with the bottom of Preserve Connector. Go right and head up Preserve Connector. The next 2 miles is an enjoyable climb through the Preserve neighborhood (though you won't notice many homes, since they are tucked away in the woods). The only sign of development will be the occasional paved road crossing.

4.4 Cross a paved road and continue on other side. Stay on Preserve Connector across a couple paved roads as it winds through this gated

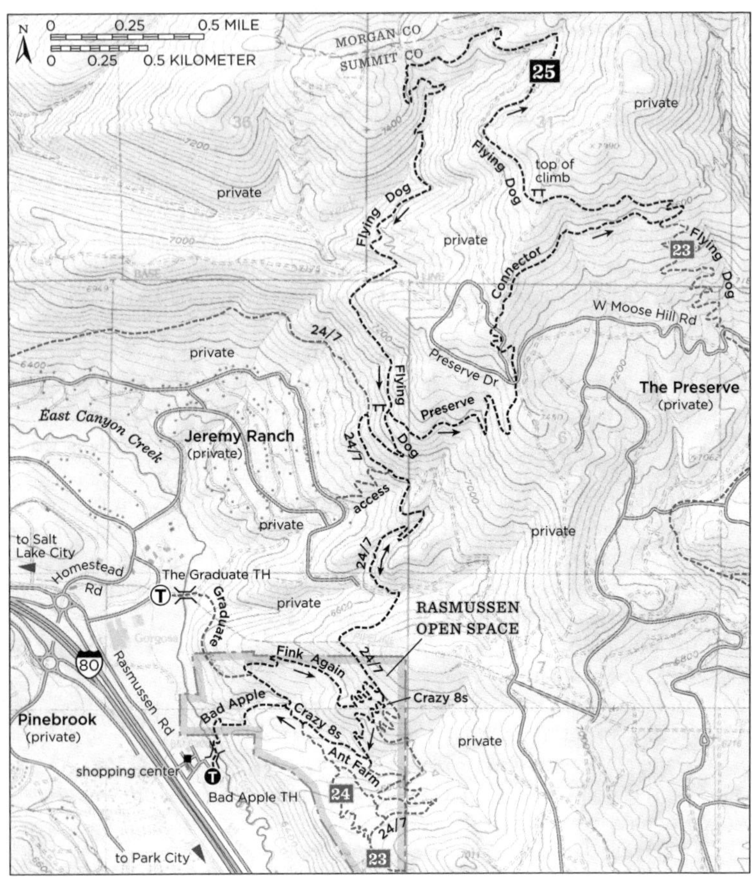

community. After crossing the final road, the trail levels out somewhat and traverses northeast through stands of aspen.

5.6 Preserve Connector ends at the east side of Flying Dog. Go left on Flying Dog and continue uphill for the counterclockwise loop.

6.2 At the top of Flying Dog, find a flat spot with a bench. Go to the opposite side to a sign that states, "Yo Dude! Slow Down." This is the start of the Flying Dog downhill. Heed the sign's advice because many riders still climb up this side and ride the loop clockwise. Be aware and be courteous to uphill traffic. Enjoy this famed section of trail and keep an eye out for moose that live in the area.

9.3 Flying Dog connects back with the bottom of Preserve Connector. Go right on Flying Dog toward 24/7.

9.8 When you reach the 24/7 Connector, go left onto it.

11.3 You're back at the top of Fink Again and the Bob's Basin trails. You can descend any of the downhill-only trails, but the featured route opts for Crazy 8s, which starts at this intersection. At the bottom of Crazy 8s, go left on Bad Apple and follow it back to the trailhead.

12.7 End of the ride at the Bad Apple Trailhead.

The Preserve Connector is a leisurely alternative to reach the Flying Dog Trail.

OPTIONS

Most riders use the Preserve Connector as the ascent for a counterclockwise descent on Flying Dog, but it's also a fun descent on its own. Use it as an out-and-back if you'd like some variety. You can also go right at the top of Flying Dog for a switchback descent that connects to the Glenwild Loop.

26 ROAD TO ARCYLON

LARIAT LOOP

Trail Type: 100% singletrack
Distance: 6.2 miles
Elevation Gain/Loss: 755/755 feet
High Point: 6959 feet
Ride Time: 1 hour
Technical Difficulty: Advanced
Fitness Intensity: Easy
Season: Spring–fall

Maps: Mountain Trails Foundation Summer Map; Adventure Maps, Salt Lake City, Park City, and the Wasatch; USGS 7.5-minute Park City West, Big Dutch Hollow
GPS: 40°45'17.21"N, 111°34'45.35"W
Land Manager: Summit County, private (managed by Basin Recreation)

OVERVIEW

Road to Arcylon ("no Lycra" spelled backward) is known for being an advanced-level, even expert-only, downhiller's domain. Located above the Woodward Park City action-sports camp at Gorgoza Park, Road to Arcylon

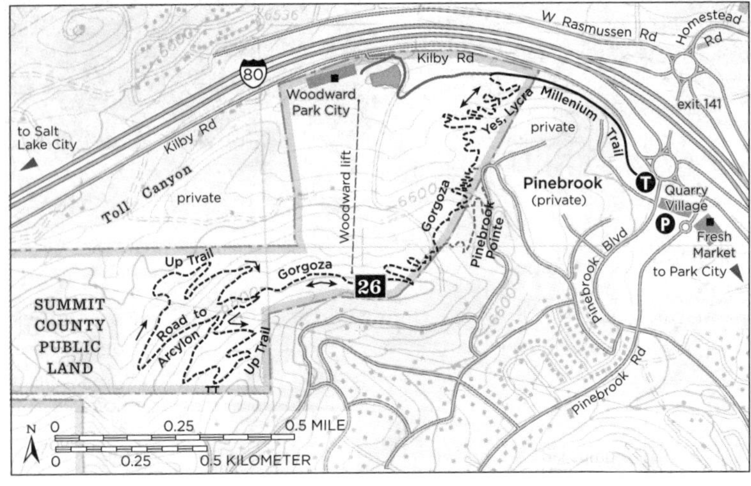

features big jumps, huge drops, giant berms, rock gardens, and massive gaps that promise a visit to the emergency room if you don't clear them.

Despite how scary that all sounds, intermediate-level mountain bikers can ride here. How is this possible? Because you don't have to attempt all of those obstacles. To be clear, Road to Arcylon is definitely technical, whether you're hitting gap jumps or not. But the biggest features all have workarounds that are more than just bypasses—they're fun rides in their own right. Not only that, but warning signs clue in lower-level riders that a big feature is coming up. That way you can plan ahead on whether you want to hit it or forget it.

As I write this, construction of Woodward Park City at Gorgoza Park has eliminated the traditional parking area and access trail. Currently there is no word on whether the old trailhead parking will be reopened. Instead, mountain bikers have been parking in the nearby Pinebrook neighborhood and riding the paved Millennium bike path for a half mile to the new ascent trailhead named "Yes, Lycra."

GETTING THERE

From the intersection of Park Avenue and Kearns Boulevard in Park City, drive north for 5.5 miles on Park Avenue (SR 224) to Kimball Junction. Get into one of the left two lanes and turn left to get on westbound I-80. In 2.1 miles, take exit 141 at Jeremy Ranch, then turn left on Homestead Road. South of the interstate, Homestead Road becomes Pinebrook Boulevard.

Drive up Pinebrook Bouevard into the Pinebrook neighborhood, where there is the Quarry Village shopping center and Fresh Market grocery store. Find parking in this area, then ride to the Millennium bike path, which is located at the intersection of Pinebrook Boulevard and Kilby Road.

MILEAGE LOG

0.0 At the paved Millennium bike path, head northwest on the path, which parallels Kilby Road.

0.5 After about a half mile on the paved trail, you'll see the Yes, Lycra Trailhead on the left (signage may call this Gorgoza Park Trail). Take this and pedal uphill. This new trail replaces the old Gorgoza Trail as access to Road to Arcylon. It's a mellow ascent with many switchbacks that wind alongside the Woodward Park City boundary.

Road to Arcylon features plenty of advanced jumps and wood ramps for riders who need a thrill. (Photo by Eric Ghanem)

1.2   At a Pinebrook access trail on the left, stay straight on Yes, Lycra.

1.4   Yes, Lycra ends at (or rather becomes) the Gorgoza Trail. You are now on the original up-track to Road to Arcylon. At this point, another Pinebrook Pointe trail enters on the left. Stay straight on Gorgoza. After more climbing, the trail heads west and traverses above the Woodward lift. Continue following the signs to Road to Arcylon and the Up Trail.

2.2   Gorgoza ends at the Up Trail. Go left and, as the name implies, head uphill.

2.7   At the top of the Up Trail there are two benches. This is the start of Road to Arcylon. You'll know you've made it based on the signs that warn riders of the difficulty of this freeride bike trail. Be sure you have the ability and bike skills to handle this sort of thing, then lower your seatpost and enjoy the exciting descent.

3.4 'At the bottom of Road to Arcylon you're at the start of the Up Trail. Take this back up for another lap (why wouldn't you?) or to return to the Gorgoza Trail to end your ride.

4.0 Back at the top of Gorgoza, go left to return down to the Millennium bike path.

5.7 After coming down Gorgoza and Yes, Lycra, which are fun descents in their own right (be aware of uphill riders), you're back at the Millennium bike path. Go right.

6.2 Arrive back at the intersection of Pinebrook Boulevard and Kilby Road, the end of your ride.

27 ROAD TO WOS

LARIAT LOOP

Trail Type: 100% singletrack
Distance: 5 miles
Elevation Gain/Loss: 800/800 feet
High Point: 7900 feet
Ride Time: 0.5–1.5 hours
Technical Difficulty: Intermediate
Fitness Intensity: Easy
Season: Summer–fall

Maps: Mountain Trails Foundation Summer Map; Adventure Maps Salt Lake City, Park City, and the Wasatch; USGS 7.5-minute Park City West
GPS: 40°44'27.87"N, 111°37'2.78"W
Land Manager: Summit Park Open Space, Toll Canyon Open Space (managed by Basin Recreation)

OVERVIEW

Summit Park, a neighborhood at Parleys Summit west of Park City, is home to what was once a little-known, but very fun mountain bike trail network. But the secret is out. This collection of maintained singletrack, including the marquee trail, Road to WOS, features smooth and tacky dirt, berms, and rolling jumps. There's nothing overly technical here—just easy, manicured flow that's great for beginners but still interesting enough for intermediate to advanced riders.

The network is located within the Summit Park and Toll Canyon Open Spaces in the Snyderville Basin Special Recreation District. Most of the ridable singletrack is on the north slope of Summit Park Peak, winding under the shade of old-growth evergreen trees. Temperatures stay cool even in

Popping a little air on No Worries, a fun option for extending the Road to WOS loop (Photo by Mason Diedrich)

the height of summer. But thanks to those trees and the cold aspect, these trails can sometimes be buried under snow until June. This area is also rife with wildlife—you can sometimes spot moose and even black bears. While it's possible to link several trails for variations, perhaps the most appealing option for mountain bikers is the Road to WOS lariat loop. It gives you the best bang for your buck both uphill and down.

You may ride the loop in either direction, but I prefer heading counterclockwise from the Short Stack Trailhead. The loop described here is different from the traditional loop that incorporates a lot of dirt roads and begins at the Road to WOS Trailhead on Matterhorn Drive, where parking space is limited. This featured loop is entirely on singletrack and includes two fun descents instead of just one. You can also choose to add in the new No Worries Trail.

GETTING THERE

From the intersection of Park Avenue and Kearns Boulevard in Park City, drive north on Park Avenue (SR 224) to Kimball Junction. In 5.5 miles, take I-80 west toward Salt Lake City. Drive five miles and get off at the Parleys Summit exit. Go left (south) under the interstate into the Summit Park neighborhood. Immediately turn right and head west on Aspen Drive, which becomes Maple Drive in half a mile. Basically, just stay right at all road intersections as you follow Maple Drive while it curves left uphill and becomes Crestview Drive. In another half mile, Crestview turns left. Again, stay right as the main road becomes Innsbruck Strasse. Soon after, the pavement turns into a dirt road. Follow it until you see the Short Stack Trailhead on the right side of the road. Park only at designated spots along the road.

MILEAGE LOG

0.0 Locate the Short Stack Trail on the south side of the road and head uphill. The trail climbs fairly steeply up through an evergreen forest. The trail is wide with well-rounded corners on every switchback, which eases difficulty. Still, going up Short Stack is one heck of a warm-up.

1.2 Near the top of the climb, the Short Ribs Trail comes in on the left. Stay right. At this point the trail is now Road to WOS, and it levels out while traversing the mountainside. You will begin to see aspen trees among the evergreens.

1.5 On the left you'll see an overgrown doubletrack that leads down to a water tank. Keep right on Road to WOS.

2.3 The climb tops out in a large meadow at 7900 feet. Unfortunately, there isn't much of a view to reward you. Stay straight on the main trail to the other side of the meadow. Turn left, keeping on Road to WOS as it goes downhill (right is a road grade popular with hikers.) This section of Road to WOS is a joy-filled descent through the trees on smooth dirt with multiple corners and fast straightaways. But check your speed as you will assuredly encounter hikers and other mountain bikers.

2.8 A trail called No Worries connects on the right in the middle of a switchback. This is a newer addition to the Road to WOS area. The trail is nearly two miles long and drops a little over 700 vertical feet into Toll Canyon, ending at St. Moritz Terrace. This bi-directional singletrack is a very fun downhill and moderate climb that provides another access point from the Summit Park neighborhood. However, there is no place to park there, so this access is best used by Summit Park residents only. I suggest doing it as an optional out-and-back if you desire more miles. Otherwise, stay left on Road to WOS for the standard loop.

3.3 At the intersection with Short Ribs, you can go right and stay on Road to WOS to continue downhill to the trailhead on Matterhorn Drive. Instead, I suggest going left on Short Ribs.

3.8 After climbing nearly a half mile on Short Ribs, you come to the intersection with Road to WOS and Short Stack. To do the loop again, go left on Road to WOS. Otherwise to return to the trailhead, turn right on Short Stack. This descent is a blast! You can dive-bomb around the many berms and even catch some air off the whoop-de-dos and water bars. But as always, be aware and careful of other trail users that you encounter.

5.0 End the ride back at Innsbruck Strasse.

OPTIONS

For a longer loop, you can follow the dirt road that connects the two trailheads. I still recommend parking at Innsbruck Strasse at the Short Stack Trailhead. From here continue on the Innsbruck Strasse dirt road on your

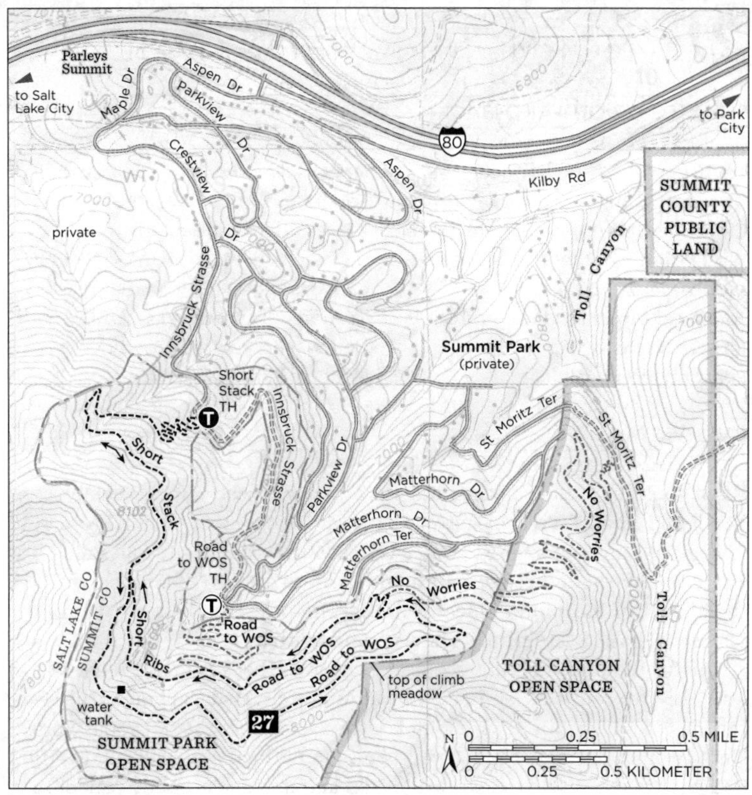

bike. Vehicles are prohibited from driving through here by a couple of cycle-around gates. After 0.75 mile, you'll reach the Road to WOS Trailhead at the intersection of Parkview Drive and Matterhorn Drive. Climb up a bit of steep trail until you see the Road to WOS singletrack on the left, and then ride the loop as described above except in a clockwise direction.

For a longer ride, tack on the No Worries Trail as an out-and-back, adding around 3.5 miles roundtrip and 700 vertical feet of ascent and descent to your ride.

28 MORMON PIONEER TRAIL

SHUTTLE OR OUT-AND-BACK

Trail Type: 100% singletrack
Distance: 12 miles
Elevation Gain/Loss: 1850/1850 feet
High Point: 7420 feet
Ride Time: 2–2.5 hours
Technical Difficulty: Intermediate
Fitness Intensity: Moderate
Season: Spring–fall

Maps: Adventure Maps Salt Lake City, Park City, and the Wasatch; USGS 7.5-minute Mountain Dell
GPS: 40°46'44.24"N, 111°41'17.99"W
Land Managers: Salt Lake City Corporation, Uinta-Wasatch-Cache National Forest (managed by National Park Service)

OVERVIEW

Want to go mountain biking and get a history lesson at the same time? You'll find what you're looking for on the Mormon Pioneer Trail. From 1846 to 1869, Mormon pioneers traveled from Nauvoo, Illinois, to Salt Lake City, Utah. It took them three to four months to travel that 1300 miles. In 1978, the historical Mormon Pioneer National Historic Trail became part of the National Trails System and is now popular with hikers.

As for mountain biking, the best section of the Mormon Pioneer Trail stretches from Little Dell Reservoir in Mountain Dell Canyon to the summit of Big Mountain Pass in the Uinta-Wasatch-Cache National Forest. This 12-mile out-and-back is very well maintained and sees a lot of foot and tire traffic. While the elevation gain and mileage are pretty moderate, you will still get a cardio workout as the trail is steep in a few sections. But overall there is little technical difficulty.

Most mountain bikers ride the trail from Little Dell Reservoir, where there is plenty of free parking. Another option to access the Mormon Pioneer Trail is a roadside trailhead between Little Dell Reservoir and Affleck Park campground. From here you'll enjoy a straightforward but steep ascent up the canyon bottom followed by switchbacks that climb up to Big Mountain Pass. At the top, you'll be treated to one of the most gorgeous, sweeping views in the Wasatch Mountains. This trail can also be enjoyed as a shuttle ride.

Retrace the steps of pioneers on the Mormon Pioneer Trail.

GETTING THERE

From the intersection of Park Avenue and Kearns Boulevard in Park City, drive north on Park Avenue (SR 224) to Kimball Junction. In 5.5 miles, take I-80 west toward Salt Lake City. Drive 10.5 miles over Parleys Summit and down into Parleys Canyon. Exit the interstate onto SR 65 and turn right (north). Drive past Mountain Dell Golf Course and continue up the highway 2.9 miles to the Little Dell Reservoir parking area. There is a fee booth, but you only have to pay for reservoir recreation or to park at the lower lots. To mountain bike, park at the free upper lot which is open from 8 AM to 8 PM. If you want to ride outside those hours, you may park along the north shoulder of the highway. The trailhead is at the southwest corner of the lot.

To park at the alternate trailhead, drive an additional 1.6 miles up the canyon until you come to a pair of dirt pullouts on both sides of the road. There is a forest service outhouse on the east side. Park here. The trailhead is located on the west side of the road.

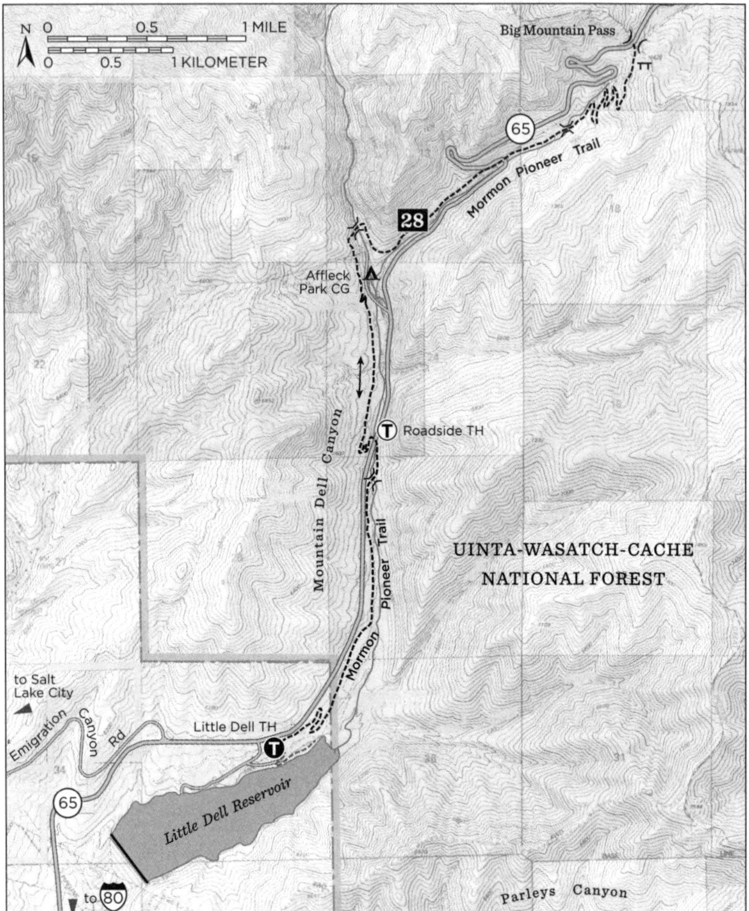

MILEAGE LOG

0.0 At the Little Dell Reservoir parking area, find the trailhead on the southwest corner of the lot next to a bench and informational signs.

Head down the trail. After only a few dozen yards there is a fork. Go left on the narrower singletrack that traverses the hillside (right is a wide and steep trail that goes down to the reservoir).

0.5 A footpath that goes to the reservoir connects on the right. Stay left on Mormon Pioneer Trail.

1.8 Cross a wood bridge that spans a creek.

2.0 The trail intersects SR 65 at the alternate trailhead. Cross the highway while staying left and locate the trail's continuation on the other side. From here the trail gets steeper as it switchbacks up the mountain then traverses above the Affleck Park campground. This is a fun section with nice flow and excellent views of nearby mountains.

3.4 A trail on the right provides access to Affleck Park campground. Stay left on Mormon Pioneer Trail and cross a bridge.

3.6 Another campground trail intersects the main trail on the right. Stay left (straight) and continue up.

4.4 The trail exits out onto the highway. Cross the road and continue on the other side. Here you will see a sign marking this as the "Original Trail."

4.8 Cross a large, wood bridge. From this point the trail challenges you with a long, steep climb. There are several switchbacks, and some are very steep and tight. It's obvious that this trail was built with hikers in mind. Look up and notice the huge communications towers on the ridgeline above. That's your destination.

6.0 At the top of Big Mountain Pass, you'll find a large parking area, historical markers, and a bench where you can take a load off. This is also the start of the ride if you're shuttling the trail as a downhill only. But before you go downhill, be sure to soak in that epic view. At this point, all you have left to do is go back downhill. It's a scary-fast, 6-mile, 1500-foot descent that I'll bet Mormon pioneers never could have imagined people doing.

OPTIONS

For a shorter ride, you can start at the alternate trailhead. This option makes the ride 7.3 miles roundtrip. If you want to shuttle the trail, leave a car at either trailhead and drive the second vehicle to the top of Big Mountain Pass, then dive-bomb the downhill back to the bottom car.

ROUND VALLEY AREA

The Round Valley area is a network of singletrack and doubletrack trails in an open space named for the valley on the east side of Park City. These rides are easygoing, well maintained, and suitable for beginner and intermediate mountain bikers. However, experts looking for an easy day will also find some technical fun. As with all rides in Park City, buffed out singletrack is the name of the game here. There are dozens of ways to link rides in this network, but this region highlights popular local loops like the Round Valley Classic (Route 30) as well as newly cut trails such as Pulp Friction (Route 31). Plus, this open space is adjacent to perhaps the very best place in Park City to learn mountain bike skills: the Trailside Bike Park (Route 32). Round Valley is also the top spot in the area for fat biking in winter. Mountain Trails Foundation maintains and grooms several trails ranging from beginner to expert. Many trails popular with mountain bikers are designated fat bike routes, including Happy Gilmor, Tin Man, PorcUClimb, and Barrel Roll. With so much variety in winter, there's no reason not to ride your bike in Park City all year long.

In addition to Round Valley, this region features a handful of trails located on the opposite side of US Highway 40, including Princess Di, South Canyon, and the Ross Creek Loop at Jordanelle State Park (Routes 33–35).

In Park City terms, trails in Round Valley and the surrounding area are at low elevations (around 6500 feet), which means they're among the first spots to open in the spring and can be ridden late into fall. The lower elevation also gives the area a different feel for Park City, as you'll be riding through scrub oak forests and over sage and rabbit brush, much like the nearby Glenwild Loop.

Opposite: *Dive-bombing down Pulp Friction (Route 31), arguably the most enjoyable downhill trail in Round Valley*

29 ROUND VALLEY EASY LOOP

LOOP

Trail Type: 50% singletrack, 50% doubletrack
Distance: 6.3 miles
Elevation Gain/Loss: 585/585 feet
High Point: 7145 feet
Ride Time: 1–2 hours
Technical Difficulty: Beginner
Fitness Intensity: Easy
Season: Spring–fall
GPS: 40°40'44.68"N, 111°28'13.55"W

Maps: Mountain Trails Foundation Summer Map; Round Valley and Trailside Area Trails Map; Adventure Maps Salt Lake City, Park City, and the Wasatch; USGS 7.5-minute Park City East
Land Manager: Round Valley Open Space (managed by Mountain Trails Foundation)

OVERVIEW

Round Valley's numerous loop options can be intimidating for beginners. This easy featured loop links equal parts doubletrack and singletrack for laid-back pedaling and maximum mileage. The coolest part, however, is the fairly new PorcUclimb ascent and Down Dog descent, both excellent introductions to singletrack riding. You will enjoy smooth, machine-cut trails, wide berms, and low-angle grades. Start by using this nontechnical loop as a baseline for mountain biking at Round Valley. Then, after you've sharpened your skills, spread out and explore more technical trails in the network, such as Rusty Shovel, Backslide, and Pulp Friction.

GETTING THERE

From the intersection of Park Avenue and Kearns Boulevard in Park City, drive northeast on Kearns Boulevard (SR 248) for 2.8 miles. When you reach Round Valley Drive, turn left. It curves back north for 0.1 mile. Then turn left on Gillmor Way. Stay on Gillmor Way for 0.5 mile as it loops around the sports fields to the Quinn's Trailhead parking, the last lot on the right near the Park City Ice Arena.

MILEAGE LOG

0.0 Locate Quinn's Trailhead across Gillmor Way from the parking lot. It is marked by a large map kiosk. Three doubletrack trails start here. Take the left trail (straight) on Fast Pitch.

0.5 At a four-way intersection, go left on Hat Trick doubletrack. These old roads gently climb up into Round Valley.

0.8 At the next four-way, you'll intersect with Fairway Hills Connector. Stay straight on Hat Trick.

1.3 Go left onto Fast Pitch.

1.5 Stay right (left takes you to a neighborhood trailhead). Immediately after, you'll come to another trail intersection. Go left on Matt's Flat, a low-grade doubletrack.

1.6 Singletrack trails intersect on both sides. Stay straight on Matt's Flat.

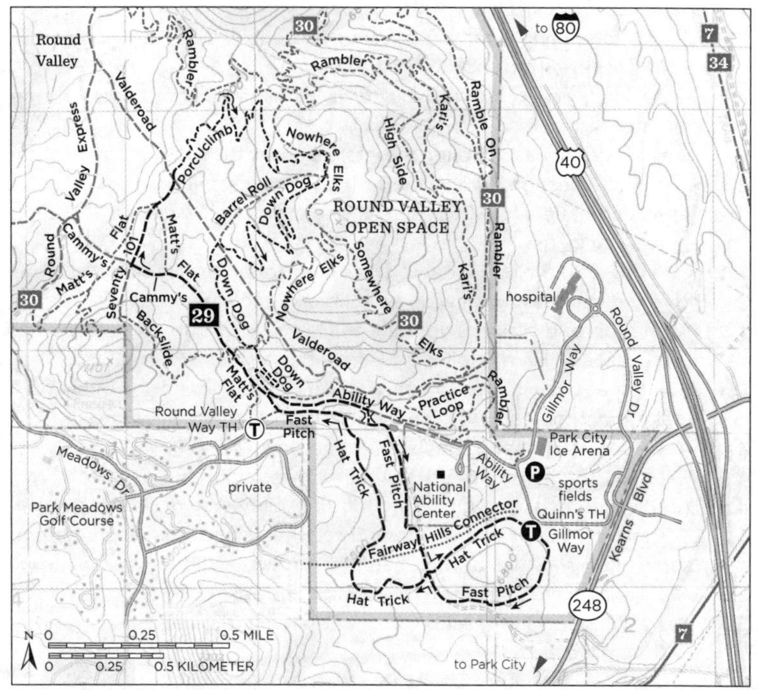

Down Dog is an ideal descent for beginners to learn cornering skills.

1.8   At the fork, hang a left onto Cammy's doubletrack. This trail gets a little steeper as it climbs to the top of a rise.

2.0   At the top, go right onto Seventy 101. This doubletrack rides a little rougher.

2.1   Stay on Seventy 101, ignoring the intersection with Matt's Flat singletrack.

2.3   At the intersection with Valderoad, go left by staying on Seventy 101. At this point Seventy 101 becomes singletrack and weaves up through sagebrush fields.

2.5   Go right onto the uphill-only PorcUclimb Trail. The climbing is steeper here but very easy with wide switchbacks and smooth dirt.

3.3   At the top of the climb, go right on Nowhere Elks. Immediately after, you'll come to Barrel Roll. Stay left on the easier Nowhere Elks.

3.4   Go right at this intersection onto Down Dog, a very fun, downhill-only trail perfect for learning cornering skills on singletrack berms.

4.2   At Valderoad crossing, stay straight on Down Dog.

4.6   Here you cross Nowhere Elks. Again, stay straight on Down Dog.

4.9   At the bottom of Down Dog, go left on Ability Way doubletrack.

5.2   Go right on a spur trail that cuts through a picnic area with a natural spring. Cross a small bridge then turn left on Fast Pitch.

5.6   At Fairway Hills Connector, stay straight on Fast Pitch.

5.7   At the four-way intersection, turn left on Hat Trick. Take it all the way to the trailhead.

6.3   Arrive back at Quinn's Trailhead.

OPTIONS

There are numerous options to ride this easy loop. You can ascend and descend the Fast Pitch and Hat Trick doubletracks in reverse. You can also stay on Matt's Flat up to Seventy 101 instead of going left on Cammy's.

30 ROUND VALLEY CLASSIC LOOP

LOOP

Trail Type: 95% singletrack, 5% doubletrack
Distance: 11.2 miles
Elevation Gain/Loss: 1395/1395 feet
High Point: 6885 feet
Ride Time: 1.5–3 hours
Technical Difficulty: Intermediate
Fitness Intensity: Moderate
Season: Spring–fall

Maps: Mountain Trails Foundation Summer Map; Round Valley and Trailside Area Trails Map; Adventure Maps Salt Lake City, Park City, and the Wasatch; USGS 7.5-minute Park City East
GPS: 40°40'53.58"N, 111°28'18.25"W
Land Manager: Round Valley Open Space (managed by Mountain Trails Foundation)

OVERVIEW

Locals consider this ride at Round Valley the "classic loop" of the area. Take a spin on this route and you'll soon see why. The Classic Loop basically circumnavigates the Round Valley Protected Open Space while staying almost totally on singletrack. This loop links together the best and most enjoyable trails in the system like Rambler, Rusty Shovel, Ramble On, La Dea Duh, Backslide, Nowhere Elks, and Somewhere Elks. Expect moderate ascents and fast, rollicking descents on manicured trails. Aside from a few rock gardens, there's nothing too technical here—just loads of fun.

There are dozens of intersecting trails along this loop, so it's easy to get confused and/or lost. If that happens, don't worry because Round Valley's trails are interconnected, and maps are located at major intersections. If you go off route, keep pedaling and you'll eventually find your way back on the loop or even back at the trailhead. No matter how you ride here, you can't go wrong with your trail choices.

GETTING THERE

From the intersection of Park Avenue and Kearns Boulevard in Park City, drive northeast on Kearns Boulevard (SR 248) for 2.8 miles. When you reach Round Valley Drive, turn left. It curves back north for 0.1 mile. Then turn left on Gillmor Way. Stay on Gillmor Way for 0.5 mile as it loops around the sports fields to the Quinn's Trailhead parking, the last lot on the right near the Park City Ice Arena. Rather than starting at the official Quinn's Trailhead, locate the Rambler Trail next to Ability Way and begin your ride here.

MILEAGE LOG

0.0 Rambler Trail starts on the right side of Ability Way. Go right as the singletrack rises up above the Ice Arena.

0.3 At the intersection with the beginner-friendly Practice Loop, keep going straight on Rambler.

0.4 Practice Loop rejoins Rambler. Stay right. Immediately after this, the trail intersects Somewhere Elks on the left. Again, stay right on Rambler.

0.7 At the next intersection, where Kari's comes in on the left, stay right on Rambler and traverse a wide bench above the hospital.

1.0 Stay right on Rambler once more (left is Ramble On).

1.2 At this four-way junction, go across Ramble On and stay on Rambler. From here the trail aggressively climbs along several switchbacks.

1.5 Stay right on Rambler (left is the top of Kari's).

1.8 At the intersection with High Side, stay right on Rambler.

2.2 This is the top of the loop's first climb and is a major intersection of Rambler, Nowhere Elks, and Rusty Shovel. Leave Rambler here and go right on Rusty Shovel, which is a very fun, flowing descent. You'll know you're on the correct path if you spot rusty shovels hanging in trees along the way.

3.8 At the bottom of the downhill, turn left on Ramble On. The trail slightly climbs through scrub oak groves until it rejoins Rambler.

4.0 At the fork, stay left on Ramble On (right is Rusty Spur).

5.0 At the fork with Round Valley Connector, stay left on Ramble On.

6.1 Ramble On meets back up with Rambler. Go right on Rambler.

6.2 Cross Round Valley Express and continue on Rambler.

6.8 At the intersection with the Rademan Ridge doubletrack, go left on the road. This is one of the few doubletracks you'll encounter on the ride.

6.9 Look for the singletrack on your right marked "La Dea Duh" off of Rademan Ridge and go right onto this trail. It descends over chunky

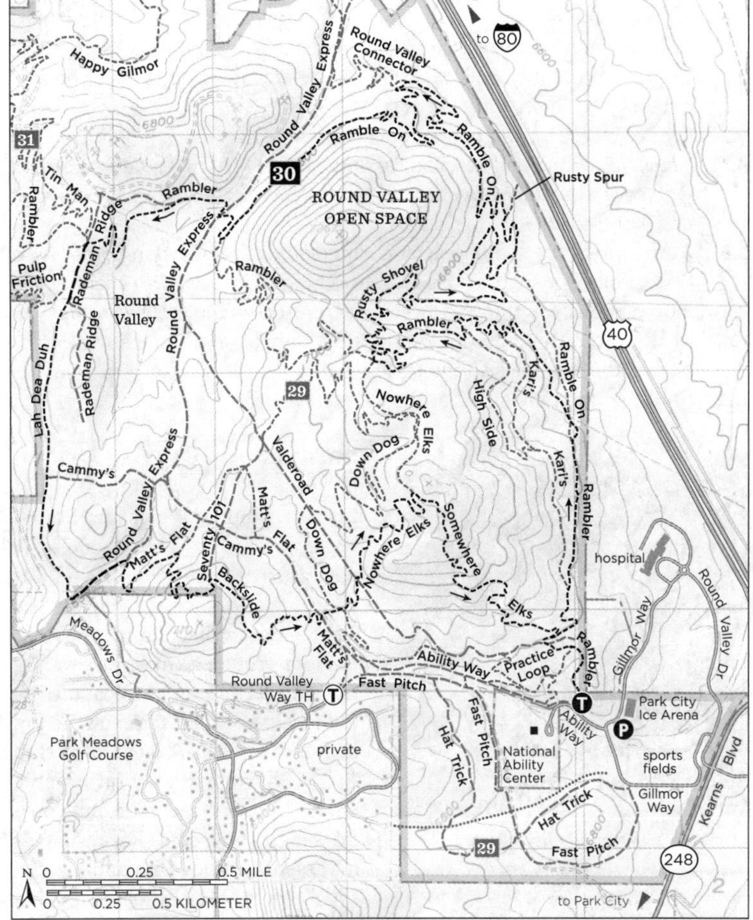

and slabby rock. This fun, technical traverse may challenge you, depending on your skill level.

7.4   When Cammy's comes in on the left, stay straight on La Dea Duh.

7.8   Go left on Round Valley Express, another short section of doubletrack.

7.9   At the trail fork, go right on Matt's Flat singletrack.

8.2   Leave Matt's Flat and go right on Backslide, the steepest ascent on the loop as the trail switchbacks up and around a small hill.

8.6   At the intersection with Seventy 101, stay straight on Backslide to descend another twisting, flowy downhill that will leave you smiling.

9.1   Cross Matt's Flat doubletrack. On the other side of Matt's Flat, the trail becomes Nowhere Elks.

9.2   Cross Down Dog and continue on Nowhere Elks.

9.3   Cross Valderoad and keep on Nowhere Elks. From here, the trail climbs with several switchbacks but it's not steep or technical. This is the final uphill of the ride.

9.8   At the top of the climb, you hit an intersection. Go right on Somewhere Elks. Drop your seatpost because this biggest, most fun descent of the loop plunges you through sweeping turns down the mountainside.

10.7   At the end of the descent, go right on Rambler and retrace the beginning of the ride back to the trailhead.

11.2   Return to the parking lot at the ice arena.

This local's favorite links several popular trails. (Photo by Lexi Dowdall)

OPTIONS

Countless options exist at Round Valley. This Classic Loop is described counterclockwise, but you can easily ride it clockwise. There are no directional trails on the loop. You can also create variations by ascending Kari's and High Side from Rambler to reach the top of Rusty Shovel. You can also skip Rusty Shovel and stay on Ramble On for a more direct loop, but you'd miss a great descent. For a shorter loop, avoid La Dea Duh and instead take Rambler to Seventy 101, then connect with Cammy's, which intersects Backslide. However ride it, make sure you enjoy the excellent descents on Rusty Shovel, Backslide, and Somewhere Elks.

31 PULP FRICTION

LOOP

Trail Type: 100% singletrack
Distance: 3 miles
Elevation Gain/Loss: 470/470 feet
High Point: 6840 feet
Ride Time: 0.75 hour
Technical Difficulty: Intermediate
Fitness Intensity: Easy
Season: Summer–fall

Maps: Mountain Trails Foundation Summer Map; Round Valley and Trailside Area Trails Map; USGS 7.5-minute Park City East
GPS: 40°70'10.57"N, 111°50'72.34"W
Land Manager: Round Valley Open Space (managed by Mountain Trails Foundation)

OVERVIEW

Pulp Friction is a newer downhill-only flow trail on the northwest end of Round Valley. The trail's completion added some much-needed excitement to the area. The descent is typical of what mountain bikers expect from a downhill-only trail. You've got banked turns, berms, and jumps. There's even impressive rock work on one of the berms—a testament to the trail builder's hard work. Pulp Friction's grade is steep enough to maintain speed but not so steep that you have to white-knuckle the brakes. Pulp Friction is 1.5 miles long and begins at the intersection of Rambler, Rademan Ridge and Tin Man. The total vertical drop is around 450 feet to the Old Ranch Road Trailhead.

There are a few ways to get to Pulp Friction to do loops, but two trailheads in particular provide the closest access via the Happy Gilmor Trail. The Old Ranch Road Trailhead is the obvious place to start and end your ride, so that's the route I describe below. But I prefer the alternative of starting at the Happy Gilmor Trailhead on Round Valley's north end. This start/end point adds additional mileage and makes me feel like I've "earned my turns." (See Options for details.)

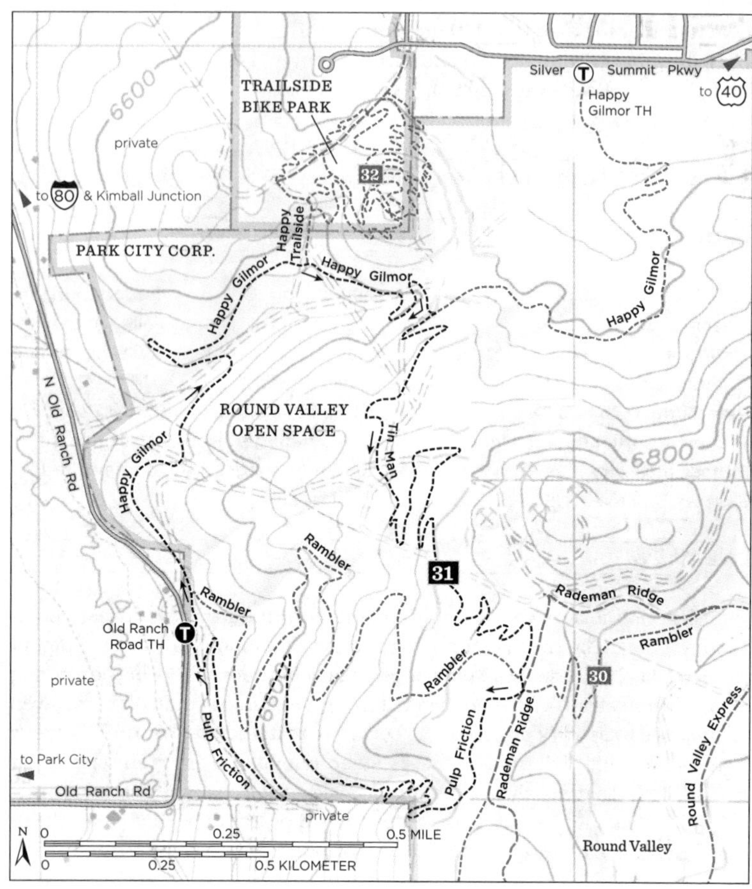

GETTING THERE

From the intersection of Park Avenue and Kearns Boulevard in Park City, drive north on Park Avenue (SR 224) for 3 miles. Turn right on Old Ranch Road and follow it north and east through a series of turns for 2.2 miles. Then turn left on N. Old Ranch Road and follow it north for 0.2 mile until you see the Old Ranch Road Trailhead on your right. Park here.

MILEAGE LOG

0.0 From the Old Ranch Road Trailhead, go left on Rambler. In just 300 feet or so, you'll come to an intersection where Rambler make a hard right turn. Veer left onto the Happy Gilmor Trail.

0.8 At the intersection with Happy Trailside, which provides access to Trailside Park, stay straight on Happy Gilmor.

1.0 After the trail makes a few switchbacks uphill, it intersects with Tin Man. Go right on Tin Man to get to the top of Pulp Friction. If you stay on Happy Gilmor for about a mile, it will take you to the alternate Happy Gilmor Trailhead. Tin Man is a slightly steeper ascent with a few rock gardens, but nothing too difficult. It's also a fun trail to ride downhill.

2.0 Tin Man ends at the top at a major trail intersection including Rademan Ridge, Rambler, and Pulp Friction. The first trail on the right is Rambler, a more old-school trail with chunky rocks and no flow. The second option on the right, Pulp Friction, is the newer flow trail in Round Valley. Pulp Friction is a smooth, downhill-only ride that has become a Round Valley destination. Enjoy descending the hillside back to the Old Ranch Road Trailhead.

3.0 You've reached the trailhead and the end of the ride.

Blasting around a berm on Pulp Friction

OPTIONS

For a longer, 5.5-mile lariat loop with Pulp Friction, start and end your ride at the Happy Gilmor Trailhead, located just east of Trailside Park. Ride up the Happy Gilmor Trail for 0.9 mile to the intersection with Tin Man and proceed as above. After descending Pulp Friction, ride Happy Gilmor all the way back to the trail's namesake trailhead.

32 TRAILSIDE BIKE PARK

NETWORK

Trail Type: 90% singletrack, 10% doubletrack
Distance: Up to 4 miles
Elevation Gain/Loss: 150/150 feet per lap
High Point: 6735 feet
Ride Time: 10 minutes per lap
Technical Difficulty: Beginner to Expert
Fitness Intensity: Easy

Season: Spring–fall
Maps: Mountain Trails Foundation Summer Map; Round Valley and Trailside Area Trails Map; Adventure Maps Salt Lake City, Park City, and the Wasatch; USGS 7.5-minute Park City East
GPS: 40°42'44.16"N, 111°30'06.18"W
Land Manager: Snyderville Basin Special Recreation District

OVERVIEW

Trailside Bike Park is a treasure for the Park City mountain bike community. Tucked between the sports fields at Trailside Park and Round Valley Open Space, this world-class bike park offers mountain bike skills training with downhill flow lines ranging from beginner to expert in difficulty. You'll find pump tracks, wood features, jumps, berms, rock gardens, and more. With five main flow trails, you can improve your riding from the ground up.

A quick and easy climb up doubletrack gets you to the top, where you can choose from the mellow rollers of The Great Gazoo to the experts-only Bamm Bamm, with its mandatory drops and big wood features. Each lap is less than a mile and takes around 10 minutes, so you can play around

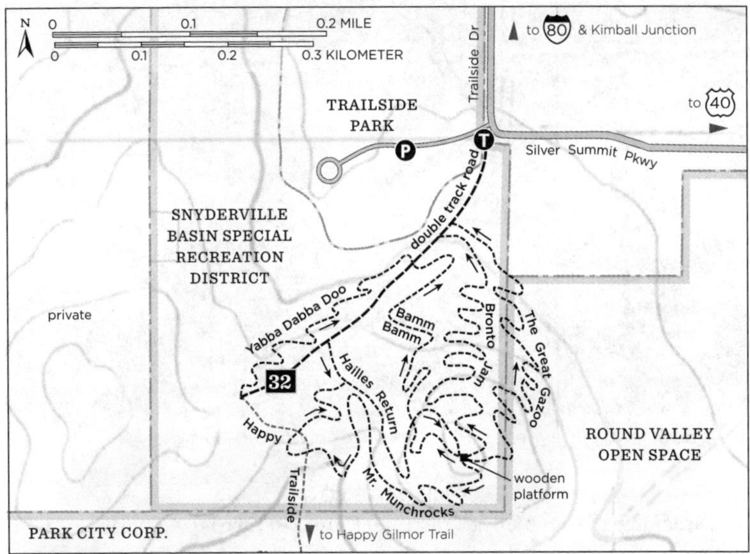

on every trail multiple times. Riding all five flow lines adds up to around 4 miles total.

Beyond the downhill-only skills trails, there's something for the whole family. At Trailside Bike Park you'll find small pump tracks for the kids and a jump course where you can practice getting air in a safe environment. This place is a must ride if you want to improve your bike-handling skills or just enjoy a quick ride after work.

GETTING THERE

From the intersection of Park Avenue and Kearns Boulevard in Park City, drive northeast on Kearns Boulevard for 3.2 miles to US 40. Turn left on the highway and follow it north for 2.4 miles. When you reach exit 2 for Silver Summit, leave the highway and go left on the off-ramp onto Silver Summit Parkway. Follow this road for 1 mile to Trailside Park, where there is a large parking lot. The trailhead for the bike park is located right at the entrance of the parking lot.

Trailside Bike Park is a great place to advance your bike-handling skills.

MILEAGE LOG

The ascent up the doubletrack road and Hailles Return is 0.4 mile long. At the top there is a large wooden platform where four of the five flow trails begin. For Yabba Dabba Doo, continue ascending past Hailles Return on the dirt road. Below are all five trails in order of difficulty.

BEGINNER

Yabba Dabba Doo This easiest trail in the park has small berms and jumps that you can just roll over. Start here to get a feel for your bike and how to manage flow-trail features.

The Great Gazoo This easy flow trail has larger, sculpted berms and a few dirt jump features.

INTERMEDIATE

Bronto Jam This trail features more large berms with the addition of wood berms and a few jumps, including a big tabletop. All features offer ride-around options.

ADVANCED

Mr. Munchrocks As the name implies, this somewhat technical trail has a lot of rock gardens and obstacles. It also has berms and jumps as well as wood bridges mixed in.

EXPERT
Bamm Bamm The most difficult trail in the park features huge wood jumps, drops, berms, gaps, and more. Only attempt it after working your way up from the easier trails.

33 PRINCESS DI

LOOP

Trail Type: 52% singletrack, 26% pavement, 22% doubletrack
Distance: 14.5 miles
Elevation Gain/Loss: 1730/1730 feet
High Point: 7300 feet
Ride Time: 2–3 hours
Technical Difficulty: Advanced
Fitness Intensity: Strenuous
Season: Spring–fall

Maps: Mountain Trails Foundation Summer Map; Adventure Maps Salt Lake City, Park City, and the Wasatch; USGS 7.5-minute Park City East, Wanship
GPS: 40°43'27.58"N, 111°28'18.05"W
Land Manager: Private (managed by Basin Recreation), Utah State Parks

OVERVIEW

The adventurous Princess Di Trail goes around the back side of gated Promontory Mountain. The singletrack segment is 7.5 miles long, with a 3-mile approach on paved trail to the trailhead and a 4-mile return on the Rail Trail. While the approach and return are easy, the Princess Di singletrack provides one hell of a ride. You can expect to find steep and loose climbing, traverses through burnt forests, sage flats, rock formations, shady aspen groves, expansive views of Rockport Reservoir, fast-and-tight descents, and a climactic end in a tunnel beneath I-80 in Tollgate Canyon.

While not very technical, narrow Princess Di tends to become overgrown in late summer. Some sections are steep with tight switchbacks that can be loose, especially if it hasn't rained in a while. But overall, advanced riders will find Princess Di suitable for a novel mountain biking experience.

The Three Mile Canyon and Princess Di Trails are entirely on private property, located within the Promontory development. But an easement allows access to the public. Stay on the trail at all times to avoid trespassing. Utah State Parks manages the Rail Trail section of this loop.

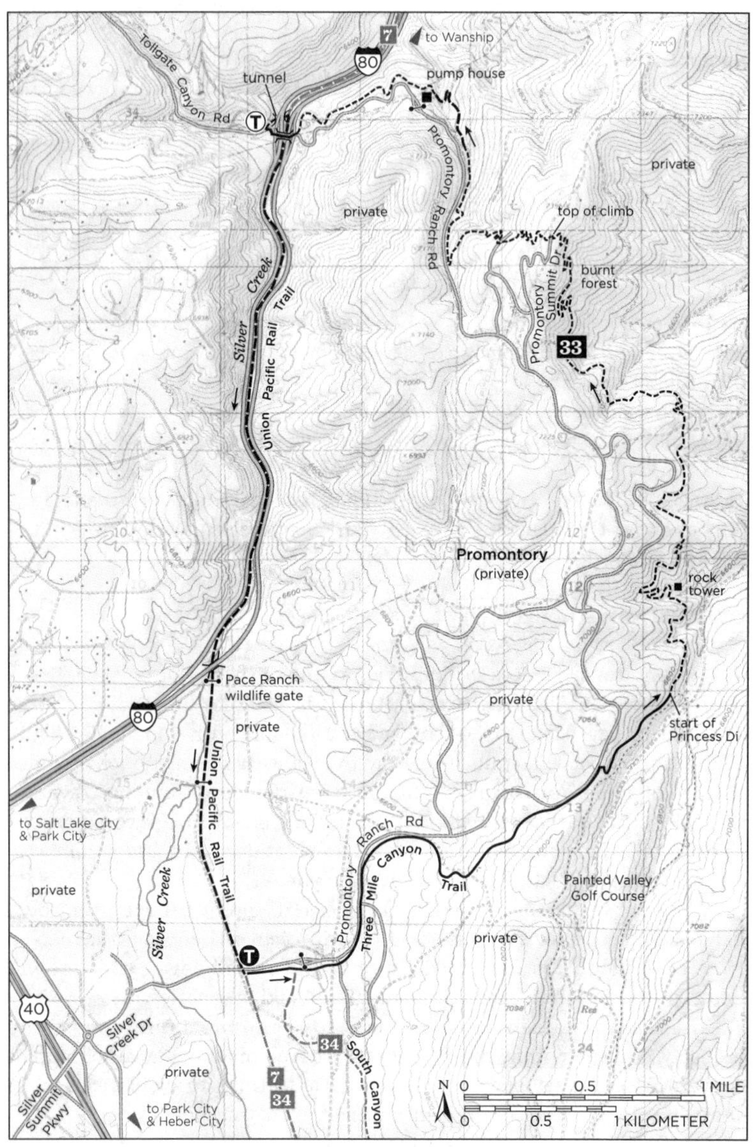
to Wanship
80
7
pump house
tunnel
T
Tollgate Canyon Rd
private
Promontory Ranch Rd
private
top of climb
Silver Creek
Union Pacific Rail Trail
burnt forest
Promontory Summit Dr
33
Promontory
(private)
rock tower
12
12
private
start of
Princess Di
Pace Ranch
wildlife gate
80
private
Union Pacific Rail Trail
to Salt Lake City
& Park City
private
13
Silver Creek
Promontory Ranch Rd
Three Mile Canyon Trail
Painted Valley
Golf Course
private
T
private
24
40
Silver Creek Dr
34
South Canyon
7
34
private
to Park City
& Heber City
Silver Summit Pkwy
N 0   0.5   1 MILE
0   0.5   1 KILOMETER

GETTING THERE

From the intersection of Park Avenue and Kearns Boulevard in Park City, drive northeast on Kearns Boulevard (SR 248) for 3.2 miles to US 40. Go left and enter the highway going north toward I-80. Drive 2.4 miles and get off at exit 2 toward Silver Summit. Go right on Silver Creek Drive. In 0.3 mile you'll come to a roundabout. Take the second exit and stay on Silver Creek Drive.

In 0.3 mile from the roundabout, turn right on Promontory Ranch Road and go east for 0.5 mile to the Promontory (Star Pointe) Rail Trail parking area on the left.

MILEAGE LOG

0.0 Go to the southeast corner of the parking lot, cross the street, and go left on the paved Three Mile Canyon Trail, which winds up into the Promontory neighborhood. Stay on this paved trail while ignoring all the dirt side trails that intersect. The paved trail soon leaves the homes behind and climbs up the mountainside. This is a great warm-up for what's to come.

2.3 At the top of the climb you're at the entrance to the Painted Valley Golf Course. At this point the paved trail goes downhill.

3.0 At a sharp turn where the pavement turns to dirt, the Princess Di Trailhead starts on the left. The singletrack is easy to find and is signed. Enter here. The path goes down and switchbacks right away before you start climbing again through several tight turns. On this stretch of trail, you'll find a large rock tower and nice views. Keep an eye out for wildlife, especially deer.

4.5 Ignore the doubletrack on the right and stay left on Princess Di. From this point the trail is a delightful traverse, downhill through scrub oak and aspen groves.

5.8 A little-used footpath connects on the left. Stay right on Princess Di. For the next few miles the trail ascends with many switchbacks through a burnt ghost forest charred by fire a few years ago. Through the blackened trunks you can see Rockport Reservoir far below.

7.1 After this final big climb you top out on the ridge at 7300 feet. Enjoy the 360-degree view and get ready for a long descent. To find it, cross the paved road (Promontory Summit Drive) and locate the singletrack on the other side. The trail is marked by a rock cairn. This downhill section is narrow with tight switchbacks. But overall, the ride is mellow,

Navigating a tight switchback on Princess Di (Photo by Justin Lozier)

smooth, and fast until you have to scrub your speed at every twisting corner.

7.7 Cross the paved road and continue the descent on the other side.

9.3 Where the trail meets up with some doubletrack, go left and take it down. A sign indicates that Princess Di continues in this direction. After a brief descent the track steeply climbs up loose rock and ends at a pump house. Take a hard right back onto singletrack. The trail falls steeply into Tollgate Canyon toward I-80. You'll be able to see and hear the traffic far below.

10.2 The trail traverses in a westerly direction above I-80 and ends at the north Promontory entrance. Turn right and cross the overpass above the interstate. On the other side, locate a pipeline sign on your right and hike down to the creek on a footpath. Once at the creek (usually dry in the summer) go right again on the creek bottom. Walk your bike through the tunnel beneath the interstate's southbound lane. On the other side, you'll be on the Union Pacific Rail Trail between the freeway lanes. Turn right and pedal the flat doubletrack back toward Park City.

12.8 Near Pace Ranch, you'll come to a wildlife gate. Go through it and close it behind you so animals don't end up on the interstate.

14.5 The rail trail returns to Promontory Trailhead and your vehicle.

OPTIONS

I've described this loop counterclockwise as I think it is the best way to experience this ride. But you can conceivably do it clockwise. Some locals also enjoy it as an out-and-back, starting from the Promontory entrance in Tollgate Canyon. This is a steeper ascent for the first 3 miles. You can turn around and descend at any point for a shorter ride.

34 SOUTH CANYON

LOOP

Trail Type: 70% singletrack, 30% doubletrack

Distance: 9 miles

Elevation Gain/Loss: 660/660 feet

High Point: 6884 feet

Ride Time: 1–2 hours

Technical Difficulty: Intermediate

Fitness Intensity: Easy

Season: Spring–fall

Maps: Mountain Trails Foundation Summer Map; Adventure Maps Salt Lake City, Park City, and the Wasatch; USGS 7.5-minute Park City East

GPS: 40°43'27.47"N, 111°28'18.20"W

Land Manager: Private (managed by Basin Recreation), Utah State Parks

OVERVIEW

Park City is home to many famous and popular mountain bike trails. South Canyon is neither. So why ride this under-the-radar singletrack? Because while everyone is dodging each other on the crowded Wasatch Crest or Mid Mountain Trails, you can assuredly find solitude here.

While the South Canyon loop is not a destination ride per se, you can use it to extend a ride on the Princess Di Trail. Both rides start at the Promontory (Star Pointe) Rail Trail parking area. After finishing your Princess Di loop, ride past your car and continue south on the Union Pacific Rail Trail to South Canyon for some added mileage.

You can ride South Canyon two ways. First, ride it as a loop that's nearly 7 miles long. Or add the out-and-back for a 9-mile lariat-style loop. The mileage log described here is for the 9-mile ride. The South Canyon Trail is on private land with access allowed under a public easement, so be respectful of the generous property owners and do not trespass off the trail.

GETTING THERE

From the intersection of Park Avenue and Kearns Boulevard in Park City, drive northeast on Kearns Boulevard (SR 248) for 3.2 miles to US 40. Go left and enter the highway going north toward I-80. Drive 2.4 miles and get off at exit 2 toward Silver Summit. Go right on Silver Creek Drive.

In 0.3 mile you'll come to a roundabout. Take the second exit and stay on Silver Creek Drive. In 0.3 mile from the roundabout, turn right on Promontory Ranch Road and go east for 0.5 mile to the Promontory (Star Pointe) Rail Trail parking area on the left.

MILEAGE LOG

0.0 From the parking lot, go south and cross Promontory Ranch Road. Continue southbound on the Union Pacific Rail Trail. It's easy pedaling on doubletrack for the next 2.5 miles. Along the way you'll pass through two cattle gates. Be sure to close them behind you so the cows don't escape. The Rail Trail is owned and managed by the State of Utah, but it's surrounded by private property.

2.5 Leave the Rail Trail and go left on the Roc Mon singletrack trail. It's not obvious, but a huge gravel pit on your right is a good landmark. Immediately after you leave the Rail Trail, ignore a dirt road on the left. Stay right on the singletrack that goes through an opening in a fence. This trail can be overgrown and difficult to see at first, but it becomes clearer once you gain some elevation. Roc Mon climbs steeply with a couple of switchbacks up the mountainside.

3.0 Roc Mon connects with the South Canyon Trail. Go right for the out-and-back (go left

You will likely find solitude on the South Canyon loop.

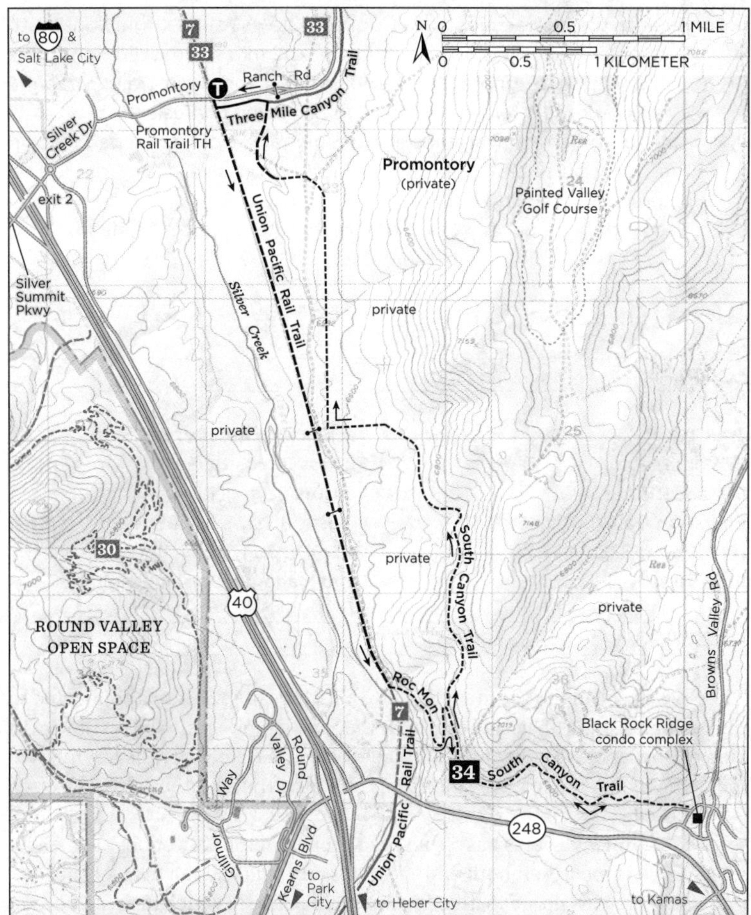

for the shorter loop) that gradually climbs as it traverses south then east. The riding is somewhat rocky with a few technical challenges suitable for intermediate riders.

4.3   South Canyon Trail descends through a scrub oak forest and ends at a fence that surrounds the Black Rock Ridge condo complex. Turn around and go back the way you came.

5.6 Back at the intersection with Roc Mon, stay straight (right) on South Canyon as it parallels a fence. In the next 2 miles, three different footpaths intersect. Ignore these and stay on the main trail. Carsonite posts mark the intersections here to avoid any confusion.

8.2 The South Canyon Trail ends at a doubletrack. Go left and pedal down the dirt road back to the Three Mile Canyon bike path. Stay left to return to the parking lot.

9.0 End of the ride back at the Promontory (Star Pointe) Trailhead.

35 ROSS CREEK

LOOP

Trail Type: 85% singletrack, 15% doubletrack

Distance: 3.2 miles

Elevation Gain/Loss: 350/350 feet

High Point: 6285 feet

Ride Time: 0.5–1 hour

Technical Difficulty: Beginner

Fitness Intensity: Easy

Season: Spring–fall

Maps: USGS 7.5-minute Park City East

GPS: 40°39'17.32"N, 111°24'49.48"W

Land Manager: Jordanelle State Park

OVERVIEW

The Ross Creek loop at Jordanelle State Park is really two loops connected to make a figure eight. The ride begins at the Ross Creek Trailhead on the north side of Jordanelle Reservoir. The Wada Way and Keetley Trails are the two loops that connect. You can ride either one for a shorty or both to bang out a 3.2-mile ride.

The technical level is easy; there isn't much in the way of obstacles. The singletrack is mostly smooth and the turns are wide enough to easily negotiate. There are also no steep hills or much vertical gain, which makes this loop great for upper-level beginners.

As you ride the loop through brushy flats and groves of scrub oak, you'll have nice views of the reservoir below. The park charges an entrance fee. If you plan to visit at least three state parks in a single year (several routes in this book are in state parks), then you may want to purchase an annual pass. If you're paying a day-use fee here, to maximize your money, I suggest you

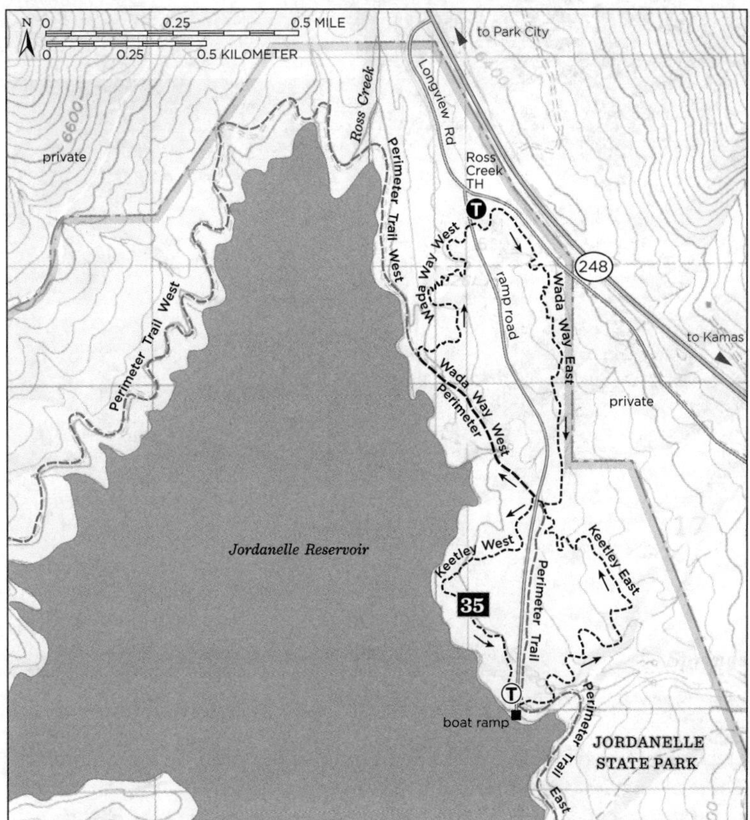

make it a multisport day by riding your bike then cooling off with a swim or stand-up paddleboarding session on the water.

GETTING THERE

From the intersection of Park Avenue and Kearns Boulevard in Park City, drive northeast on Kearns Boulevard (SR 248) for 3.2 miles to US 40. Continue straight going under the highway on SR 248. In another 3.2 miles, turn

Meandering along the mellow Ross Creek loop at Jordanelle State Park

right onto Longview Drive across from the Deer Mountain development. Follow Longview for 0.7 mile and stay right at a fork onto a road that enters the state park and heads down to the lakeshore, where there is a boat launch. Park at the Ross Creek Trailhead lot on the left. There is ample parking, a bathroom, and a state park payment kiosk.

MILEAGE LOG

0.0 Locate the trail next to a metal gate across the boat-launch road, just beyond the restrooms. The trails begin on either side of the road. For this recommended clockwise figure-eight loop, go left (up) on the Wada Way singletrack. The sign on a post says, "Wada Way East." This section of trail winds with many curves through scrub oak groves.

0.8 Cross the paved road, then go left onto Keetley West. The trail dives down into sagebrush flats along the reservoir's shoreline.

1.4 Keetley West comes out at the Ross Creek boat ramp parking area where boaters launch kayaks and stand-up paddleboards. This is another option for parking to mountain bike as well, but it costs a little more than the trailhead parking, so maximize your dollars and park here if you plan on a multisport day. To continue the figure eight, cross the ramp road. On the other side is a four-way trail intersection. The far right is Perimeter Trail to Rock Cliff; left is Perimeter Trail to the Ross Creek parking lot. On the second trail from the right, go straight on Keetley East.

2.3 Keetley connects with Perimeter Trail. Go right onto Perimeter. Immediately after, cross the paved boat-launch road. You are now back at the middle of the figure eight. On the other side of the road, stay right on Perimeter Trail/Wada Way West. This section of doubletrack dips up and down and allows for a ton of speed.

2.7 Leave Perimeter Trail and get onto the Wada Way West singletrack on the right. This next section is the most climbing of the ride as the trail switchbacks up to the road.

3.2 End your ride back at the Ross Creek parking lot.

OPTIONS

You can do this figure-eight loop counterclockwise as well. You can also ride both the Wada Way and Keetley loops individually. For a much longer ride, go for a pedal on the Perimeter Trail. It's not very interesting mountain biking, as it is all doubletrack with a lot of steep, rolling terrain requiring strong legs and a granny gear, with downhill sections of loose rock. But the reward is a view of the reservoir from beginning to end.

Both the east and west sections of the Perimeter Trail are out-and-backs. You can go as far as you'd like before turning around, but if you do the entire section, it's nearly 30 miles and over 2000 feet of total climbing.

GUARDSMAN PASS

At an elevation of 9717 feet, Guardsman Pass is one of the highest passes in the Wasatch Mountains. The road that runs east-west over the pass connects Park City and Big Cottonwood Canyon. Deep snow keeps the pass closed in winter, but come summer, Guardsman Pass is one of the busiest recreational spots in Utah. One reason is that it's the start of the famed Wasatch Crest Trail (Route 36). Parking is prohibited on the pass and for about a mile on either side, as vehicle congestion has reached critical levels. Taking a commercial shuttle is pretty much the only way to ride the Wasatch Crest from the top down.

Pine Canyon Road, which connects the town of Midway to Guardsman Pass, is the starting point for another epic ride. The WOW Trail (Route 38) drops from Bonanza Flat nearly 2500 feet to the campground in Wasatch Mountain State Park. Like the Wasatch Crest, WOW is another epic descent that is fast becoming a popular shuttle ride. For both the Wasatch Crest and WOW, you can reserve a shuttle service. Try Fox 'N Rox at www.foxnroxshuttle.com. Or contact Big Rack Shuttles at www.bigrackshuttle.com.

Guardsman Pass will soon have more new trails to ride. Mountain Trails Foundation has big plans for Bonanza Flat, including a big loop that circumnavigates the area. Be sure to ride them once they are complete. Check www.mountaintrails.org for the latest news.

The mountain bike trails at Solitude Mountain Resort (Route 37), located at the bottom of the pass in Big Cottonwood Canyon, are also worth exploring. Leave the Park City crowds behind on Solitude's narrow singletrack, steep climbs, and chunky descents. You may choose to pedal uphill or ride the Sunrise chairlift to maximize descent time.

Opposite: *Mountain bikers cruise the epic WOW Trail (Route 38), a 2500-foot descent on the Wasatch Back.*

36 WASATCH CREST

SHUTTLE

Trail Type: 90% singletrack 10% doubletrack

Distance: 14 miles

Elevation Gain/Loss: 1175/3800 feet

High Point: 9843 feet

Ride Time: 2.5–4 hours

Technical Difficulty: Advanced

Fitness Intensity: Moderate

Season: Summer–fall

Maps: Mountain Trails Foundation Summer Map; Adventure Maps Salt Lake City, Park City, and the Wasatch; USGS 7.5-minute Brighton, Park City West

GPS: 40°36'24.65"N, 111°33'17.95"W

Land Manager: Uinta-Wasatch-Cache National Forest, Park City Mountain

OVERVIEW

If one trail in Park City is considered *legendary*, it is the Wasatch Crest. The crest takes mountain bikers from Guardsman Pass to the top of the ridgeline between Park City Mountain and Big Cottonwood Canyon. From there, it's an unparalleled pedal with 360 degrees of the most jaw-dropping views in Utah. Heck, the Wasatch Crest is so famous that "Puke Hill" and "The Spine" (names for sections of the trail) are household names in the mountain biking community. Basically, it comes down to this: If you go mountain biking in Park City, riding the Wasatch Crest is mandatory.

There are three ways to ride this classic, test-piece shuttle. The start is at Guardsman Pass, but you can either descend the crest into Mill Creek Canyon to the Salt Lake Valley for the longest ride, or you may take Mill D North Fork into Big Cottonwood Canyon for a shorter shuttle. But since this is a Park City guidebook, the descent goes down the Canyons Village side of Park City Mountain. Plus, I think it's the best way to ride the Wasatch Crest.

This advanced ride is technically difficult because it has some aggressive, rocky sections, especially the steep drop known as "The Spine." Less experienced riders can walk all of these sections, so don't let being an intermediate mountain biker dissuade you from experiencing this phenomenal ride.

Parking is prohibited at Guardsman Pass and within 1 mile on either side of it, and the place is a traffic nightmare. The only sane way to get there is to

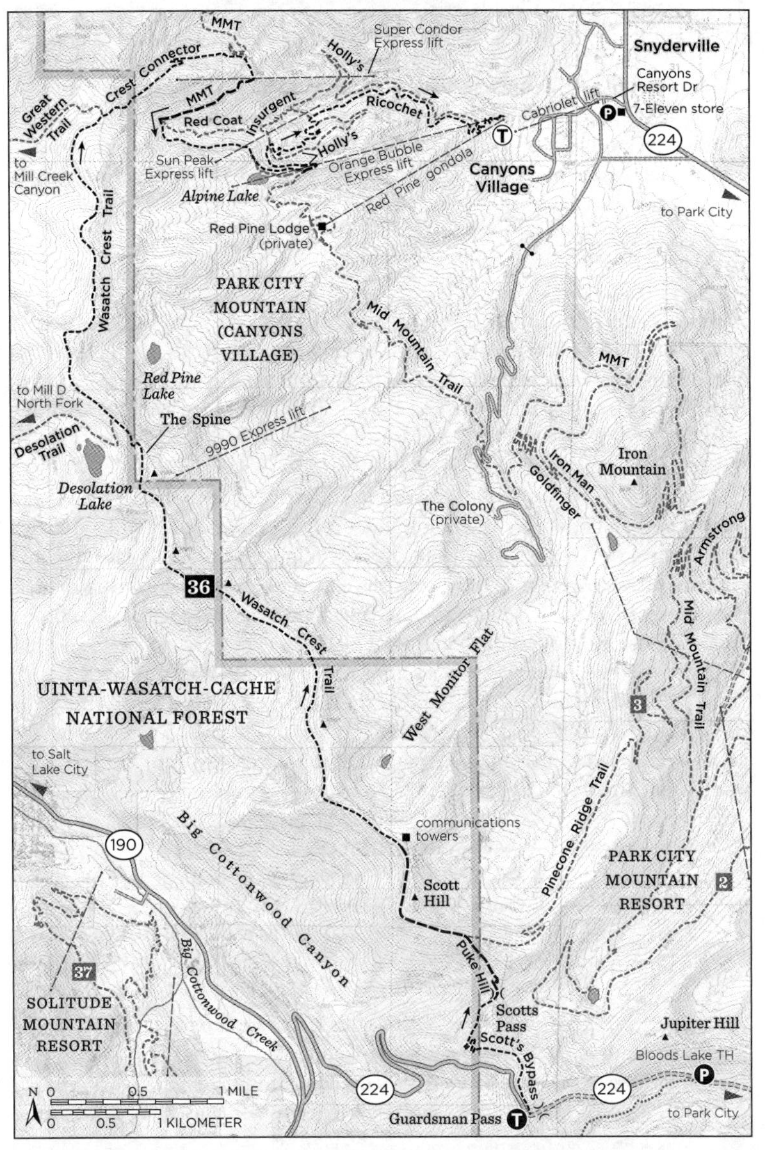
MMT
Super Condor
Express lift
Snyderville
Crest Connector
Holly's
Canyons
Resort Dr
7-Eleven store
Great Western Trail
MMT
Red Coat
Insurgent
Ricochet
Cabriolet lift
224
to Mill Creek Canyon
Sun Peak Express lift
Holly's
Orange Bubble Express lift
Red Pine gondola
Canyons Village
Wasatch Crest Trail
Alpine Lake
to Park City
Red Pine Lodge (private)
PARK CITY MOUNTAIN (CANYONS VILLAGE)
Mid Mountain Trail
to Mill D North Fork
Red Pine Lake
MMT
The Spine
9990 Express lift
Iron Mountain
Desolation Trail
Iron Man
Desolation Lake
The Colony (private)
Goldfinger
Armstrong
36
Wasatch Crest Trail
Mid Mountain Trail
UINTA-WASATCH-CACHE NATIONAL FOREST
West Monitor Flat
3
to Salt Lake City
190
communications towers
Pinecone Ridge Trail
PARK CITY MOUNTAIN RESORT
Big Cottonwood Canyon
Scott Hill
2
Big Cottonwood Creek
37
Puke Hill
SOLITUDE MOUNTAIN RESORT
Jupiter Hill
Scotts Pass
Bloods Lake TH
Scott's Bypass
N 0   0.5   1 MILE
0   0.5   1 KILOMETER
224
Guardsman Pass
224
to Park City

use a shuttle service. Fox 'N Rox Shuttle and Big Rack Shuttle both provide transportation from Park City to Guardsman Pass for a reasonable fee. Go to www.foxnroxshuttle.com or www.bigrackshuttle.com to book your ride.

Local mountain bikers ride this must-do trail at least once every season. The scenery, quality of the trail, various options of descent, and the overall experience make mountain biking the Wasatch Crest Trail a sweet way to spend a summer day in the mountains of Utah.

GETTING THERE

If you insist on shuttling the Wasatch Crest with your own vehicles, here's how to do it. First, leave a car at the Cabriolet lot behind the 7-Eleven store at the Canyons Village base area. To get there from the intersection of Park Avenue and Kearns Boulevard in Park City, drive north on Park Avenue (SR 224) for 2.8 miles to Canyons Resort Drive. Turn left and leave a car in the lot adjacent to the Cabriolet lift.

From there, go back to Park Avenue and drive south for 3.1 miles. Turn left onto Deer Valley Drive while following the signs to Deer Valley Resort. In 1.1 miles, you'll come to a traffic circle. Follow it to the opposite side and continue straight, leaving the circle on Marsac Avenue. Follow this road as it winds up through a canyon and into the mountains for 3.6 miles to a traffic circle at Deer Valley's Empire Canyon Lodge.

Take the circle all the way around and continue up Marsac (SR 224) toward Guardsman Pass. Stay on this road and in 2.7 miles you'll reach the Bloods Lake Trailhead on the right. Park here. You'll have to pedal your bike another mile on the steep, paved road to get to Guardsman Pass. Trust me, it's best to just hire a shuttle service.

MILEAGE LOG

0.0 At Guardsman Pass, find the Scott's Bypass Trailhead on the north side of the road. There is an old dirt road here that goes up the mountainside. The singletrack is on the left of this road. Scott's Bypass is a nice entry to the Wasatch Crest as it dips and weaves through an evergreen forest.

1.3 Scott's Bypass exits onto a meadow with a dirt road going down the middle of it. Go straight across and up the road. This is the start of the infamous Puke Hill. Dig deep and find the strength in your legs because this ascent is steep, loose, and unrelenting as it climbs straight up the mountain. If you attempt to pedal up it without taking a breather, you may find out why it's called Puke Hill.

1.8 At the top of Puke Hill, take a well-deserved rest and breathe in the view—you are now standing on the Wasatch Crest. When you're ready, go left (northwest) on the Wasatch Crest doubletrack as it traverses the ridge.

2.2 Pass the communications towers on Scott Hill. At this point the doubletrack ends and the singletrack begins. This next section is among the most scenic, as you're treated with views of Big Cottonwood Canyon's row of high-alpine peaks. It's mostly a mellow, rolling downhill save for one decent climb (I call it the "red dirt climb"). Don't forget to stop and take in the scenery from time to time.

5.6 You've reached The Spine. This fin of sharp, steep rocks descends to a saddle between the 9990 lift area of Park City Mountain on one side and Desolation Lake on the other. Only the best and bravest mountain bikers ride the crest of The Spine. There is an easier route to the left

As you admire the view on the Wasatch Crest Trail, you'll realize why it's legendary. (Photo by Adam Symonds)

but it's still very technical. Most riders choose to walk this part, and there is no shame in doing so.

5.9   At the bottom of The Spine, go right at a fork to stay on the Wasatch Crest Trail toward Mill Creek Canyon and Park City Mountain. The left fork travels to Desolation Lake and the Desolation Trail, which leads to Mill D North Fork for an alternate descent that ends in Big Cottonwood Canyon. After taking the right fork, you climb a bit then descend over several technical rock gardens that are challenging but nowhere as scary as The Spine.

8.1   The Wasatch Crest Trail ends in a large meadow at a three-way intersection. Left is the Great Western Trail, which falls into Mill Creek Canyon (open to mountain bikers on even days only). Instead, go right on the Crest Connector (also called Ridge Connector) into Park City Mountain.

9.2   The Crest Connector ends at the Mid Mountain Trail (MMT). Go right on MMT.

9.6   Mid Mountain Trail intersects a doubletrack. Go left (downhill) on the doubletrack, which is still technically Mid Mountain Trail.

9.9   At the bottom of the hill, you'll see Red Coat on the left. This downhill-only trail takes you to the Canyons Village base. It is less used and can be loose. Plus, your only option at the bottom of Red Coat is to ride down the advanced Insurgent Trail, which is steep with jumps and drops. It eventually ends at Holly's, which takes you to the bottom. For this route, stay right instead on MMT as it becomes singletrack again to get to Ricochet.

10.6   Mid Mountain Trail runs into a dirt road near the Alpine Lake fishing pond beneath the Orange Bubble Express chairlift. Stay left on the MMT singletrack.

10.9   Mid Mountain Trail makes a sharp right turn where it once again ends up on a dirt road. Leave MMT and stay left. You are now on Holly's. The intersections are a bit confusing here so when in doubt, follow the signs pointing the way to Holly's and Ricochet.

11.2   Reach a three-way intersection where you get to choose your own adventure. To the left is Insurgent, which is an advanced, downhill-only trail. The middle is Ricochet—a moderate, downhill-only trail with fun rollers, jumps, and berms. To the right is Holly's, which is bi-directional and is used by a lot of hikers and uphill mountain bikers. Take the middle fork (which I personally prefer) on Ricochet to avoid the uphill traffic on Holly's.

14.0 Ricochet ends on a dirt road above a golf course. Go right and pedal into the Canyon's Village base area. Grab a post-ride beer at the Umbrella Bar before cruising down the road back to the Cabriolet Lot where your vehicle awaits.

OPTIONS

As noted above, you can descend into Big Cottonwood Canyon via Mill D North Fork from Desolation Lake. At the meadow where Wasatch Crest Trail ends at Crest Connector, a left on Great Western Trail goes down to Mill Creek Canyon and eventually Salt Lake City. This is the classic way to ride the Crest, but it can only be done on even-numbered days. (All trails in Mill Creek are closed to bikes on odd-numbered days.)

You can also ascend to Wasatch Crest from Park City by way of Armstrong and Pinecone for either a short shuttle or to complete the long IMBA Epic loop.

37 SOLITUDE MOUNTAIN RESORT

LOOP

Trail Type: 85% singletrack, 10% doubletrack, 5% paved

Distance: 6 miles

Elevation Gain/Loss: 1645/1645 feet

High Point: 8939 feet

Ride Time: 1.5–2.5 hours

Technical Difficulty: Advanced

Fitness Intensity: Moderate

Season: Summer–fall

Maps: Adventure Maps Salt Lake City, Park City, and the Wasatch; USGS 7.5-minute Brighton

GPS: 40°37'24.24"N, 111°35'48.69"W

Land Manager: Uinta-Wasatch-Cache National Forest, Solitude Mountain Resort

OVERVIEW

Solitude Mountain Resort, located in Big Cottonwood Canyon just over Guardsman Pass from Deer Valley, has some great trails for mountain biking, including lift-serviced rides. With only 20 miles of trails, the 'Tude may not have the massive network that Park City boasts, but what Solitude lacks in trail miles, it makes up for in spectacular views, lung-busting climbs, and some ripping, technical descents. Best of all, it's relatively uncrowded, so you rarely have to compete with other riders and hikers on the singletrack.

The easiest way to mountain bike at Solitude is to ride the Sunrise lift with your bike, then rally the advanced-level Kruzr Trail. But if you enjoy a workout like I do, the ascent is where it's at. This 6-mile loop is my favorite way to pedal to Kruzr. Basically, you ascend Serenity from the Moonbeam Lodge, traverse and climb to the other side of the mountain on doubletrack, then return to the base on Kruzr.

Solitude offers quality, hand-cut mountain biking. I highly recommend it not just for the exercise, but for the actual solitude you'll find compared to other resorts with lift-served mountain biking.

GETTING THERE

From the intersection of Park Avenue and Kearns Boulevard in Park City, drive south on Park Avenue for 0.3 mile. Turn left onto Deer Valley Drive while following the signs to Deer Valley Resort. In 1.1 miles, you'll come to a traffic circle. Follow it to the opposite side and continue straight, leaving the circle on Marsac Avenue. Follow this road as it winds up through a canyon and into the mountains for 3.6 miles to a traffic circle at Deer Valley's Empire Canyon Lodge.

Take the circle all the way around to the third exit and continue up Marsac (SR 224) toward Guardsman Pass. Just 2.1 miles later, stay right on SR 224 where SR 222 (Pine Canyon Road) connects on the left. In the next 4.8 miles you cross over Guardsman Pass then switchback down to Big Cottonwood Canyon Road (SR 190). Go right and head down canyon 1.6 miles to the Moonbeam entrance to Solitude Mountain Resort. Go left and park near the Moonbeam Lodge.

MILEAGE LOG

0.0 Locate the trailhead at the southeast corner of the parking lot just below the Link chairlift bottom station. Ride a few switchbacks uphill. Go right on Serenity (the trail on the left is Down-N-Out, which goes to Solitude Village). The trail climbs steeply then traverses west under the Moonbeam chairlift. This portion of trail has many embedded rock gardens to navigate.

Taking a break on the Summit Express chairlift while climbing to the Kruzr Trail

0.3 At a fork, stay left on Serenity (right is Queen Bess Lower, which goes back down). From here, Serenity meanders up several switchbacks across ski runs and underneath the Eagle Express chairlift.

1.2 At a four-way intersection, leave Serenity and go straight on Queen Bess. If you go right on Queen Bess you will end up down at the Honeycomb Canyon dirt road. For this loop, left on Upper Serenity is an option. Both trails get you to Raptor Road at basically the same place.

1.8 After Queen Bess climbs a dozen switchbacks, it goes straight down a dive-bombing run to the paved Raptor Road. Go right and climb the road.

1.9 The road tops out at the Roundhouse Restaurant (closed summers) and becomes dirt. Continue following Raptor Road as it traverses across the resort.

2.6 At a fork, stay right on Raptor Road (left is Easy Out, a place to bail if you need to cut the ride short). At this point you are now on Summit Road. The climb gets steep and loose as the road goes directly up. It's a serious cardio workout intensified by high altitude.

Cold mountain streams have a chilling effect on Kruzr.

2.9 The Upper Kruzr singletrack connects on the left. Leave the road and go left up the trail. The climbing does not get any easier, since the trail is also steep and has rock and root gardens.

3.2 At a four-way intersection, go left on Kruzr. Straight ahead is Sunrise Connector, which is what connects you to trails if you ride up on the Sunrise lift. The trail on the right goes to Lake Solitude and is popular with hikers. Kruzr is an advanced-level trail with technical rock features, tight corners, large roots, and steep inclines. Don't go too fast, and be aware of hikers coming up Kruzr.

3.6 At a tight switchback, stay left on Kruzr. On the right a hiking trail goes to Silver Lake. Stay on Kruzr as it continues down, crosses a creek, and climbs back uphill for a short bit.

4.7 Easy Out enters on the left. If you've had enough of the technical Kruzr, make your escape here. There is also a fun creek crossing to splash through at this point.

5.0 Lookout comes in on the left. This is another short trail that you can use to escape Kruzr and get on Raptor Road. If you're up for more punishment, stay right on Kruzr.

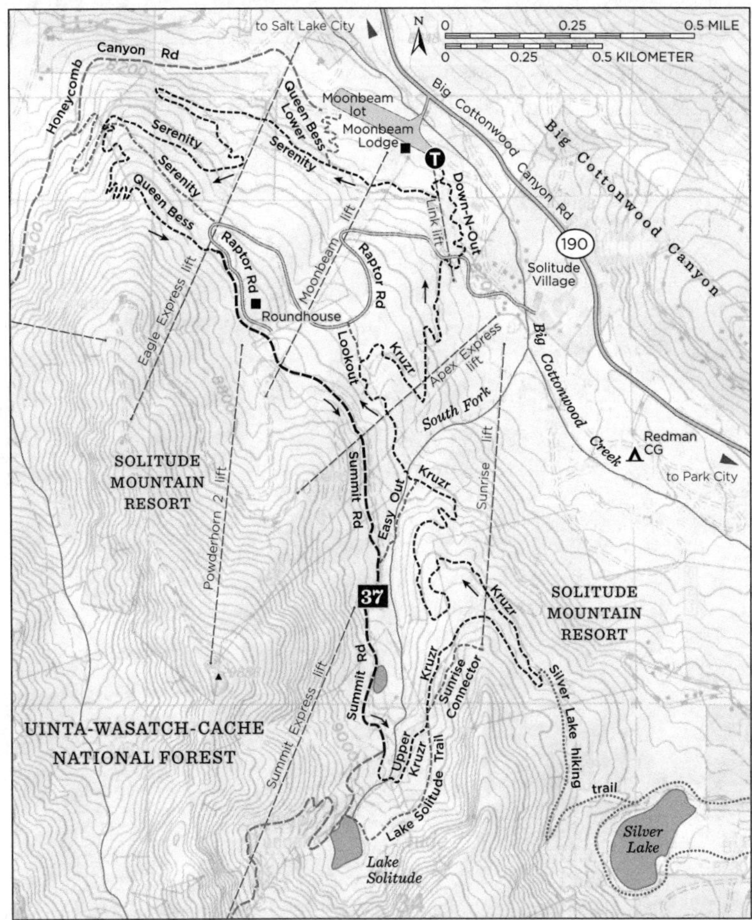

5.5 Relax your brake fingers, because Kruzr ends at the pavement on lower Raptor Road. Go right, around a switchback, then right again onto the Down-N-Out singletrack. This fun bit of downhill that dumps you back at Moonbeam Lodge features nice flowy berms.

6.0 End where you started.

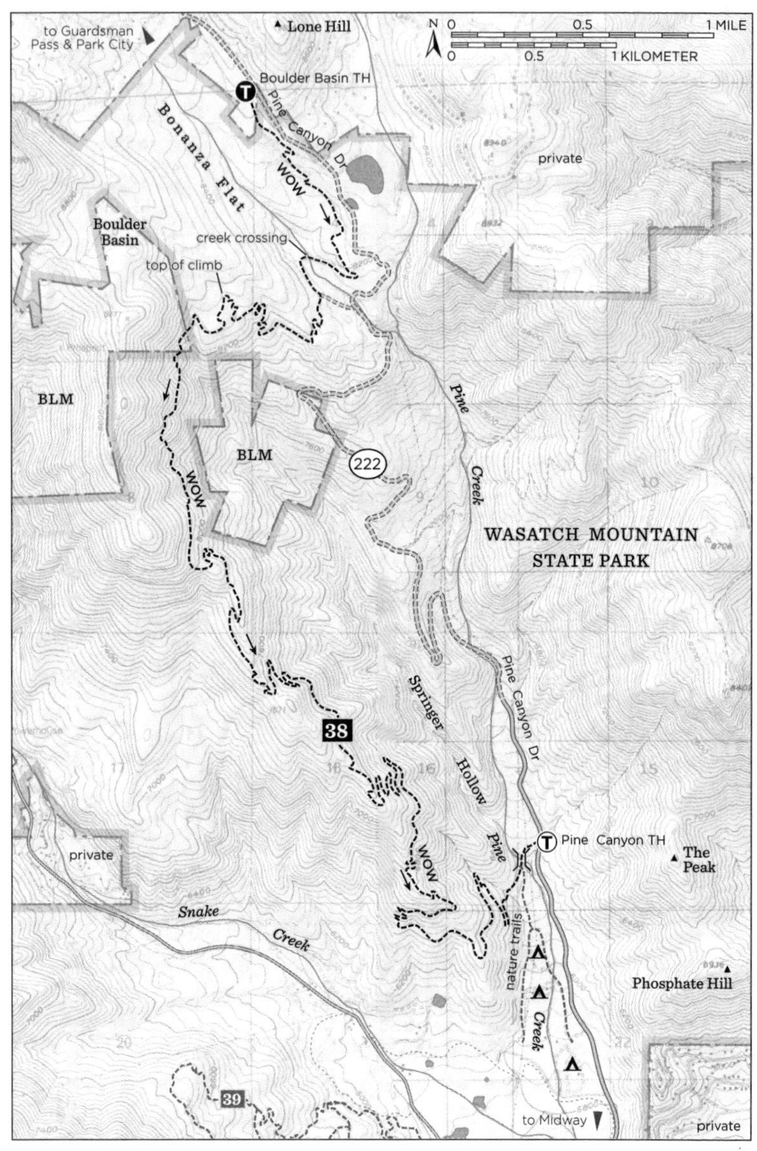

to Guardsman Pass & Park City
Lone Hill
Boulder Basin TH
N
0
0.5
1 MILE
0
0.5
1 KILOMETER
private
Bonanza Flat
Pine Canyon Dr
WOW
Boulder Basin
creek crossing
top of climb
Pine
Creek
BLM
BLM
WOW
222
WASATCH MOUNTAIN STATE PARK
Springer
Hollow
Pine Canyon Dr
38
WOW
private
Pine
Pine Canyon TH
The Peak
Snake
Creek
nature trails
Creek
Phosphate Hill
39
to Midway
private

OPTIONS

Of course, you can ascend the Sunrise lift to ride down Kruzr or go downhill on more moderate trails like Serenity and Queen Bess. For current lift rates, operating hours, and opening and closing dates, visit the resort's website, www.solitudemountain.com.

38 WOW TRAIL

SHUTTLE

Trail Type: 100% singletrack

Distance: 10 miles

Elevation Gain/Loss: 420/2440 feet

High Point: 8368 feet

Ride Time: 1–2 hours

Technical Difficulty: Intermediate

Fitness Intensity: Moderate

Season: Summer–fall

Maps: Adventure Maps Salt Lake City, Park City, and the Wasatch; USGS 7.5-minute Brighton, Heber City

GPS: 40°35′37.16″N, 111°30′37.85″W

Land Manager: Wasatch Mountain State Park

OVERVIEW

WOW, short for Wasatch Over Wasatch, is a massive work in progress. In the future, the trail will connect the campground at Wasatch Mountain State Park with the trail system at Deer Valley Resort, eventually linking Wasatch and Summit Counties. So far around 10 miles have been completed, but WOW is already a local favorite.

Over those 10 miles, mountain bikers descend nearly 2500 vertical feet through high-alpine aspen forests, old growth pines, vast open space, ridge-top cedars, and stands of scrub oak at lower elevations. From the Boulder Basin Trailhead at the top to the Pine Canyon Trailhead at the bottom, you'll experience fast straightaways, well-built switchbacks, and some of the best views of any trail in the Wasatch. There's nothing overly technical save for some small rock gardens and exposed roots, making for a very enjoyable ride.

The vast majority of riders arrange a shuttle to pedal WOW, but it is not exclusively a downhill trail. You can opt to climb it for a 20-mile out-and-back that will test your endurance and lung capacity. However you choose to ride it, you're sure to exclaim, "Wow!" at the end.

Be sure to stop and enjoy the scenery on the WOW Trail.

WOW is entirely in Wasatch Mountain State Park, which charges a recreation fee for each vehicle you park at either trailhead. Check the state park website, www.stateparks.utah.gov, for day-use rates. If you think you'll ride WOW multiple times, you may want to purchase an annual state parks pass, especially if you plan to ride any other trails on state park land described in this guide.

GETTING THERE

To begin your ride on the WOW Trail, you'll first need to drop off your shuttle vehicle. From the intersection of Park Avenue and Kearns Boulevard in Park City, drive south on Park Avenue for 0.3 mile. Turn left onto Deer Valley Drive while following the signs to Deer Valley Resort. In 1.1 miles, you'll come to a traffic circle. Follow it to the opposite side and continue straight, leaving the circle on Marsac Avenue. Follow this road as it winds up through a canyon and into the mountains for 3.6 miles to a traffic circle at Deer Valley's Empire Canyon Lodge. Take the circle all the way around and continue up Marsac (SR 224) toward Guardsman Pass. Just 2.1 miles later, turn left on Pine Canyon Drive (SR 222). Drive 5.9 miles down the mountain to the Pine Canyon Trailhead parking area on the left. Leave your shuttle car here.

To get to the start, drive back up Pine Canyon Drive for 4.7 miles until you see the Boulder Basin Trailhead on the left. Turn here into a large dirt lot with plenty of parking spaces and a forest service outhouse.

MILEAGE LOG

0.0   After coughing up your park fee at the pay tube, find the WOW Trailhead at the southeast end of the lot. The trail meanders through aspens and wildflowers on a slight incline.

1.2   There is an easy creek crossing, though it may be deep and fast flowing during spring runoff. Right after splashing through the water, you'll encounter a jeep road on the left, the old start to the WOW trail. Ignore it and stay right on singletrack to climb 400 vertical feet over a few switchbacks and an easy grade.

2.5   You've reached the top of the short climb. It's all downhill from here for the next 2400 vertical feet. You'll find speedy sections, a lot of berms, root drops, rocky stretches—WOW has the works. Navigation is easy as there are no trail intersections for the next seven miles.

9.4   Near the bottom, when you're riding in a large stand of scrub oak, a nature trail enters on the right. Ignore it and stay left on WOW.

9.6   Go across a wood bridge that spans a small creek, then stay left at another nature trail intersection.

10.0 Cross Pine Canyon Drive (SR 222) to the Pine Canyon Trailhead where you left your shuttle car.

OPTIONS

Instead of shuttling, you can ride WOW as an out-and-back for a 20-mile epic. The Pine Canyon Trailhead is also the start point for the Upper Canal Trail, which ties into Phosphate and the Dutch Hollow trail system in the town of Midway. Link these up for an even bigger ride.

Some of the mountain bike shuttle services in Park City offer services for the WOW Trail (see Resources for contact information).

HEBER VALLEY AND KAMAS

The Heber Valley, about 16 miles south of Park City, sports an impressive number of trails. In Heber City, the River View and Coyote Canyon Loops (Routes 42–43) are very popular and offer long, epic rides with stunning views of Mount Timpanogos. The town of Midway is home to Wasatch Mountain State Park and the Dutch Hollow network (Routes 39–41), where you'll often find families, high school mountain bike teams, and local shredders sharing trails with hikers and equestrians. To the east are Kamas and Oakley, both of which recently got into the singletrack game with networks of their own. Kamas is where you'll find the highly regarded High Star Ranch network (Routes 45–46). Oakley Trail Park (Route 47) is smaller and very family friendly.

The Heber Valley trails are more than 1000 feet lower than Park City, so the riding season is longer. The Dutch Hollow trails dry out and are ready to ride in early spring, since there is generally little snowpack. The terrain itself is also different, since the singletrack meanders through sagebrush and scrub oak. There is very little shade, and the area is hot during the summer. Be sure to slather on the sunscreen and carry extra water on your ride.

Trail building, led by Wasatch Trails Foundation, has exploded on the Wasatch Back. A number of projects are in the works, including the Pine Canyon bike park in Wasatch Mountain State Park and the eventual expansion of the WOW Trail. South Summit Trails Foundation is also building a 5-mile loop in the Uinta Mountains near the town of Samak. The Slate Creek Trail will be the first mountain bike–specific singletrack in the area.

Opposite: Rock hopping down Whip It (Route 46) at High Star Ranch

39 WASATCH MOUNTAIN STATE PARK

LOOP

Trail Type: 85% singletrack, 15% doubletrack
Distance: 4.7 miles
Elevation Gain/Loss: 1080/1080 feet
High Point: 6783 feet
Ride Time: 1.5–2.5 hours
Technical Difficulty: Intermediate
Fitness Intensity: Strenuous

Season: Summer–fall
Maps: Adventure Maps Salt Lake City, Park City, and the Wasatch; USGS 7.5-minute Heber City, Brighton
GPS: 40°31′59.48″N, 111°29′25.80″W
Land Manager: Wasatch Mountain State Park

OVERVIEW

Wasatch Mountain State Park in Midway is huge in terms of acreage. From Soldier Hollow to WOW Trail to Dutch Hollow, and everything in between, there are many miles of trails to mountain bike. But the singletrack network above the Wasatch Mountain State Park visitor center and golf course often gets overlooked. This series of loops allows riders a variety of mileage options. From the visitor center, you can ride anything from a 1-mile beginner loop, up to the intermediate-level, nearly 5-mile Crow's Nest loop.

The trails here are of the old-school, hand-cut variety. The singletrack is more suited for hiking, and it's obvious when you're grinding straight up the mountain while coughing up a lung. Yes, the trails are steep, narrow, and sometimes overgrown, but that's part of the allure. If you want to remember (or learn) what mountain biking was like in the 1980s and '90s, this is a good place to reminisce. That steepness also means you'll be getting a tougher workout than the mileage and vertical feet suggest. Therefore, I have rated the fitness intensity as strenuous.

While there are a few good options to ride this network, the route described here is my favorite. It incorporates what I consider to be the less steep ascent route combined with the most fun downhill section to make a long, clockwise loop.

Note that there is a per-car Utah State Park fee. For more information or to check for current pricing, visit the park's page on the Utah State Parks website, https://stateparks.utah.gov. If you'll be riding other routes on state park land (there are several in this guide), then you may want to buy an annual state parks pass.

GETTING THERE

From the intersection of Main Street and Center Street in Midway, head west on Main Street. In 0.2 mile, turn right (north) on 200 West. In another 0.2 mile, turn left (west) on 200 North. Follow this street for 0.8 mile until it curves and heads north.

After the curve the street becomes Homestead Road. Continue north on Homestead Road for 1 mile, following the signs to Wasatch Mountain State Park. Homestead curves west and becomes Snake Creek Road. On the right you'll see the state park visitor center. Turn right and park in the lot.

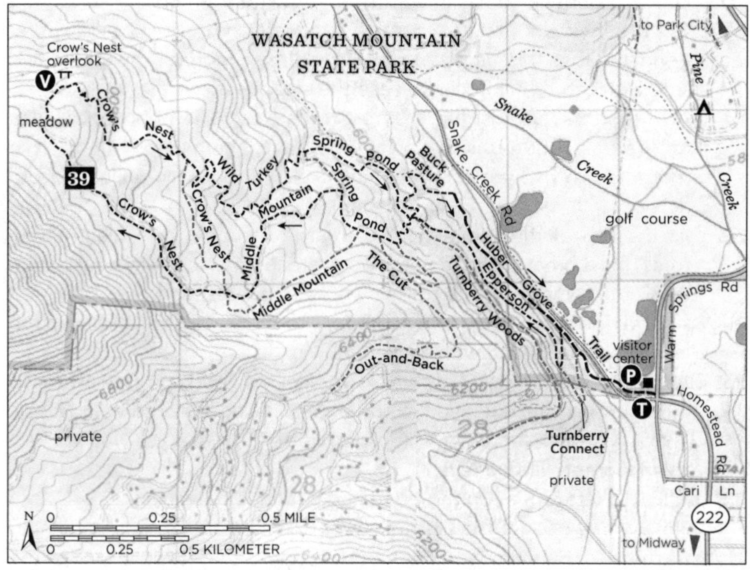

MILEAGE LOG

0.0   At the visitor center, pay your parking fee. Then find the trailhead on the opposite side of the lot from the building. This is the start of the Huber Grove Trail, a well-manicured, wide path. Soon after the trailhead, you'll cross Snake Creek Road and continue on the other side.

0.2   Leave Huber Grove and turn left onto the Epperson singletrack.

0.3   Stay right on Epperson at a switchback. The trail on the left is called Turnberry Connect.

0.5   At a fork, stay left on Epperson (right goes back down to Huber Grove). At this point the ascent starts to get steep.

0.7   You come to a four-way intersection where Epperson, Buck Pasture, Turnberry Woods, and Spring Pond Trails meet. Go straight on Spring Pond as it makes several switchbacks up the mountainside.

0.9   At the next intersection with Out-and-Back, stay right on Spring Pond. Immediately after, a trail called The Cut enters on the left. Again, stay right on Spring Pond.

1.0   Middle Mountain comes in on the left. Stay right on Spring Pond.

1.2   The other side of Middle Mountain connects on the left. Leave Spring Pond and take this Middle Mountain. It climbs aggressively up the hillside with few switchbacks to ease the steepness.

1.7   At a four-way, stay straight onto Crow's Nest. The right fork is also Crow's Nest, but this is the lower loop. To do the full upper loop, take that left Crow's Nest fork. The steep climbing levels out a bit from here.

2.3   At the top of the climb there is a large meadow with giant aspen trees. It's a great place to catch your breath after the vigorous climb. Beyond the meadow, the trail slowly starts to descend.

2.4   As you ride down, keep an eye out for the Crow's Nest overlook on the left. There is a bench with a killer view.

2.9   At a fork, you can stay right on Crow's Nest to head up for another lap of the upper trail. But if you're one-and-done, go left onto Wild Turkey. This is the most fun downhill portion of the ride, and yes, you're likely to encounter wild turkeys.

3.5   Take the left fork of Spring Pond and continue downhill.

3.8   Now you're back at the first four-way intersection near the beginning of the ride. This time, take a hard left onto the left-most fork of the Epperson Trail (Buck Pasture).

Gliding through a meadow on Buck Pasture at Wasatch Mountain State Park

4.1 Buck Pasture ends at Huber Grove. Go right onto the wide bike path and head back toward the visitor center.

4.5 Back at the Epperson start, stay left on Huber Grove, cross the road, and coast back into the parking lot.

4.7 You've reached the end of your ride.

OPTIONS

There are numerous loop configerations in this trail network. You can do a short lower loop on Spring Pond. If you want to try a middle loop on Middle Mountain, counterclockwise involves a less steep climb. You may also loop Crow's Nest as many times as you'd like or use the lower part of the Crow's Nest loop to shortcut directly to the top of Wild Turkey.

40 DUTCH HOLLOW SHORT LOOP

LOOP

Trail Type: 100% singletrack

Distance: 4.4 miles

Elevation Gain/Loss: 600/600 feet

High Point: 5991 feet

Ride Time: 1–2 hours

Technical Difficulty: Beginner

Fitness Intensity: Easy

Season: Spring–fall

Maps: Adventure Maps Salt Lake City, Park City, and the Wasatch; USGS 7.5-minute Heber City

GPS: 40°32'43.09"N, 111°27'12.28"W

Land Manager: Wasatch Mountain State Park

OVERVIEW

Dutch Hollow boasts perhaps the most complex trail network in the Heber Valley, with more than 20 miles of singletrack to explore. The system is located inside Wasatch Mountain State Park just northeast of the town of Midway. It offers a multitude of options from very easy beginner trails to steep and tight, advanced bruisers. Figuring out the best way to link all these trails can be confusing, especially if it's your first time riding here. These short, interconnected trails can be pieced together to create either very short "lunch" rides or longer loops. There is no wrong way to mountain bike this network of trails. You can choose your own adventure at least a half dozen times and not ride the same loop twice.

A good introduction to the network, this counterclockwise loop begins at the main trailhead and connects beginner and lower intermediate trails together for a mellow ascent up Sage Loop and fun descent with a lot of corners on Dutchman Way. Plus, you'll get to see a ton of nice views along the way. This network is easy to navigate, as most intersections are well signed.

Dutch Hollow is inside a state park. There are fee envelopes at the trailheads to deposit the entrance fee if you park within the state park boundary. If you'll be riding at least a few of the routes on state park land in this guide, you may want to purchase an annual state parks pass. Many locals start the ride from their surrounding neighborhoods.

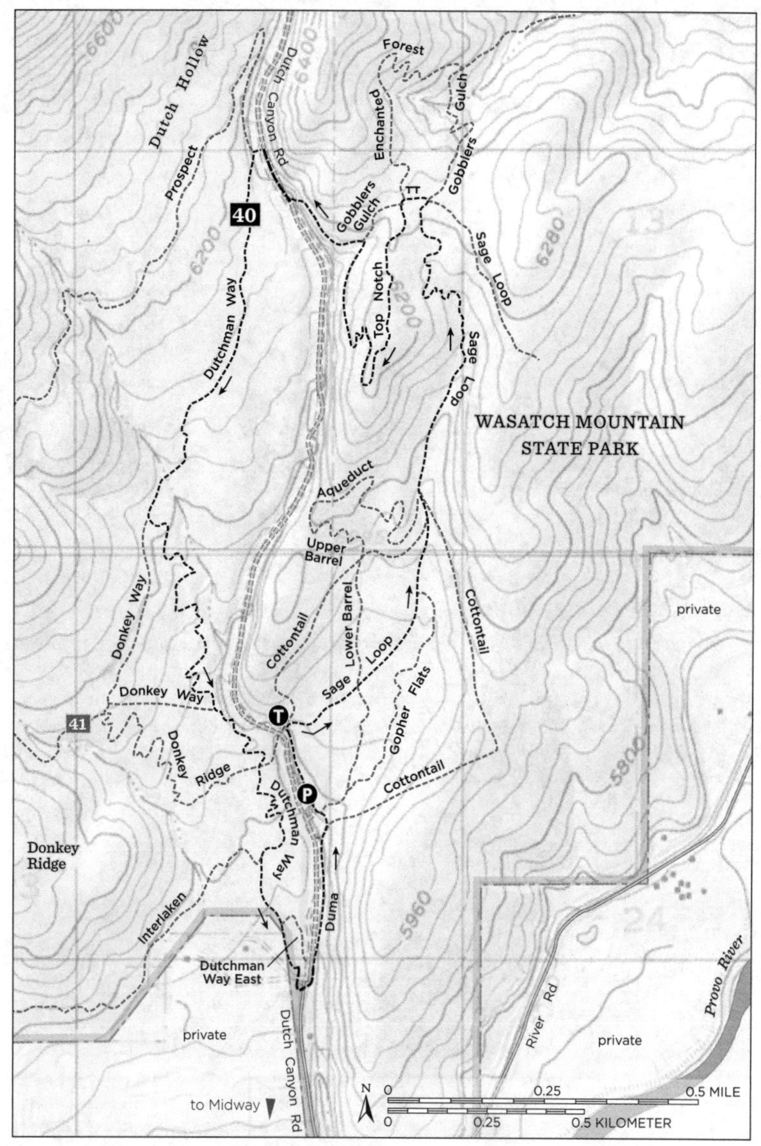
6600
Dutch Hollow
Forest
Enchanted
6400
Dutch Canyon Rd
Prospect
Gobblers Gulch
Gobblers Gulch
TT
40
6200
Sage Loop
6280
1.3
Dutchman Way
Top Notch
Top Notch
6200
Sage Loop
Sage Loop
WASATCH MOUNTAIN
STATE PARK
Aqueduct
Upper
Barrel
Donkey Way
private
Cottontail
Lower Barrel
Sage Loop
Cottontail
Donkey Way
Gopher Flats
41
Donkey
Ridge
T
Cottontail
5800
P
Dutchman Way
Donkey
Ridge
Interlaken
Duma
5960
24
Dutchman
Way East
River Rd
private
Provo River
private
Dutch Canyon Rd
to Midway
N
0
0.25
0.5 MILE
0
0.25
0.5 KILOMETER

Dutch Hollow has options for riders at every skill level.

GETTING THERE

From the intersection of Main Street and Center Street in Midway, drive east on Main Street for a half mile to River Road. Turn left and head north for 1.2 miles. At the traffic circle, take the second exit and continue on River Road as it goes northeast. After 0.8 mile from the traffic circle, turn left onto Dutch Canyon Road.

Drive north into Wasatch Mountain State Park. In 0.8 mile the road turns to dirt. Stay right and park in the large, dirt parking area. There is an outhouse and information kiosk as well as a fee station.

MILEAGE LOG

0.0 Locate the Sage Loop singletrack on the north end of the parking lot. Go right on Sage Loop as you leave the dirt road.

0.1 At a fork, stay right on Sage Loop (Donkey Ridge is on the left). After one switchback up, there is another fork with Cottontail. Stay right on Sage Loop.

0.3 At the intersection with Lower Barrel, stay straight on Sage Loop.

0.5 Gopher Flats Trail comes in on the right. Stay straight on Sage Loop.

0.6 At a four-way intersection with Cottontail, stay straight on Sage Loop.

1.3 You come to a large area where many trails collide. There is a wood bench overlooking a view of the Heber Valley. Go left to remain on Sage Loop. Immediately after making this left-hand turn, Sage Loop ends at another four-way. Make a hard turn left and down on Top Notch (right is Enchanted Forest and straight is Gobblers Gulch).

2.0 Cross Gobblers Gulch Trail, which goes straight down a narrow gully. Continue on Top Notch on the other side.

2.1 Top Notch ends at Dutch Canyon Road. Go right and up the dirt track.

2.2 Leave the road by crossing a dry creek bed on the left. You'll find the Dutchman Way Trail on the other side. Go left on this singletrack, which is a very fun, beginner downhill ride. But don't go too fast because hikers, other mountain bikers, and equestrians may also be on the trail.

2.9 At the intersection with Donkey Way, stay left on Dutchman Way. Continue straight when Donkey Way rejoins.

3.5 At the intersection with Donkey Ridge, stay left on Dutchman Way (though you can go left on Donkey for a shortcut to the parking lot).

3.8 You come to Interlaken Trail on the right. Stay left on Dutchman Way.

3.9 At this next intersection, go straight through while staying on Dutchman Way (a hard left on Dutchman Way East is another shortcut back to the trailhead).

4.0 Dutchman Way ends at Dutchman Road. Go left and pedal up the road. On your right is a singletrack called Duma. Climb up this trail because it's more interesting than the road up to the parking lot.

4.4 Return to the parking lot to end the ride.

OPTIONS

For a more advanced version of this short loop, ride it clockwise by climbing Dutchman Way, but instead of descending Sage Loop, come down the bobsled-style downhill of Upper and Lower Barrel. Get there by first riding down Sage Loop then going right on Cottontail to Aqueduct to get you to Upper Barrel.

41 DUTCH HOLLOW BIG LOOP

LOOP

Trail Type: 100% singletrack

Distance: 9.5 miles

Elevation Gain/Loss: 1440/1440 feet

High Point: 7420 feet

Ride Time: 2–3 hours

Technical Difficulty: Intermediate

Fitness Intensity: Moderate

Season: Spring–fall

Maps: Adventure Maps Salt Lake City, Park City, and the Wasatch; USGS 7.5-minute Heber City

GPS: 40°32'43.09"N, 111°27'12.28"W

Land manager: Wasatch Mountain State Park

OVERVIEW

Dutch Hollow has enough connected trails for any number of longer rides. This featured loop is a good overview as it circumnavigates the network borders. It traverses a long mountainside and climbs a ton of vertical on trails like Donkey Ridge, Phosphate, and Prospect. Along the way you'll find vast views of the Heber Valley and Wasatch Mountains. The fast and flowing descent on Upper Barrel and Lower Barrel trails completes the ride.

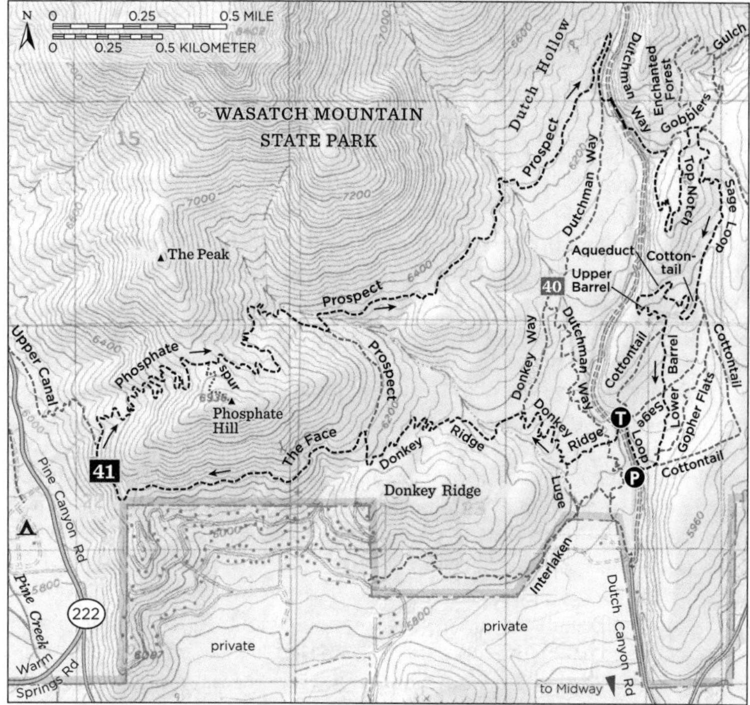

Dutch Hollow is inside a state park. There are fee envelopes at the trailheads to deposit the entrance fee if you park within the state park boundary. If you'll be riding at least a few of the routes on state park land in this guide, you may want to purchase an annual state parks pass. Many locals start the ride from their surrounding neighborhoods.

GETTING THERE

From the intersection of Main Street and Center Street in Midway, drive east on Main Street for a half mile to River Road. Turn left and head north for 1.2 miles. At the traffic circle, take the second exit and continue on River Road as it goes northeast. After 0.8 mile from the traffic circle, turn left onto

Dutch Canyon Road. Drive north into Wasatch Mountain State Park. In 0.8 mile the road turns to dirt. Stay right and park in the large, dirt parking area. There is an outhouse and information kiosk as well as a fee station.

MILEAGE LOG

0.0 Go to the northwest corner of the parking lot, and ride up the dirt road for a short distance. At the end, pedal onto the Sage Loop Trail that goes into the scrub oak forest. Almost immediately after this, take your first left onto Donkey Ridge. You'll cross Dutch Canyon Road and continue on the singletrack on the other side.

0.2 At the intersection with Dutchman Way, stay straight.

0.3 The Luge Trail comes in on the left. Stay right on Donkey Ridge.

0.8 At another intersection with Dutchman Way, stay left. At this point Donkey Ridge switchbacks up the hillside, but it's a pleasant ascent on smooth singletrack.

1.7 At this intersection, Donkey Ridge makes a very hard left turn and goes into a neighborhood. Instead, go right (straight) on Prospect. Almost immediately after making this right turn, go left on a trail called The Face. This is an easy trail that traverses west across the south face of Phosphate Hill.

2.7 At the fork with Upper Canal, go right. This is the start of Phosphate and is a trail notorious for the ungodly amount of switchbacks as it climbs to nearly the top of Phosphate Hill. This ascent is the most cardio you'll do on the whole loop, but the corners are pretty wide and easy to negotiate.

4.0 At the top of the Phosphate climb, you come to a saddle. There is a spur trail on the right to the top of Phosphate Hill. It's only 0.3 mile but it's not suitable for bikes. If you want to "bag the peak," it's a short hike with a stunning view of the Heber Valley. Otherwise, continue riding Phosphate as it drops down the east side. This steepish drop into a narrow hollow has a lot of tight turns. Still, it's a ton of fun.

5.1 At the bottom of the Phosphate Trail, you intersect with Prospect. You can go right to reconnect to Donkey Ridge and return to the trailhead the way you came. But to do the big loop, go left on Prospect.

6.5 Dutchman Way enters as a hard right. Take this right and go downhill. At the bottom, the trail spits you out at a dry wash. Go left across the wash onto Dutch Canyon Road. Go right (downhill) on the road and keep an eye out on the left for your next singletrack connection.

6.8 Top Notch Trail appears on the left. Take this trail as it ascends up a hillside. Cross Gobblers Gulch and continue straight.

7.7 At the intersection with Enchanted Forest, stay right on Top Notch. Immediately after you come to a three-way intersection. Take the right-hand trail on Sage Loop.

8.4 At a complicated-looking four-way intersection with Sage Loop and Cottontail, go hard right onto Cottontail. Right after taking this turn, you'll come to a fork. Go right onto Aqueduct. Follow this trail as it switchbacks up a short distance to the top of Upper Barrel.

Rounding one of many switchbacks on Phosphate in Dutch Hollow

8.8 At the top of Upper Barrel, go left and hang on for the fastest and most flowing descent of the loop. This first part is more advanced, with big natural berms that swoop up the sides of a steep gully.

8.9 At the intersection with Cottontail, stay straight on Lower Barrel. At this point, Upper Barrel becomes Lower Barrel. From here the descent is a bit tamer, but it's still a good time, with easy berms in a dry wash.

9.4 At the bottom of Lower Barrel, go right on Cottontail. It drops down into the parking lot for the end of the ride.

9.5 Return to the parking lot.

OPTIONS

Dutch Hollow is such a complex network with so many intersecting trails that your options are limitless. You can shorten or lengthen this featured loop or add variety by choosing different or easier descents than Lower Barrel. Even if you get lost at the sometimes-confusing intersections, every trail will eventually bring you back to either where you were before or where you eventually want to go.

42 RIVERVIEW LOOP

LOOP

Trail Type: 90% singletrack, 10% doubletrack
Distance: 13.1 miles
Elevation Gain/Loss: 1575/1575 feet
High Point: 6325 feet
Ride Time: 2–3 hours
Technical Difficulty: Intermediate
Fitness Intensity: Moderate

Season: Spring–fall
Maps: Adventure Maps Salt Lake City, Park City, and the Wasatch; USGS 7.5-minute Heber City
GPS: 40°32'48.28"N, 111°24'43.77"W
Land Manager: Private (managed by Wasatch Trails Alliance)

OVERVIEW

The Riverview Loop in Heber City lives up to its namesake, with a nice view of the Provo River as well as the Wasatch Mountains and Heber Valley. The ride isn't half bad either. This loop is more of a figure eight that utilizes the Upper Riverview and Lower Riverview Trails, with a connector in the middle that acts as both ascent and descent. In this way you can do an actual loop, a counterclockwise figure eight, or just half-loops if you're short on time.

This loop is very popular among Heber City mountain bikers. Access it right in town with a trailhead at the Utah Valley University (UVU) Wasatch Campus. The fun, flowing singletrack has only a few short sections of rock gardens to negotiate. The loop is mostly on private land owned by Utah Valley University and the Sorenson family. The public is allowed access to the trails, so be courteous and respect the trails and the land. Also be aware that you may encounter sheep and their human herders on horseback.

The Riverview Loop can be ridden from about April to November. But this lower-elevation ride gets brutally hot in the summer and there is little to no shade. Ride early or late in the season or mornings and evenings for maximum enjoyment. And don't forget to carry extra water and sunscreen.

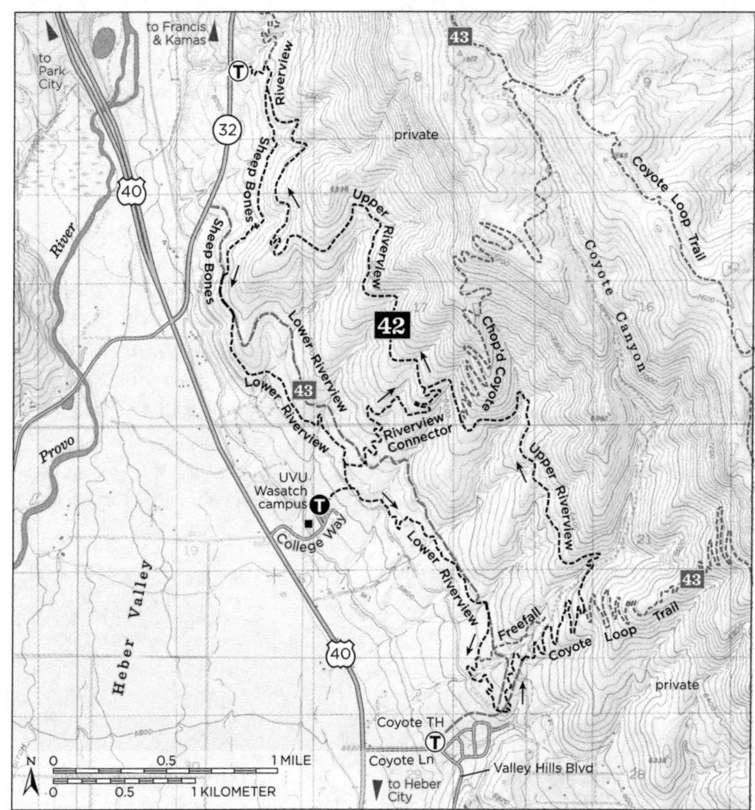

GETTING THERE

From the intersection of Main Street and Center Street in Heber City, drive north on Main (US 40) for 2.7 miles. Turn right onto College Way and drive up into the UVU Wasatch Campus. Continue up all the way to the upper parking lot at the Riverview Trail System Trailhead. Park at the very top of the lot where the trailhead is located.

MILEAGE LOG

0.0   The trailhead is marked by a large kiosk. Walk your bike under a wooden arch and go straight up the singletrack. This trail is called many different names: College Connector, Riverview Connector, or UVU Connector. I'll use Riverview Connector here.

0.1   At the intersection with Lower Riverview Trail, go left.

0.2   At the fork, go right.

0.4   At a four-way intersection with Lower Riverview doubletrack, continue straight on Riverview Connector. At this point the trail ascends with several switchbacks. It's a nice climb ending at a big rock that's a great place to stop and enjoy the view.

1.5   At the top of Riverview Connector, go left on Upper Riverview. For the next 3 miles the trail traverses the mountainside north on undulating singletrack. There are a few punchy, rocky climbs, but this section is mostly moderate in difficulty.

Enjoying the view of Mount Timpanogos and Heber Valley from the top of Riverview Connector

4.3   At the trail fork, take a hard left onto Sheep Bones. While this rocky descent may test your mettle, it shouldn't be too difficult for intermediate riders.

5.2   At the bottom of Sheep Bones, go left onto lower Sheep Bones doubletrack, which almost immediately ascends a giant rock slab and then levels out.

5.4   At the fork, leave the doubletrack by going right onto Lower Riverview singletrack (Lower Riverview North). This section starts out rocky but soon becomes smooth and flowing.

6.4   Here you are back at the intersection with Riverview Connector. Keep going straight (right at fork) as if you are returning to the trailhead.

6.5   Back at the first trailhead intersection, stay straight on Lower Riverview.

7.4   Here the singletrack rejoins the old doubletrack. Go right onto the doubletrack road (Lower Riverview).

7.5   Right after the road dips into a wash and goes back up, turn right where Lower Riverview singletrack continues. The sign here directs riders to the Coyote Trailhead.

7.8   At this intersection with Freefall, stay right on Lower Riverview.

8.0   Here you come to a T intersection. Go right on Lower Riverview as if you are going to the Coyote Trailhead.

8.2   At this point you come to two doubletrack roads that lead down to a concrete bridge en route to Coyote Trailhead. Go straight across the dirt roads and locate the singletrack on the other side. This is the start of the Coyote Loop Trail and it climbs up through the sagebrush.

8.4   At the intersection, go right. A wooden sign that says "trail" points the way.

8.6   Cross a doubletrack and continue on singletrack on the other side.

9.6   Leave Coyote Loop Trail and go left onto Upper Riverview Connector. Much like the north section of Upper Riverview, this south section traverses on undulating terrain interspersed with fun, short descents and a few short, rocky climbs.

9.8   Cross the doubletrack and rejoin the singletrack trail on the other side.

11.3   At the intersection with Chop'd Coyote, stay straight (left fork).

11.6   Here you rejoin the top of Riverview Connector. Go left and head downhill. This is your reward. Enjoy the fun descent that features tight corners and fast straightaways all the way back down to the parking lot.

12.8   At the intersection with Lower Riverview, stay straight and continue going downhill.

13.0 Stay right and cross the concrete bridge. Continue down for a final section to the UVU trailhead.

13.1 Reach the parking lot and the end of your ride.

OPTIONS

There are many possible variations. You can make a shorter ride by doing only one of the two loop halves using Riverview Connector. You can also connect this ride with the longer Coyote Loop by ascending either Coyote or Chop'd Coyote to the top of the mountain. Or perhaps you would enjoy the featured loop clockwise instead.

43 COYOTE CANYON

LOOP

Trail Type: 100% singletrack

Distance: 19.5 miles

Elevation Gain/Loss: 2500/2500 feet

High Point: 7537 feet

Ride Time: 3–4 hours

Technical Difficulty: Advanced

Fitness Intensity: Strenuous

Season: Spring–fall

Maps: Adventure Maps Salt Lake City, Park City, and the Wasatch; USGS 7.5-minute Heber City

GPS: 40°34'23.60"N, 111°25'13.26"W

Land Manager: Private (managed by Wasatch Trails Alliance)

OVERVIEW

One of the premiere mountain bike trails in Heber City, Coyote Canyon Loop is located entirely on private land owned by the Sorenson family, who operate a sheep ranch on it. Stay on the trail and be respectful of their generosity at offering a public easement. You'll likely have a memorable ride as you pedal through herds of sheep while tipping your helmet to a horse-mounted cowboy (sheep boy?) overseeing the flock.

As for the trail, this classic, must-ride loop begins with a rolling traverse on Upper Riverview to the Coyote Loop Trail. Once there, you grind up a long set of switchbacks to the mountaintop, where you encounter advanced-level rock obstacles. But the reward is breathtaking views of Mount Timpanogos and the Wasatch Back. The ride ends with a fun descent through aspen

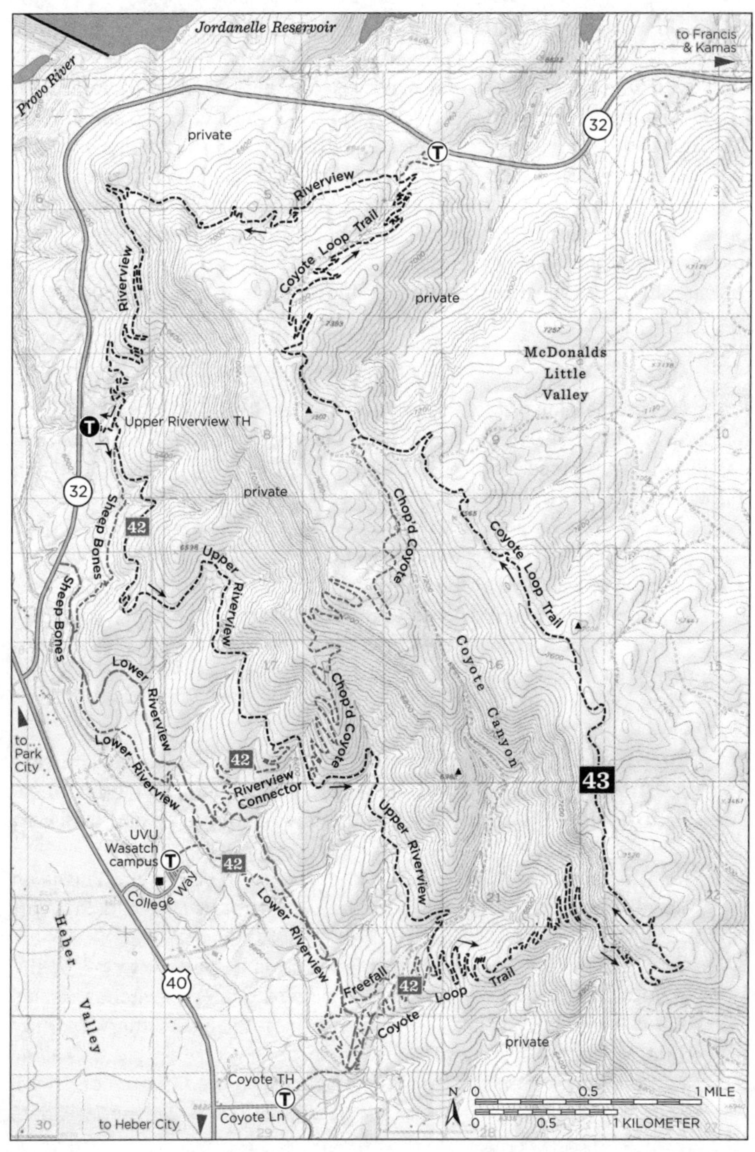

Jordanelle Reservoir
Provo River
to Francis & Kamas
private
32
Riverview
Coyote Loop Trail
private
McDonalds Little Valley
Riverview
Upper Riverview TH
32
Sheep Bones
42
Sheep Bones
Upper Riverview
Chop'd Coyote
Coyote Loop Trail
Lower Riverview
Coyote Canyon
Lower Riverview
Chop'd Coyote
to Park City
42
43
Riverview Connector
Upper Riverview
UVU Wasatch campus
42
College Way
Lower Riverview
40
Heber Valley
Freefall
42
Coyote
Loop Trail
private
Coyote TH
to Heber City
Coyote Ln
N
0   0.5   1 MILE
0   0.5   1 KILOMETER

groves above Jordanelle Reservoir. The trail can be technical, with several chunky rock gardens, making it unsuitable for beginners.

The Coyote Canyon Loop can be accessed from four different trailheads: Upper Riverview, Lower Riverview (on the UVU Wasatch Campus) off Coyote Lane to the south, and a new one on Highway 32 off the north side of the mountain. By starting at the Upper Riverview Trailhead and riding counterclockwise, the featured route allows for a more flowing descent back to the car, but you can start from either of the other three trailheads if you prefer— just be aware that the access trails from each will add some distance, and in the case of the southernmost trailheads, more climbing and descending.

GETTING THERE

From the intersection of Main Street and Center Street in Heber City, drive north on Main (US 40) for 3.7 miles. After leaving town, you'll come to a traffic light at the intersection of SR 32 and River Road. Go right on SR 32 and follow it uphill for 1 mile to a large, dirt pullout on the right.

MILEAGE LOG

0.0 Locate the trailhead at the entrance to the dirt pullout by the highway. The trail immediately comes to a barbed wire fence. Carry your bike over a ladder that goes over the fence. You are now on private property. Continue pedaling up a few switchbacks that are at times steep and rocky.

0.2 At a fork, go right on the Upper Riverview Trail.

0.4 The next fork is an intersection with Sheep Bones. Go left and stay on Upper Riverview. At this point you have a long, winding traverse south. The trail is mostly level with a few hairpin turns and rock gardens to negotiate.

3.1 An intersection with Riverview Connector is on your right. This is an alternate access to the loop from the UVU campus trailhead. Stay left on Upper Riverview.

3.4 Chop'd Coyote intersects on the left. This is a shortcut to get to the Coyote Loop atop the mountain via dozens of steep switchbacks. It's is a great option if you're looking for less mileage. Otherwise, stay right on Upper Riverview for the long loop.

5.1 Upper Riverview ends where it intersects with the Coyote Loop Trail. Going right takes you down to the alternate Coyote Canyon Trailhead.

Rock gardens and plenty of elevation gain—Coyote Canyon is a challenging day trip on a bike.

Instead, go left on Coyote Loop and breathe deep for a long climb. From here the trail ascends right up the mountain with many switchbacks interspersed with rock gardens. When you finally reach the flat mountaintop, the trail enters a forest of scrub oak where the most advanced rock gardens on the loop are found. If you find them too difficult, they are easily walked.

9.5 Where the scrub oak opens into large meadows, you'll have spectacular views of Mount Timpanogos and the Heber Valley. These are awesome spots to take a rest and have a snack. At this point, the trail continues through more scrub oak.

12.4 The top of Chop'd Coyote enters on the left. It's unmarked and somewhat vague, so you'll probably not even notice it as you pedal past it. Soon after this point, you'll descend through aspen groves on the mountain's north side. I think this is the most enjoyable part of the ride. The dirt is soft and loamy, there is ample shade, and the singletrack flows through stands of trees. It's not a fast or steep downhill, but a nice, mellow ride with bits of flow. As you descend, you'll see Jordanelle Reservoir to the north.

15.0 At the bottom of the aspen-grove descent, you come to an intersection. This is the end of Coyote Loop Trail. Going right takes you to another alternate trailhead on SR 32. Instead, go left onto Riverview Trail. From here, you'll climb up to the top of a ridge, just when you thought you were done with climbing. Once you gain the ridge, the trail descends back down to the Upper Riverview Trailhead. It's a rocky downhill with tight corners and a few fast sections—an exciting way to end your ride.

19.5 Return to the Upper Riverview Trailhead.

OPTIONS

Change the character of this loop by starting at any of the other trailheads or by riding it clockwise. The ascent is easier clockwise (and shadier in those aspens), but the descent on the south side of the mountain is a slow, technical brake-fest. If 19 miles isn't enough to wear you out, you can also connect this loop with the Lower Riverview Loop.

44 ROCKY TOP

OUT-AND-BACK

Trail Type: 98% singletrack, 2% doubletrack

Distance: 8 miles

Elevation Gain/Loss: 890/890 feet

High Point: 6974 feet

Ride Time: 1–2 hours

Technical Difficulty: Intermediate

Fitness Intensity: Easy

Season: Spring–fall

Maps: USGS 7.5-minute Francis

GPS: 40°36'7.72"N, 111°19'42.34"W

Land Manager: Victory Ranch (managed by South Summit Trails Foundation)

OVERVIEW

This nice, mellow trail starts at the east side of Jordanelle Reservoir and ends on a rocky summit overlooking the Kamas Valley. Difficulty is lower-intermediate, almost easy, with just a few rocky sections to navigate. The climb is mostly gentle with few switchbacks. Navigation is even easier, as it doesn't cross or connect to any other trails.

Taking in the scenery is a good reason to ride Rocky Top. The ride starts with cool cliffs. Once you gain the summit ridge, spectacular views of the Wasatch Back unfold below your front tire. At the end, the boulders of Rocky Top serve as picnic furniture from where you can take in the view. Since

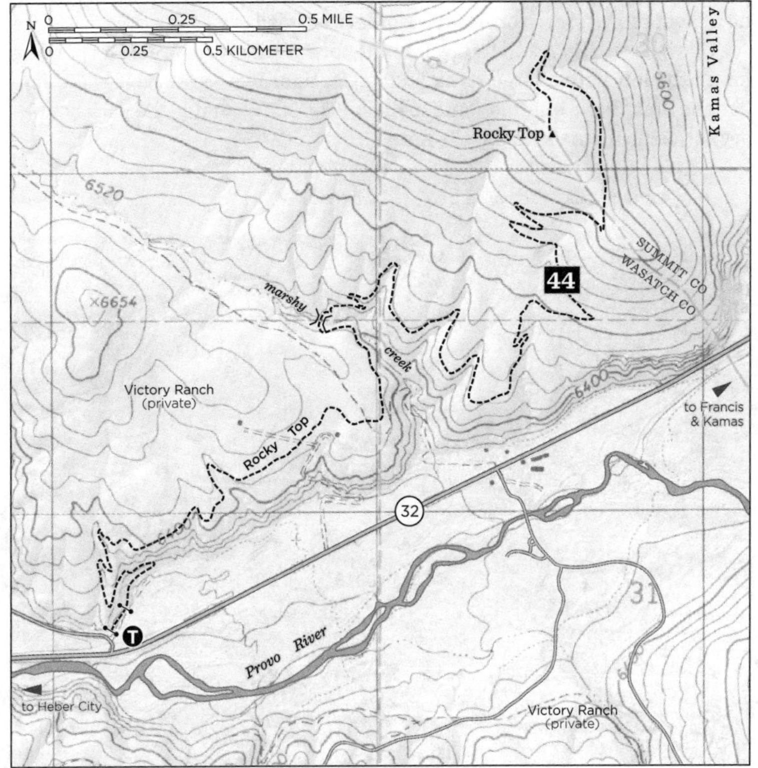

there are few turns in the trail, the descent can be fast, but so few mountain bikers come here, you shouldn't have to worry about much user conflict.

The trail is located entirely on Victory Ranch, but the public is allowed access through an easement managed by the South Summit Trails Foundation. Public access will continue as long as riders stay on the trail and don't trespass beyond it, so be respectful. Also, because the land is a working ranch, you may encounter cows. Give them a wide berth.

GETTING THERE

From the intersection of Main Street and Center Street in Heber City, drive north on Main (US 40) for 3.7 miles. After leaving town, you'll come to a traffic light at the intersection of SR 32 and River Road.

Go right on SR 32 and follow it uphill for 7.7 miles to a large, dirt parking lot on the left with a large kiosk and fee station. The fee station is for Jordanelle State Park, but this route to Rocky Top stays outside the park boundary so you do not need to pay the fee.

On aptly named Rocky Top, large boulders serve as perches for soaking in the scenery.

MILEAGE LOG

0.0 Go to a kiosk on the west side of the lot and sign the register. Then ride to a cattle gate by a Provo River stream; a dirt road runs alongside it. Go through the gate and be sure to close it behind you so the cows don't escape. Ride up the doubletrack. About 400 feet later, go through another gate on the left. The singletrack on the other side is the Rocky Top Trail.

0.5 After climbing a few switchbacks beneath some cliffs, the trail levels out and traverses across an expanse of sagebrush flats. Eventually it angles down into a small canyon where the trail curves north and runs alongside the edge.

1.5 Cross a wooden bridge that goes over a tiny, marshy creek bed. Beyond the bridge, the trail climbs more steeply up the mountainside. The smooth trail also gets a bit more technical with loose stones to navigate.

3.3 The trail tops out onto a ridge overlooking the Kamas Valley.

4.0 The Rocky Top Trail ends at a sort of indistinct summit. The most prominent feature is a collection of large boulders (where the trail gets its name). These rocks are an excellent place to sit and take in the view. When you've had your fill of scenery, turn your bike around, then descend the way you came up. It's a fun descent that you can get decent speed on due to the long, straight stretches of trail with few tight corners to slow you down.

8.0 End your ride back at the Provo River bottom and the parking lot.

45 HIGH STAR RANCH ADVANCED LOOP

LOOP

Trail Type: 95% singletrack, 5% doubletrack

Distance: 8.2 miles

Elevation Gain/Loss: 1565/1565 feet

High Point: 7963 feet

Ride Time: 2–3 hours

Technical Difficulty: Advanced

Fitness Intensity: Moderate

Season: Spring–fall

Maps: Online at www.highstarranch.com, USGS 7.5-minute Kamas

GPS: 40°39'40.12"N, 111°16'30.69"W

Land Manager: High Star Ranch

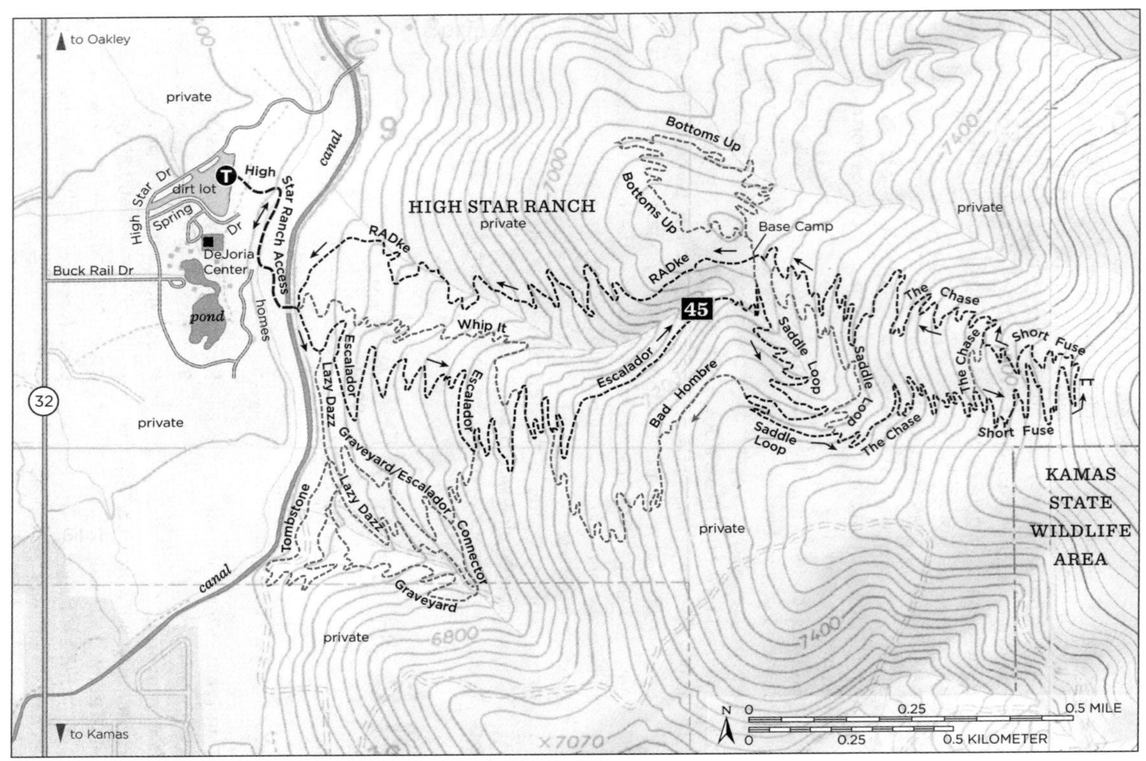

to Oakley
private
High Star Dr
dirt lot
Spring
High
T
Dr
DeJoria Center
Buck Rail Dr
pond
homes
canal
Star Ranch Access
RADke
HIGH STAR RANCH
private
Bottoms Up
Bottoms Up
Base Camp
RADke
private
45
Whip It
Escalador
Escalador
Escalador
Escalador
Bad Hombre
Saddle Loop
Saddle Loop
Saddle Loop
The Chase
The Chase
The Chase
The Chase
Short Fuse
Short Fuse
T
Lazy Dazz
Graveyard/Escalador Connector
Tombstone
Lazy Dazz
Graveyard
private
private
private
32
canal
to Kamas
KAMAS STATE WILDLIFE AREA
7000
7400
7400
6800
x 7070
N
0   0.25   0.5 MILE
0   0.25   0.5 KILOMETER

OVERVIEW

Mountain biking on the Wasatch Back became a lot more interesting with the addition of the High Star Ranch trails in Kamas. Located on a mountainside above the DeJoria Center, High Star Ranch has miles of excellent, machine-cut singletrack. This network consists of loops both low on the mountain and higher up, so you can create as long (or short) of a ride as you'd like. Radiating out from the main loops, connecting trails allow you to choose your own adventure. Each trail was born with the DNA of modern mountain biking, with berms, rock drops, and even directional trails to maximize the fun factor.

While there are many ways to ride High Star Ranch, this advanced loop is arguably the best way to experience the most (and best) trails in a single, connected route. This loop encounters a bit of everything, from smooth, ascending climbs and flowing downhills to steep, technical trails covered with unavoidable rock features. This loop is ridden counterclockwise, but because of the numerous shortcuts, you can exit the loop and head back down from various points in the ride.

This working ranch is being subdivided into housing developments, which means these trails are on private property. While the public is allowed to use the trails, do everything possible to keep the property pristine. It is great that we are allowed to enjoy this trail network for free—let's keep it that way.

GETTING THERE

From the intersection of Center Street and Main Street in Kamas, drive north on Main (SR 32) for 1.1 miles. Just after exiting town, you'll see the DeJoria Center on the right. Turn right on Buck Rail Drive and go east for 0.2 mile toward the DeJoria Center. Turn left onto High Star Drive, and follow it for 0.2 mile to a large dirt parking lot. Park on the east side of the lot where the trailhead is located.

MILEAGE LOG

0.0 From the trailhead, climb up a singletrack called High Star Ranch Access that soon becomes doubletrack as it levels. Follow the signs pointing the way to the trail network. You'll traverse above the DeJoria

Center when the track crosses over a canal and ends at a sort of log fence. Cross through the space in the fence.

0.3 The singletrack begins after the fence. Stay right and climb up the easy Lazy Dazz Trail.

0.4 At a fork, Lazy Dazz continues on the right. Instead, go left and climb up Escalador. As the name implies, this trail is the main highway to ascend the mountainside. It's a fairly easy uphill with wide corners, a mellow grade, and only a few rocks to pedal over.

1.4 Intersect with the Graveyard/Escalador Connector here, an alternate way to ascend to this point. Stay left on Escalador.

1.7 Escalador intersects with the top of the Whip It Trail on the left. This is an intermediate downhill-only flow trail that you can descend from here for a very short loop. Instead, stay right and continue uphill.

2.0 The exit point for the intermediate Bad Hombre Trail comes in on the right. This is another downhill-only trail. Stay left on Escalador.

2.6 At a three-way intersection, go right, following the sign for Saddle Loop. Officially this intersection is the start of the Saddle Loop Trail. You have the option of going left on Saddle Loop to descend the advanced, downhill-only RADke Trail or to do the intermediate Bottoms Up lariat loop.

3.2 On the right you'll find the start of the Bad Hombre downhill trail. Stay left on Saddle Loop.

3.4 The start of The Chase Trail is on the right (left is the continuation of the Saddle Loop Trail). For the advanced loop, go right and head up The Chase. At this point the climb becomes a bit more steep, rocky, and technical, but overall, it's intermediate in difficulty.

4.1 The Chase intersects with Short Fuse on the right. For a shorter loop, go left on The Chase. Otherwise, go right onto Short Fuse. This trail is more advanced as the climb gets even steeper with tighter corners. It's also more technical, with large rock features to navigate.

5.0 You reach the top of Short Fuse and the highest point of the High Star Ranch trail system. There is a rough stone bench where you can take a breather. When ready, continue on Short Fuse as it now goes down. This advanced, technical descent has a lot of unavoidable rock gardens. It's fun, though, as the rocks alternate between fast berm sections.

5.3 Short Fuse ends at The Chase. Go right on The Chase and continue down. This next section is my favorite bit of trail at High Star Ranch. It's fast, flowing singletrack with perfectly sculpted berms and intermediate rock gardens. Try not to smile as you sweep through corners.

6.4 The Chase ends at Saddle Loop. Go right and continue down a single switchback to a large flat. The High Star Ranch map calls this "Base Camp." It is the meeting point of three trails: Saddle Loop, Bottoms Up, and RADke. If you want to add 1.25 miles to your ride, go right on Bottoms Up. It's a side-trip lariat loop of cross-country singletrack. There are a few rock gardens and a bit of flow, but it's mostly a pedaling diversion. To complete this advanced loop, go west on the downhill-only RADke Trail, the most technically advanced trail at High Star Ranch. Expect steep sections paired with large rock and boulder obstacles requiring excellent bike-handling skills. The lower section swoops in and out of a small drainage as you bobsled back and forth with a bit of speed.

7.9 At the bottom of RADke, take the High Star Ranch Access doubletrack.

8.2 You're back at your car and at the end of the ride.

Bombing down RADke, the most technical trail at High Star Ranch

OPTIONS

As detailed above, you can shorten this ride by either shortcutting Saddle Loop or The Chase. In addition, that Bottoms Up diversion will add another 1.25 miles to the ride.

46 HIGH STAR RANCH INTERMEDIATE LOOP

LOOP

Trail Type: 95% singletrack, 5% doubletrack
Distance: 5.6 miles
Elevation Gain/Loss: 930/930 feet
High Point: 7156 feet
Ride Time: 1–2 hours
Technical Difficulty: Intermediate

Fitness Intensity: Easy
Season: Spring–fall
Maps: Online at www.highstarranch .com, USGS 7.5-minute Kamas
GPS: 40°39'40.12"N, 111°16'30.69"W
Land Manager: High Star Ranch

OVERVIEW

Bad Hombre, Whip It, Graveyard. Do these trails sound intimidating? Despite having ominous names, these intermediate-level, downhill-only flow trails at High Star Ranch are suitable for many mountain bikers. What makes the High Star Ranch network so great is that you can customize the intensity of your ride. This intermediate loop is a sort of figure eight that combines the best downhill-only trails of moderate difficulty with an easy climb.

The ascent has you pedaling up the easy Escalador, but you don't come to this place to pedal. The two trails that you'll descend, Bad Hombre and Whip It, are both considered flow trails. And they do indeed feature berms and rollers, but like all the trails at High Star Ranch, they also have rock gardens galore to keep you on your toes. Equal parts fast on smooth singletrack and slow on chunky rock features, this loop has tons of variety.

This working ranch is being subdivided into housing developments, which means these trails are on private property. While the public is allowed to use the trails, do everything possible to keep the property pristine. It is great that we are allowed to enjoy this trail network for free—let's keep it that way.

GETTING THERE

From the intersection of Center Street and Main Street in Kamas, drive north on Main (SR 32) for 1.1 miles. Just after exiting town, you'll see the

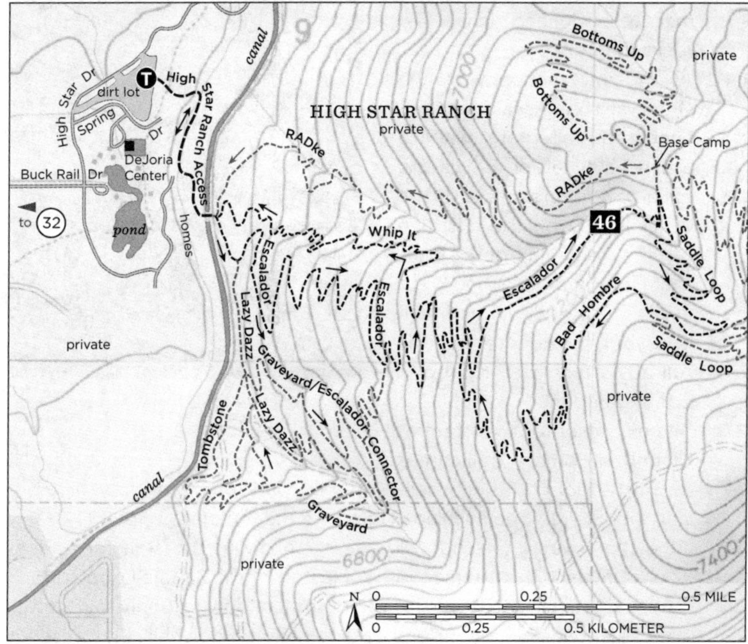

DeJoria Center on the right. Turn right on Buck Rail Drive, and go east for 0.2 mile toward the DeJoria Center. Turn left onto High Star Drive, and follow it for 0.2 mile to a large dirt parking lot. Park on the east side.

MILEAGE LOG

0.0 From the trailhead, climb up the singletrack called High Star Ranch Access that soon becomes doubletrack as it levels. Follow the signs pointing the way to the trail network. You'll traverse above the DeJoria Center when the track crosses over a canal and ends at a sort of log fence. Cross through the space in the fence.

0.3 The singletrack begins after the fence. Stay right and climb up the easy Lazy Dazz Trail.

0.4 At a fork, Lazy Dazz continues on the right. Instead, go left and climb up Escalador. As the name implies, this trail is the main highway to ascend the mountainside. It's a fairly easy uphill with wide corners, a mellow grade, and only a few rocks to pedal over.

1.4   At the intersection with the Graveyard and Escalador Connector, an alternate way to ascend, stay left on Escalador.

1.7   Escalador intersects with the Whip It Trail on the left, one of the downhill-only trails that you will descend. For a really short loop you can end your climb here. For the full adventure, stay right and continue uphill.

Approaching a small rock drop on Bad Hombre

2.0   The exit point for the intermediate Bad Hombre Trail comes in on the right. This is where you will come out from your first big descent. Stay left on Escalador to get to the top of it.

2.6   At a three-way intersection, go right, following the sign for Saddle Loop. Officially this intersection is the start of the Saddle Loop Trail.

3.2   On the right, find the start of the Bad Hombre downhill-only trail. Lower your seatpost, check your brakes, and head on downhill. This descent is not terribly technical, with easy berms, small rock features, and a few obstacles where you can practice bike-handling skills.

4.2   Bad Hombre ends when it intersects with Escalador. Go left and down a few switchbacks, as Whip It is your next destination.

4.4   Go right and head down Whip It. This trail is very similar to Bad Hombre, only with a bit more flow, larger berms, and fun rock drops. When you reach the bottom, you're back on the access trail. Go back up for another lap or if you're finished, head to the car.

5.6   Take the access trail back to the car and the end of the ride.

OPTIONS

For a beginner loop at High Star Ranch, you can follow Lazy Dazz for a half mile to Tombstone, then ride the Tombstone loop back to Lazy Dazz. This smooth, mostly flat trail doesn't have any rocks, making it a great option for newbies and kids. Alternately, ride Lazy Dazz to Graveyard/Escalador

Connector and continue to Graveyard, an intermediate downhill trail that connects with Tombstone. Both Graveyard and Tombstone are less than a mile. Some riders like to bag them as a warmup before hitting the big stuff.

47 OAKLEY TRAIL PARK

NETWORK

Trail Type: 90% singletrack, 10% doubletrack

Distance: Up to 3 miles

Elevation Gain/Loss: 240/240 feet

High Point: 6904 feet

Ride Time: 0.5–1 hour

Technical Difficulty: Intermediate

Fitness Intensity: Easy

Season: Summer–fall

Maps: Online at www.south summittrails.org/maps/, USGS 7.5-minute Kamas

GPS: 40°43'19.18"N, 111°15'17.60"W

Land Manager: City of Oakley (managed by South Summit Trails Foundation)

OVERVIEW

Built in 2018 on City of Oakley land at the mouth of Seymour Canyon, the Oakley Trail Park network features short, easy-to-intermediate rides built for leisurely climbing and fun, downhill mountain biking. The trails may not seem like much of a destination because the park is small and features little vertical gain. But for the South Summit Trails Foundation, this network is a big addition to part of the valley that did not have mountain bike trails.

Two-way trails are open to multiuse, including hikers and equestrians, but those trails lead to downhill-only flow trails with manicured berms and jumps. This is a great place for beginner riders to learn some skills in an accessible and low-key environment. I've highlighted three different loops ranging from 0.5 mile to 1.3 miles. Each varies in difficulty, length, and vertical gain/loss, but you may as well experience the whole shebang by riding all three loops for a total of 3 miles.

GETTING THERE

From the town of Oakley, drive south on SR 32 for 1 mile and turn left (east) on Boulderville Road. In 1.2 miles, Boulderville Road makes a sharp turn

Feeling the flow on Lower Rodeo at the Oakley Trail Park

left and heads north. In another mile the road makes a right-hand bend and becomes Pinion Lane. Drive another 0.3 mile and park at a large, dirt pullout on the west side of the road near the Oakley Artisan Water plant. The trailhead is on the east side of the road.

MILEAGE LOG

Buckaroo

This is the easiest and shortest loop in the trail park. From the trailhead, climb up Lower Lariat for 0.2 mile. At a four-way intersection, go right onto Buckaroo Connect. At 0.25 mile, cross a dirt road and enter the Buckaroo downhill-only trail on the other side. This quarter-mile trail descends 75 vertical feet. Perfect for beginners! At the bottom, turn right at Lower Lariat to circle back to the trailhead for a nearly half-mile ride.

Barrel Racer

Here's another quarter-mile downhill, only this one jacks up the difficulty to intermediate. But at least it takes more pedaling to get there. From the trailhead, proceed on Lower Lariat as above, only at the four-way intersection, go left and continue on Lower Lariat. It's a pretty easy climb with only a few punchy switchbacks. In 0.7 mile, you come to the top of Barrel Racer. This flow trail has bigger berms and jumps but only falls for 120 feet of elevation loss. At the bottom, go right for another lap, or left to return to the four-way intersection. If you go back to the trailhead, it's a total of 1.2 miles.

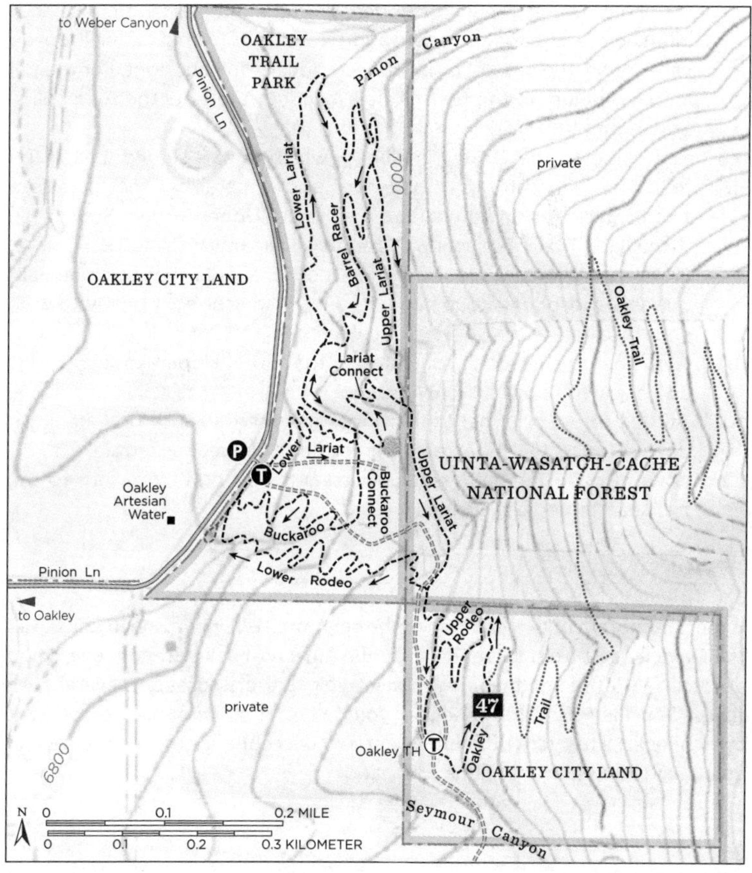

Rodeo

This loop is the biggest and most difficult in the network. It can be ridden two ways: the Upper Rodeo Loop and the Lower Rodeo Loop.

0.0   From the trailhead, ride up Lower Lariat to the four-way, then go left and immediately right to continue uphill on Lariat Connect.

0.3   Connect with Upper Lariat. You can go left for an alternate route to the top of Barrel Racer. For Rodeo, go right. Soon after, Upper Lariat intersects a dirt road. Go left and pedal up the road. After a dozen yards or so, the top of Lower Rodeo appears on your right. For the full loop, continue up the road. A half mile into the ride, the road splits. Stay right at this fork.

0.6   You come to the Oakley Trailhead, which is well-signed. Leave the road here and carry your bike over a low, metal bar that acts as a sort of gate. A sign here shows the way to Upper Rodeo. Soon after, the Oakley Trail intersects with the Seymour Trail. Stay left on Oakley. From here you can attempt to ride a boulder field that has been laid out as a sort of flagstone path. It's a bit technical, so it's okay to walk your bike.

0.7   After the boulder field, you come to the top of Upper Rodeo. Go left and enjoy the downhill-only descent.

0.9   At the bottom of Upper Rodeo, cross the dirt road and continue down Lower Rodeo, which features tighter turns on steeper terrain.

1.2   Lower Rodeo terminates at Lower Lariat. Go right to return to the trailhead to end the 1.3-mile loop.

OPTIONS

Expert mountain bikers can ride to the beginning of Upper Rodeo and climb the Oakley Trail from there. It's a 2-mile out-and-back with just over 1000 vertical feet of steep, technical singletrack that crisscrosses several rock fields. You may have to maneuver your bike up stone steps on the tight switchbacks. This very difficult ascent and descent adds some mileage and spiciness to an otherwise tame trail park.

ACKNOWLEDGMENTS

No mountain bike trail would exist without the tireless work of trail builders, volunteers, and the nonprofit organizations that make singletrack happen. My humble thanks to Mountain Trails Foundation, Basin Recreation, South Summit Trails Foundation, and Wasatch Trails Foundation. Park City and the Wasatch Back have the best mountain biking in the world because of you.

Huge thanks to my friends who joined me on "research rides" for this book. You endured countless hours and many miles of stopping at every intersection for me to log mileage and take photos.

The biggest thanks go to my wife, Callista, for her patience and understanding as I disappeared every weekend to ride. And of course, thanks to my mom, for teaching me how to ride a bike in the first place.

Catching big air on Bamm Bamm at Trailside Bike Park (Route 32)

RESOURCES

SHUTTLE SERVICES

Big Rack Shuttle
www.bigrackshuttle.com
(801) 882-7225

Fox 'N Rox Shuttle Service
www.foxnroxshuttle.com
(801) 560-9804

GUIDE SERVICES

All Seasons Adventures
www.allseasonsadventures.com
1555 Lower Iron Horse Loop Road
Park City, UT 84060
(435) 649-9619

Destination Sports
www.destinationsports.com
1025 Empire Avenue, Suite 3
Park City, UT 84060
(435) 649-8092

Wasatch Adventure Guides
www.wasatchadventureguides.com
3551 North Escala Court
Park City, UT 84098
(435) 200-4885

White Pine Touring
www.whitepinetouring.com
1790 Bonanza Drive
Park City, UT 84060
(435) 649-8710

BIKE SHOPS

Park City

Cole Sport
www.colesport.com
1615 Park Avenue
Park City, UT 84060
(435) 649-4806

Contender Bicycles
www.contenderbicycles.com
1352 White Pine Canyon Road
Park City, UT 84060
(435) 214-7287

Jans
www.jans.com
600 Park Avenue
Park City, UT 84060
(435) 649-4949

Park City Bike Demos
www.parkcitybikedemos.com
1500 Kearns Boulevard
Park City, UT 84060
(435) 659-3991

Silver Star Ski and Sport
www.silverstarskiandsport.com
1825 Three Kings Drive, #85
Park City, UT 84060
(435) 645-7827

Storm Cycles
www.stormcycles.net
1153 Center Drive, G140
Park City, UT 84098
(435) 200-9120

Switchback Sports
www.switchbacksports.com
1245 Deer Valley Drive
Park City, UT 84060
(435) 615-1555

White Pine Touring
www.whitepinetouring.com
1790 Bonanza Drive
Park City, UT 84060
(435) 649-8710

Heber City

Slim & Knobbys Bike Shop
www.slimandknobbys.com
84 S. Main Street
Heber City, UT 84032
(435) 654-2282

TRAIL ORGANIZATIONS

Basin Recreation
www.basinrecreation.org

Mountain Trails Foundation
www.mountaintrails.org

South Summit Trails Foundation
www.southsummittrails.org

Wasatch Trails Foundation
www.wasatchtrails.org

SKI AND MOUNTAIN BIKE RESORTS

Deer Valley Resort
www.deervalley.com
2250 Deer Valley Drive S
Park City, UT 84060
(435) 649-1000

Park City Mountain
www.parkcitymountain.com
1345 Lowell Avenue
Park City, UT 84060
(435) 649-8111

Solitude Mountain Resort
www.solitudemountain.com
12000 Big Cottonwood Canyon Road
Solitude, UT 84121
(801) 534-1400

LAND MANAGERS

US Forest Service
Uinta-Wasatch-Cache
National Forest
www.fs.usda.gov/uwcnf
857 West South Jordan Parkway
South Jordan, UT 84095
(801) 999-2103

Heber-Kamas Ranger District
2460 South Highway 40
Heber City, UT 84032
(435) 654-0470

Salt Lake Ranger District
6944 South 3000 East
Cottonwood Heights,
UT 84121
(801) 733-2660

Bureau of Land Management
Utah State Office
440 West 200 South #500
Salt Lake City, UT 84101
(801) 539-4001

Utah State Parks

www.stateparks.utah.gov

Jordanelle State Park
515 SR 319
Heber City, UT 84032
(435) 649-9540

Wasatch Mountain State Park
1281 Warm Springs Road
Midway, UT 84049
(435) 654-1791

Other Parks

High Star Ranch
www.highstarranch.com
218 Buck Rail Drive
Kamas, UT 84036
(435) 783-3515

Trailside Bike Park
www.basinrecreation.org/parks/trailside
5715 Trailside Drive
Park City, UT 84098
(435) 649-1564

INDEX

ABOUT THE AUTHOR

Jared Hargrave is a freelance outdoors writer and author of *Backcountry Ski & Snowboard Routes: Utah*, published by Mountaineers Books, and his articles have appeared in *Backcountry Magazine, Ascent Backcountry Snow Journal, Utah Adventure Journal,* and the *Mountain Gazette.* He is the founder and editor of UtahOutside.com, an outdoor adventure website featuring trip reports, recreation guides, gear reviews, and outdoor news for the state, with an emphasis on mountain biking, skiing, and hiking. In addition, he produces *KSL Outdoors,* a half-hour television show broadcast on Utah's NBC affiliate, KSL 5.

Callista Pearson

An avid mountain biker, Hargrave hits the singletrack trails in Park City every week from April through October and has used his expertise to write several feature articles about mountain biking in various local publications. Find out what he's up to on www.utahoutside.com, @utahoutside on Instagram, and Utahoutside.com on Facebook.

MOUNTAINEERS BOOKS including its two imprints, Skipstone and Braided River, is a leading publisher of quality outdoor recreation, sustainability, and conservation titles. As a 501(c)(3) nonprofit, we are committed to supporting the environmental and educational goals of our organization by providing expert information on human-powered adventure, sustainable practices at home and on the trail, and preservation of wilderness.

Our publications are made possible through the generosity of donors, and through sales of more than 800 titles on outdoor recreation, sustainable lifestyle, and conservation. To donate, purchase books, or learn more, visit us online:

MOUNTAINEERS BOOKS

1001 SW Klickitat Way, Suite 201 • Seattle, WA 98134
800-553-4453 • mbooks@mountaineersbooks.org • www.mountaineersbooks.org

An independent nonprofit publisher since 1960

Leave No Trace strives to educate visitors about the nature of their recreational impacts and offers techniques to prevent and minimize such impacts. Leave No Trace is best understood as an educational and ethical program, not as a set of rules and regulations. For more information, visit www.lnt.org or call 800-332-4100.

YOU MAY ALSO LIKE: